BREAKPOINTS

Breakpoints

How Managers Exploit Radical Business Change

Paul Strebel

HARVARD BUSINESS SCHOOL PRESS   Boston, Massachusetts

Printed in the United States of America
96 95 94 93 92   5 4 3 2 1

Library of Congress Cataloging-in-Publication Data

Strebel, Paul.
    Breakpoints : how managers exploit radical business change / Paul Strebel.
        p.   cm.
    Includes bibliographical references and index.
    ISBN 0-87584-369-7 (alk. paper)
    1. Organizational change.   2. Corporate reorganizations.
  3. Strategic planning.   4. Industrial management.   I. Title.
  HD58.8.S77   1992
  658.4'06—dc20   92-10438
                                                                        CIP

The paper used in this publication meets the requirements of the American
National Standard for Permanence of Paper for Printed Library Materials
Z39.49—1984

Contents

Preface

Gyrating markets, mushrooming technologies, and shifting political frontiers are changing the face of the world, creating sudden radical changes in business conditions that take the form of business discontinuities, or breakpoints: industry growth rates jump or fall, the rules of the competitive game shift, market shares move around, and companies are reorganized.

The importance of breakpoints became apparent while I was working with colleagues on a series of international consulting projects. We noticed a surprising number of companies that did not see, or could not cope with, a breakpoint in industry or company conditions. A review of eighty-seven projects from a variety of industries revealed that half of them were directed at strategic issues and, of these, most involved problems caused by shifts in competitive behavior. The companies were asking for advice, so it was not surprising that only one-sixth of them were able to deal with the shifts in some way, and only two actually participated in creating a shift. What was surprising was that so many of them faced essentially the same problem: an organization that had been unable to cope with the breakpoint.

During the same period many of the excellent American companies identified by Thomas Peters and Robert Waterman fell from grace.[1] At least one observer suggested that in most cases the fallen companies did not see, or were unable to cope with, sudden shifts in market conditions. Unfortunately, dramatizing the need to be alert and to change continuously is not enough to improve corporate adaptability. After more than half a decade on the road trying to incite companies to change continuously, Peters was reported by the *Boston Globe* to be "downbeat, telling clients in a recent newsletter that, when it comes to corporate change, 'I must declare myself . . . a pessimist.'"[2]

Part of the problem is that consultants often lump all types of change into the same category. They present most new approaches to change as if they could be applied to all companies, no matter what the specific industry and corporate circumstances might be. But continuous incremental change, for example, is not appropriate for all companies, nor even for one company all the time. Some way of differentiating among different types of change is essential.

A second problem is the tendency in too many quarters to develop unidimensional strategies such as product innovation or cost leadership. Or strategies are developed for industries that are within a single phase—emerging, growth, fragmenting, or decline. Business breakpoints, however, often mark the shifts between industry phases. Shifting business conditions require a concept of strategy that is dynamic.

With respect to breakpoints, there is a third problem. In the models and frameworks used by executives, consultants, and business schools, typically the content of the strategic choice framework is not linked to the management of the change process. As a result, strategic decisions are often made without consideration for the change process. In the case of discontinuous change, this can be disastrous: the change process may completely subvert the best of strategic decisions.

With its emphasis on equilibrium, the economics literature has little to say about different types of change, or about the process of shifting between moving equilibria in particular. To the best of my knowledge, the only work that might be considered somewhat relevant to the management of breakpoints is Joseph Schumpeter's analysis of the entrepreneurial process[3] and Richard Nelson and Sidney Winter's description of economics as an evolutionary process.[4] But neither of these is of much practical use to executives who must deal with business discontinuities. More relevant is the notion of gradual evolution punctuated by quantum leaps and Danny Miller and Peter Friesen's distinction between incremental, dramatic, piecemeal, and quantum changes.[5]

For managers, the literature on technology management is useful; in particular the work by Richard Foster on the transition between technology cycles[6] and the suggestion by Modesto Maidique and Robert Hayes that successful high-tech firms alternate between "periods of consolidation and discontinuity with sharp reorientation."[7] Henry Mintzberg echoes this theme, contrasting deliberate and emerging strategy, and with the notion of brief quantum leaps to strategic reorientation.[8] Little is said, however, about the timing or management of these shifts.

One place where discontinuities, as well as different types of change, are analyzed is in the mathematics of the catastrophe models and the more recent and more complex theory of chaos. Both show how simple mathematical expressions can generate discontinuous solutions. The former in particular shows how the interaction between two independent, or causal, variables can result in sudden jumps in the response of a system.[9] In application, the two causal variables usually involve a driving force of change on the one hand and some resistance to change on the other. But these models cannot be used in management because the variables cannot be measured precisely.

Nevertheless, a qualitative exploration of how forces of change may interact with resistance turns out to be fruitful. By the late 1940s, Kurt Lewin had already demonstrated how tension between environmental forces of change and psychological resistance can be used to explain human behavior.[10] In this book I present a simple framework based on the interplay between the forces of business change and resistance. I contrast basic types of business change, select appropriate corporate responses to sudden radical change, and point out efforts that have been successful in creating change. Readers will understand the kinds of change that are appropriate under certain conditions, and how to successfully manage breakpoints.

The framework goes beyond the experience of any single company in the IMD management consulting projects; it represents a new, yet simple way of looking at change, contingent on what's happening in the business environment. The versatility of the approach and the ease with which practitioners take to it indicate its broad appeal. In cases where the rules of confidentiality permit, I use examples from the IMD consulting projects, and from my own personal experience, to illustrate how the framework can be applied. Examples are supplemented by others taken from case studies in the public domain, ones written by colleagues at IMD, the Harvard Business School, and elsewhere, and other published sources.

Apart from those whose work is cited, I am indebted to the faculty and executive participants at IMD for the international perspective, the opportunity to integrate across all the management disciplines, and the continual interaction that makes the institute so provocative an environment for exploring managerial issues. Access for me as a project director and for research purposes to the consulting projects that are set up and coordinated by Jan Kubes was key, not only to seeing the difficulty managers have coping with breakpoints, but also to developing insight about their successful management. The projects led first to the concept of outpacing strategies that was developed in several joint papers with Xavier Gilbert, then to competitive turning points, and finally to the notion of discontinuities and how to anticipate, exploit, and create breakpoints.

Derek Abell, dean of IMEDE, was a continual source of encouragement during the early part of the work. After the merger between IMEDE and IMI to create IMD, Juan Rada, the new director general, allocated the resources for my sabbatical. The Harvard Business School provided the ideal environment for testing and fine-tuning the framework and conclusions. Henry Reiling, in particular, facilitated innumerable discussions with his colleagues. I would like to thank Howard Stevenson and Chris Bartlett for especially spirited and insightful conversations.

Carol Franco and her team at the Harvard Business School Press have been the most constructive of editors, prodding me to come up with improvements like the user-friendly change arena diagram and to highlight crucial notions like that of leapfrogging the competition. An anonymous reviewer of the manuscript also provided a valuable perspective on the importance of the central theme in the book: the way in which the interplay between the forces of change and resistance shapes radical business change. Per Jenster suggested that the awkward word, "discontinuity," be replaced by the more evocative, "breakpoint." The manuscript itself was typed and corrected several times by Carine Barraud, Amy Griffith, and Anne-Catherine Glaus, while the diagrams and exhibits were prepared by Michèle Mayer and Max Thommen. Little would have been possible, however, without the continuing support and affection of my immediate family: Biff, Chris, and Heidi.

Introduction

> The final plunge of the most powerful and dreaded firm on Wall
> Street in the Roaring Eighties came with astonishing speed. Like
> the abrupt fall of the Berlin Wall thousands of miles away, the col-
> lapse suddenly confirmed what everyone in the financial world
> could already feel in the wind: A new era had arrived.

This is how *Business Week* introduced its cover story on February
26, 1990. The story began in 1983 when Drexel Burnham Lambert
first promoted junk bonds for leveraged buyout financing.

Junk bonds were not merely another new financial instrument.
By changing the rules of the acquisition game, junk bonds actually
created financial breakpoints. They made it possible for any Wall
Street deal maker with enough flair and daring to launch multibil-
lion dollar offers for Main Street companies. Between the fourth
quarter of 1987 and the second quarter of 1988, junk bonds grew
from 20 to 60 percent of new corporate debt financing in the United
States, before peaking out. In the process, Drexel was transformed
from a second-tier institution into a Wall Street powerhouse. The
fall of Drexel marked the end of the leveraged buyout junk bond
cycle, another breakpoint, during which the 152-year-old Drexel
filed for bankruptcy, the investment banking industry went into
recession, and the corporate takeover game shifted away from
highly leveraged deals.

Breakpoints, or sudden radical shifts in the rules of the business game, may shape the course of an industry, or of a company,

1

but they need not be as dramatic as the junk bond story. Nor are they necessarily linked to corporate failure, or to a product cycle. They may originate far more prosaically in the form of a change in international politics, government policy, or the economy, a shift in life-style, or the emergence of a new technology. A breakpoint may be a price war, a new competitive approach, or, in the company itself, a radical reorganization or the succession between chief executives.

Coping with shifts in business conditions is one of the most difficult tasks facing management. Many excellent companies have gone under, not because they ignored their customers, or the commandments of so-called excellent management, but because business conditions shifted under their feet. When business conditions change, the formula for success must inevitably change. Whenever a major breakpoint occurs, trends and patterns are broken and forecasts collapse, making a mockery of immediate experience. Recognizing and then managing these breakpoints is not easy.

In the mid-1980s a U.S. manufacturer of grinding tools, a worldwide leader in its segment, was confronted with the entry into the market of Japanese and other Far Eastern competitors. As did so many other companies and industries that had to deal with low-price competitors from the Far East, it decided to stick to its knitting, in this case, pursue its expansion in the U.S. market with high-quality products. Only belatedly did the company realize that the Japanese had created a sharp shift toward low-cost competition. Its response was as confused and unfocused as any other.

The difficulty of dealing with discontinuity is not restricted to manufacturing companies. A major second-tier Swiss bank, primarily for business clients, was busily cutting costs to cope with shrinking spreads between borrowing and lending rates. At the same time, foreign banks were slowly introducing new financial instruments and other innovations into the Swiss market. Then suddenly the big three Swiss banks followed suit. The second-tier bank was unable to respond. In the space of a few years, a once highly profitable operation was on its knees, struggling to survive.

What emerges from cases like these is that

- companies have difficulty seeing the breakpoint,
- they fail to exploit it, and
- only rarely do they create a competitive breakpoint.

The tool manufacturer didn't see the breakpoint. Management didn't appreciate the significance of the Japanese entry; it refused to believe that Far Eastern competition could possibly threaten high-quality products. In the same vein, General Joffre, the French commander-in-chief during World War I, believed the Germans would attack France by the most direct route, across the border in Alsace and Lorraine. He was so convinced of the logic of this that he dismissed all reports of German armies and French casualties on the northern Belgium border as obvious diversionary tactics. It was only when the hospitals were overflowing that Joffre went north to look for himself. The main German armies were only 70 km from Paris. The French almost lost their capital city as a result of Joffre's preconceived ideas.

The second-tier bank saw the breakpoint but was unable to exploit it. It worried about the impact of financial innovation; but the cost reduction program had eliminated the human resources needed to cope with the shift to higher-value-added services. Many overly diversified companies in the 1980s had a related problem. They knew their market value had dropped well below their breakup value. And yet they couldn't bring themselves to take the necessary steps to refocus on their core business. As a result, they were easy targets for leveraged buyouts.

Could the managers have done better in coping with sharp shifts in the business environment? If their companies had been prepared, almost certainly. For organizations that are prepared, breakpoints provide some of the best opportunities for outpacing the competition. Whereas smooth change provides little room for altering the balance of competitive power, discontinuous change redistributes the competitive cards.

Breakpoints distinguish business leaders from managers. When the waters are calm, management keeps the ship on course. However, when the wind comes up, when the forces of change begin to build and confront resistance, leadership becomes critical. Executives who are aware of the potential in a breakpoint can change the course of their companies. But real commitments of time, effort, and money have to be made. As timid managers let go, true leaders take hold.

Companies that are sensitive to potential shifts in the environment are best positioned to trigger a competitive breakpoint. They have new product prototypes in reserve, a cost structure that is continually improving, and a flexible organization. These capabilities cannot be acquired overnight. Their development involves deep, gradual changes in organizational behavior and repeated cycles of learning. These companies, in most cases, have been working at it for years, and are able to systematically create break-points in their industries.

But even the best-managed companies are subject to external breakpoints beyond their control. These, and they are increasing in number, come from other social institutions, those determining demand and supply, or from national and global events. Technological change, and the accompanying deregulation and globalization, are increasing the interconnectedness between previously isolated spheres of social influence. As a result, disturbances and disconti-nuities in, say, the politics of world peace will often trigger sharp shifts down the line, say, in a second- or third-tier manufacturing industry.

To deal successfully with radical change, executives and their teams need to anticipate business breakpoints as early as possible. When anticipating late, they need to exploit breakpoints to produce radical internal change in order to catch up with and leapfrog the competition; when anticipating early, they need to create compet-itive breakpoints by developing the company's ability to capitalize on the interplay between forces of change and resistance.

In this book I describe how managers and their companies can anticipate, exploit, and create breakpoints. The core idea is that the key to taking advantage of radical change is in the interplay between the forces of change and resistance. The basic message is that

1. Managers can learn to anticipate breakpoints by identifying the forces of change, assessing the resistance, and building scenarios based on a limited number of ways in which the balance between these forces might change.
2. Managers can exploit breakpoints by choosing an intervention path, strategy, organization structure, and implementation style that is consistent with the interplay between the forces of change and resistance.
3. Managers can create competitive breakpoints by drawing on a limited number of organizational capabilities, each appro-priate for capitalizing on a different configuration of change forces and resistance.

ANTICIPATING BREAKPOINTS

To anticipate breakpoints, the key is to look for typical pat-terns in the interplay between the forces for change and resistance.

For example, when the forces are growing and the resistance is high, a discontinuity is possible. If the forces keep growing, at a certain point the resistance is likely to crack and collapse, causing discontinuous change. Not that people suddenly change in a fundamental way, but rather that the structures around them change sharply and they get shunted aside.

Breakpoints are seldom inevitable. Managers can always intervene to alter the balance between forces of change and resistance. And relatively minor events may trigger or delay the breakpoint. To cope with this uncertainty, it is useful to explore scenarios that include breakpoints and that reflect typical patterns in the interplay between the forces of change and resistance over time.

When the forces of change in the leveraged buyout market were growing in the late 1980s, with increasingly overvalued assets and the continued use of high leverage, Frederick Joseph and his team at Drexel should have been thinking through scenarios and developing strategic options. When government regulators started closing in, and the rate of sale of new junk bonds turned down in 1989, it was already too late. Making an organization more resilient to alternative scenarios has to be done in good times. But in the hubris of success, the psychological resistance to negative change is often so great that it is difficult to think through a reverse.

Thousands of miles away, West German Chancellor Helmut Kohl hinted in several TV interviews that he had been dreaming about German reunification for years. When the Berlin Wall finally collapsed, he must have known that the forces of change were in the ascendancy over Soviet resistance. Far better than many both inside and outside West Germany, Kohl sensed that he could capitalize on Gorbachev's "perestroika" breakpoint; he piggybacked on Gorbachev's notion of a common European house to argue for a unified Germany. And he rode the rising tide of East German refugees to far more rapid unification than was possible even in the dreams of others.

EXPLOITING BREAKPOINTS

Even when anticipation is poor, or difficult, a breakpoint still can be exploited. Breakpoints initiated by others, or beyond the control of a company, provide special opportunities. The Japanese frequently use external breakpoints (such as "endaka," the rising of the yen) to drive even more radical internal change to avoid or leapfrog the competition. The experience of successful players indicates that, to leapfrog, the latecomer must be able to buy time and sequence a series of strategic steps chosen from a limited repertoire of intervention paths.

Had Drexel understood the forces confronting it, its management would have pondered alternative scenarios, chosen an intervention path, reorganized accordingly, and developed alternative ways to create breakpoints—instead of simply reacting to them. By contrast, learning at Drexel Burnham Lambert apparently was restricted to the development of new financial instruments, with little consideration for risk management, let alone the notion of adding capabilities to manage change. Even if the executives had clearly seen the breakpoint coming, it is doubtful whether much could have been done with the existing organization.

CREATING BREAKPOINTS

A company is truly topflight when it cannot only anticipate or react to, but also create, competitive discontinuities. This way, it resolves the uncertainty about the direction of the industry. It relieves the pressure on its own organization ahead of time and maximizes pressure on its rivals, forcing them to change if they want to keep up. Emerging management practice suggests that the key to creating breakpoints is an organization that can capitalize on the change patterns available for creating a discontinuity.

The emphasis in the chapters that follow is on breakpoints within the environment of a business unit or company. I focus on anticipating breakpoints primarily at the level of the market or industry, and exploiting or creating them from inside the firm. Although the framework presumably can be adapted for use in other areas, such as society or the economy, breakpoints there are considered forces of change but not subjects of discussion in their own right. Crises like the Bhopal explosion, the Alaskan oil spills, or the Schweizerhalle fire on the Rhine are not considered. Neither are bankruptcies and liquidations.

The ultimate test of the overall framework is its usefulness to practicing executives. Keys to practice close each chapter, providing a brief summary of how the content of the chapter can be applied. Taken together, the keys and their background constitute a practical approach to dealing with discontinuity. With this approach companies can outpace less nimble competitors by more systematically anticipating, exploiting, and creating breakpoints.

PART **I**

Anticipating
Breakpoints

ANTICIPATING BREAKPOINTS is foremost a question of being able to read the signs. To do so requires knowing what the signs are and an ability and willingness to read. The chapters in Part I describe the signs that precede and characterize a business breakpoint, and explain how they can be read.

To anticipate breakpoints, managers need to consider three key variables: rate of change, forces for (or of) change, and resistance to change. The first three chapters are devoted to these key variables. In Chapter 1 are examples of how to describe the rate of business change. Chapter 2 defines the forces of change as well as some of their leading indicators. Chapter 3 considers the resistance to change, including the unwillingness of executives to read the signs and the difficulty that organizations have in changing. The basic variables are brought together in Chapter 4 to map out different change scenarios. In Chapter 5, the interplay between forces and resistance is used to generate strategic change scenarios, especially those that involve breakpoints.

CHAPTER 1

Describing Breakpoints

THE SMALL SWISS TOWN of Wohlen in the canton of Aargau is home to an impressive turn-of-the-century building that was once the headquarters of Georges Meyer & Co., one of the world's leading straw hat manufacturers. The company originated in the straw plaiting industry which emerged from the European countryside in the late sixteenth century. A major breakthrough occurred in 1860 when Georges Meyer and his partner introduced plaiting machines. By the 1950s, their company employed more than 1,000 people, occupied a sprawling site that included manufacturing and dyeing facilities, and had agencies and representatives around the world. Georges Meyer's success attracted other competitors, primarily three Swiss companies, Dreyfuss, about half its size, and Breitschmid and Jacques Meier, each about a quarter of its size.[1]

In the 1960s the industry was confronted unexpectedly with a major breakpoint: hats were out of fashion. The confined spaces inside automobiles and airplanes had been making hats more and more cumbersome for some time. The ever accelerating life-styles left less and less time for the careful dressing and stately occasions so appropriate for hats. When these forces finally culminated in a shift in fashion, the impact on the straw braid industry was disastrous. Demand hit bottom.

Georges Meyer's competitors began moving into different but related activities. Dreyfuss exploited its agency network to distribute other products, especially those of 3M Corporation with whom it developed a link. Breitschmid used its braiding know-how to manufacture cable sleeves and in the process came up with the curl to the telephone handset cable. Jacques Meier moved into cellophane bags, capitalizing on the plastic film technology that had been used to encase the straw before braiding.

At Georges Meyer itself, rivalry between the three managing directors prevented the company from focusing on a single response to the discontinuity. Strong financial reserves allowed for several diversification attempts, including, for example, the manufacture of stuffed straw animals, all of which failed. By the early 1970s, business was so bad the company had to be liquidated. Georges Meyer converted to a property holding and investment company designed to manage the remaining assets, including the stately head office, and distribute the proceeds to the shareholders.

The demise of Georges Meyer illustrates how a breakpoint in the business environment, in this case a radical shift in fashion, triggered a breakpoint in demand, which turned into a strong force for change in the industry. The result was a sharp shift in the competitive rules of the game and a major breakpoint in the performance of the leading company.

Business discontinuities can be best recognized relative to recent trends and behavior in the industry, company, or business unit. The quantitative signs of a breakpoint take the form of shifts in performance trends. These are sharp changes in direction, up or down, in the quantitative performance of the industry, company, or business unit. When plotted on a graph, a performance shift generates a jump, a sudden rise or fall in the growth rate of the trend. The qualitative signs take the form of shifts in the competitive or organizational behavior of the industry, company, or business unit. These shifts involve qualitative changes in the rules of the industry or company game, which are reflected in the set of viable strategies.

This chapter describes the characteristics of

- Industry breakpoints in the form of shifts in industry performance and shifts in competitive behavior.
- Corporate breakpoints using shifts in corporate performance and shifts in organizational behavior.

It then provides a summary contrast of

- Breakpoints versus turning points, that is, sudden radical change versus gradual radical change.

INDUSTRY BREAKPOINTS

Shifts in Industry Performance

The sales and profit data of industries and competitors, if broken down sufficiently, usually can be used to visualize the impact of a breakpoint. A Princeton statistician is said to have remarked often that a simple graph is worth the output from a thousand equations. To identify quantitative shifts in performance, one does not need to engage in complex statistical analysis. Rather one should decide on the key quantitative measure of performance for the business and find a way of graphing it that most simply reflects what is happening.

Consider the example in Exhibit 1-1 of the Dutch audio-video market, radio and hi-fi equipment, tape recorders, TV, video recorders and cameras, compact discs, and so forth.[2] Industry sales in millions of guilders are shown on the vertical axis. The overall shape of the curve reflects the early growth, followed by gradual maturing, of the Dutch audio-video market. (The slope of the line gives a direct indication of the industry's growth rate, because a log scale has been used on the vertical axis.)

Over the forty years, distinct periods of rapid and low growth can be distinguished. During the 1950s, the audio technology developed during World War II was adapted to civilian use. Rapid growth rates, averaging 20 percent per annum, persisted until 1960. The saturation of the market, combined with an economic slowdown, triggered a breakpoint in the growth of demand, followed by sharply lower growth rates during the early 1960s. Although interrupted by the introduction of the compact cassette and hi-fi stereo in 1964 and 1965, the slow growth continued until 1968, at an average annual rate of 6.6 percent.

In 1969, the surging sales of color TVs triggered another sharp breakpoint, this time in the direction of higher growth rates averaging almost 25 percent annually for six years. The oil price crisis hit in 1974, producing the next breakpoint in the direction of lower growth rates. Despite the success of video recorders and compact discs, the average growth rate was less than 4 percent during the

EXHIBIT 1–1   **Sales Growth Rate Shifts in the Dutch Audio-Video Industry**

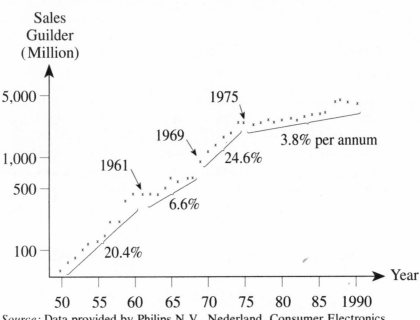

Source: Data provided by Philips N.V., Nederland, Consumer Electronics Division.

1980s. Without these new products the growth rate probably would have been negative.

The point is that industry performance trends do not necessarily change smoothly, nor randomly. Rather an industry's performance may exhibit a sudden upturn or downturn which persists for some time. These shifts in industry performance are typically jumps in the growth rate of the performance measure.

Performance curves are often too aggregated to reflect key breakpoints which are important to managers. When industries or companies are complex and more mature, new product breakpoints, for example, may be obscured by overlapping product life cycles. The video recorder and compact disc were of the same order of importance to competitors in the Dutch audio-video market as color TV. Yet the aggregate performance displayed merely a blip in its growth rate. To reflect these breakpoints, more detailed market segment data are necessary.

Shifts in Competitive Behavior

Industry growth rate breakpoints are often accompanied by sharp shifts in competitive behavior. These breakpoints may be stimulated by external factors, such as the shift in fashion that affected the straw braid industry, or by internal life cycle developments.[3]

No matter where they originate, competitive shifts involve transitions between two well-known ways of competing.[4] The two ways are illustrated by a value–cost diagram of the evolution of the personal computer industry (see Exhibit 1-2). One possibility, shown with the vertical arrows, is to make the product better, by increasing the value of a personal computer as perceived by the market; the other alternative, shown with the horizontal arrows, is to make the product cheaper, by reducing the delivered cost of a given set of PC functions. Since the introduction of the PC, a progressive evolution has taken place toward increasing perceived value at declining delivered cost. Although competition takes place continually on both dimensions, in terms of growth, greater or lesser emphasis may be on perceived value or on delivered cost at different times.

EXHIBIT 1–2 **Competitive Shifts in the Personal Computer Industry (Simplified View)**

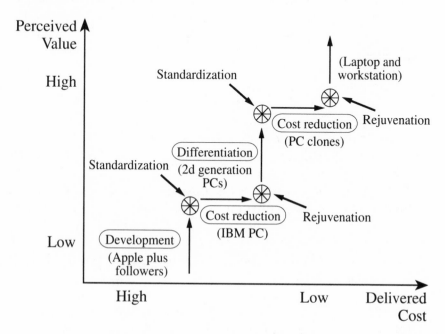

During the development phase, competitive behavior re-volved around attempts to develop the value of the product. Hundreds of small firms were competing with Apple to define the form and content of a personal computer. This value-based com-petition continued until IBM introduced what eventually became the market standard. The sudden entry of IBM triggered a break-point, toward an emphasis on matching the IBM standard and then reducing the delivered cost. Those firms unable to manage the shift in competitive emphasis, and unprotected by niche segments, went out of business in the shake-out that followed. To manage this breakpoint, Apple was forced to oust its founders and bring in a consumer marketing expert.

Competition on lower delivered costs was dominant, espe-cially with the entry of competitors from the Far East, until the leading competitors came out with a second-generation product. The emphasis on hard discs, better graphics, and greater speed triggered a second shift in market behavior back to competition around the value of the PC. To survive this shift, even the clone manufacturers in the Far East were forced to follow suit. Compet-itive behavior continued to revolve around value enhancement until the clone manufacturers caught up and switched the emphasis back to process cost reduction.

In the late 1980s, the PC industry went through yet another important shift back to value competition. In the growth segments, the product's function shifted toward the laptop and integrated workstations. As a workstation, the PC has become part of more complex information system networks with specialized applica-tions for different end-users.

Competitive shifts change the rules of the competitive game. They add a fundamentally new dimension to the competitive mix. Standardization shifts involve a move toward increasing competi-tion around rationalization and delivered costs. Rejuvenation shifts involve a move toward competition around product development, differentiation, or customization, designed to increase perceived value. In effect, competitive shifts add a new layer of value, or lower cost, which significantly improves the product offering. As a result, over time, the industry progresses up along the diagonal in Exhibit 1-2 toward product offerings with more perceived value per unit of real delivered cost.

Actual market cycles do not necessarily manifest a neat sequence of shifts. Several rejuvenations may succeed one another before a standardization occurs. Some market segments, such as designer clothing, which mostly depends on art or fashion, may rarely undergo standardization. Conversely, markets for commodities may experience successive price declines, based on process standardizations incorporating new technology, with few if any rejuvenations of the product or the service's perceived value.

With the shortening of product life cycles in today's markets, standardization shifts often follow closely on rejuvenation shifts. In fact, product innovation is not complete until the competitive formula has been standardized and the delivery system streamlined.[5] This is needed to ensure that the fully augmented product reaches the market in a cost effective manner. In the consumer electronics industry, for example, and in many service industries, new product introductions involve the immediate launching of a complete, standardized competitive formula. Therefore, it often makes no sense to talk about separate innovation and standardization shifts at the product level.

Competitive shifts only make sense at the industry sector level, when examining the behavior of competitors as a group. At this level, one can identify competitive breakpoints followed by periods of innovative activity, with a continuous stream of new products that have more or less fully standardized competitive formulas. Alternatively, breakpoints are followed by an emphasis on rationalization, characterized by a continual spate of cost reduction moves.[6]

CORPORATE BREAKPOINTS

Shifts in Corporate Performance

Shifts in competitive behavior almost inevitably have repercussions on corporate performance, at least at the business unit level. No matter where they originate, corporate breakpoints can be described in terms of shifts in performance measures like sales, profits, volume, or market share.

A striking example, described in several case studies, especially the one written by Dominique Turpin,[7] occurred during the late 1980s in the Japanese beer industry. In 1986, the Kirin Brewery Co. dominated the Japanese beer market with its German-style pasteurized lager sold under the brand name of Kirin Beer. Lager beer drunk at home was the most popular beer in Japan. Since 1888, a benevolent creature called "Kirin," from a Chinese legend, was featured on the bottles of the company's lager beer. With close to a 90 percent share Kirin had a virtual lock on the market. However, it had not always been this way.

In 1872, Shozaburo Shibuya set up the first full-scale brewery in Japan. But beer didn't begin to make inroads into Japanese drinking habits until the breakpoint created by the Sino-Japanese War (1937–1941) and World War II, when millions of Japanese soldiers tasted beer for the first time. At the outbreak of World War II, Dai Nippon Breweries had two-thirds of the market and Kirin one-third. After the war, General MacArthur created another breakpoint in the beer industry when, in breaking up the zaibatsu, he split Dai Nippon in half—Asahi in western Japan with 39 percent of the total market and Sapporo in the east with 36 percent, both leading Kirin with 25 percent.

Despite its smaller size, Kirin gained significant market share at the expense of both Asahi and Sapporo during the rapid growth after the war. Kirin targeted its pasteurized lager beer at the home market, while Asahi and Sapporo focused their draft beer on the popular beer halls, restaurants, and bars. With the spread of refrigerators throughout Japan, home consumption soared. By contrast, drinking in public places stagnated.

Kirin continued to gain share until a breakpoint, marking market maturity, occurred in the middle 1970s (see Exhibit 1-3). Volume growth dropped to below 3 percent per year. Costs became critically important. Kirin's market share stabilized above 60 percent, and Sapporo's at 20 percent. Asahi continued to lose share, albeit more slowly than before. The manager of Asahi Breweries explained it this way:

> In the 1970s, our company was the prisoner of a vicious circle . . . since consumers did not have a high image of our products, retailers did not push our products, no matter how much effort our salesmen were putting in. Salesmen were blaming the engineers for not turning out good products and, in turn, engineers were blaming the salesmen for not selling a product which they thought was as good as the competitors'.

In 1982, in order to stem the erosion, the Asahi board of directors initiated a major change. At the suggestion of Sumitomo Bank, Tsutomu Murai, a sixty-five-year-old executive vice president of the bank, took over as president of Asahi. Although many organizational improvements were introduced, Asahi's market share continued to erode. In 1986, Murai was replaced by Hirotaro Higuchi, the bank's vice president of international affairs. Higuchi concen-

Exhibit 1–3   **Market Share Shifts in the Japanese Beer Industry**

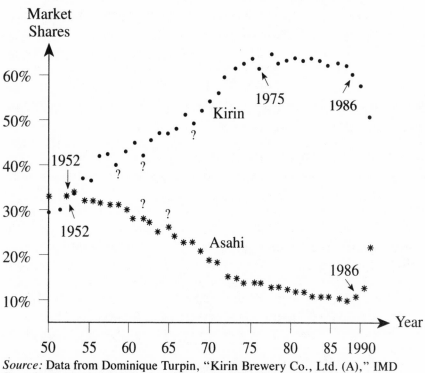

Source: Data from Dominique Turpin, "Kirin Brewery Co., Ltd. (A)," IMD Case Study M366 (Lausanne, Switzerland: IMD International, 1990).

trated on the development of a new corporate philosophy, more market research and promotion, a "Quality First" program, and new product development. Among other new products, the R&D department developed a "dry" draft beer, with less residual sugar and slightly more alcohol, targeted at heavy drinkers. After some debate, Higuchi supported the younger executives who wanted to develop this beer into a "truly different product." A new logo and label were developed; TV commercials were aired, and a huge advertising campaign, spread over three weeks, took place. In addition, free sales samples were distributed to a million people all over Japan and 1,000 "field ladies" were added to the sales force at the retail level to promote the new product and collect feedback data. The new Asahi "Super Dry" was launched on March 17, 1987.

In late October 1987, Hideyo Motoyama, president of Kirin Brewery, commented to his executives:

The launching of Super Dry by Asahi Breweries last spring has put a kick in a market that had been calmly growing at 3 percent annually. I suppose all of you have seen the figures that I circulated to you yesterday morning. In 1987, the market has grown 7.5 percent and is apparently racing ahead at an 8 percent clip. Asahi's sales leaped 33 percent in 1987. Meanwhile, Kirin's share has sagged from 60 percent to 57 percent. What's going on?

After some debate, and under strong consumer pressure, Kirin launched its own dry beer on February 22, 1988. A few days later, Sapporo and a fourth competitor, Suntory, also introduced dry beers. By the end of 1988, the four Japanese brewers had introduced sixty-eight new products and packagings, compared to thirty-three the previous year.

Asahi was the clear winner of the 1988 "dry war." Asahi Super Dry was positioned mainly as a draft beer drunk outside the home where the company had a strong distribution network. As a result, the company's share swelled by 7.2 percentage points in 1988 to 20.6 percent. The other shifts in market share that accompanied the dry war breakpoint are shown in Exhibit 1-4. The breakpoint showed up in all the performance figures. Asahi's sales increased by 58 percent in 1988, while Kirin's profits dropped by 15 percent.

The history of the Japanese beer industry illustrates the close link between market share data and competitive dynamics, between shifts in market share performance and breakpoints in competitive behavior. Several surveys of Japanese executives have confirmed the popular belief that many Japanese companies give higher priority to market share than to return on investment, or

EXHIBIT 1–4 **Market Share Shifts during the Japanese Dry Beer Breakpoint**

| | Market Share | | | |
	Kirin	Asahi	Sapporo	Suntory
1986	60%	10%	21%	9%
1987	57	13	21	9
1988	50	21	20	9

Source: Data from Dominique Turpin, "Kirin Brewery Co., Ltd. (A)," IMD Case Study M366 (Lausanne, Switzerland: IMD International, 1990).

other financial measures of performance. Indeed, the Japanese business press carries daily listings of market shares in numerous industries, in addition to the typical financial information.

The question marks in Exhibit 1-3 flag fluctuations in market share that did not signal a longer-term break in the trend. In most cases, they reflected new product introductions by Asahi which captured share and then collapsed. In general, if breaks in a trend are to be more than random fluctuations, they must be accompanied by enduring shifts in the competitive or organizational game.

Shifts in Organizational Behavior

Sharp shifts in corporate performance typically go hand in hand with organizational breakpoints—sharp changes in strategy, structure, and/or systems. The collapse of corporate sales in the Swiss straw braid industry precipitated breakpoints in the organizations of the main players. Those that survived made major adjustments in their strategies, structure, systems, staff, and skills. Because of entrenched resistance to change, Georges Meyer was unable to do so. Georges Meyer's final adjustment, the liquidation of its main business, was therefore all the more abrupt.

For large players in the Dutch audio-video industry, like Philips, the breakpoints in the 1980s occurred mainly at the business unit level. New units were set up and old ones restructured to cope with the emergence of video and tape recorders, color TVs, and so on. Similarly, in the Japanese beer industry, the emergence of dry beer spawned a spate of restructuring at the business unit level in the four main competitors.

Japanese companies especially are aware of key events and breakpoints in their corporate history. Shiseido, the leading Japanese cosmetics company and third largest in the world, traces its 118-year corporate history on five dimensions in "The Shiseido Story": corporate growth (24 main events), products (25 key new products), advertising (4 main periods), Shiseido and society (14 events), and scientific achievements (18 breakthroughs and events).[8]

Some corporate events create breakpoints on more than one dimension. The Shiseido advertising story in particular is marked by three breakpoints which had ramifications throughout the company. The first was triggered in 1916 by the return from the United States and France of Shinzo Fukuhara, the founder's son. Fukuhara initiated a major shift from pharmaceuticals to cosmetics with advertising based on "European, and particularly French, culture. . . . Corporate advertising had the unmistakable savor of an intriguing, alien culture." The growing isolation of Japan in the 1930s and the outbreak of the Sino-Japanese War marked the second breakpoint, which broke the European connection in 1936–1937 and ushered in tighter management and an "individual Shiseido style." The third breakpoint occurred at the end of the postwar era, when Shiseido teamed up with Serge Lutens of France in 1964 to reenter Western markets with the creation of the Zen product line and photographic/TV-based advertising.

Organizational breakpoints seem to fall into two general categories. In my experience, companies that miss an industry shift to a more standardized competitive approach invariably have cost control problems; they typically are advised to tighten up their organizations. Those that miss the industry's divergence to a more differentiated competitive approach invariably have problems keeping up with the market, being more innovative or entrepreneurial; they are advised to loosen up their organizations.

This simplified classification is consistent with Larry Greiner's well-known argument that companies go through a series of revolutions that mark the transitions between the classic forms of corporate organization: organic, functional, divisional, matrix, and network (see Exhibit 1-5).[9] Of these, the organic, divisional, and network forms are relatively loose, whereas the functional and matrix forms are tighter. Greiner has been criticized because companies do not necessarily all go through the same sequence of restructurings, nor are the organizational forms necessarily pure, nor the changes always revolutionary and discontinuous. Indeed, organizations never repeat their history; an organic organization is quite different from a divisional one. Nevertheless, what matters is that restructurings often are discontinuous, and many of the transitions display similar features that are useful for the description of organizational shifts.

A single organizational breakpoint may contain a mix of tightening and loosening dimensions. The survivors of the collapse of the straw braid market not only tightened up their remaining braid operations, but more important, made their organizational style loose enough to adopt a new strategic direction. Georges Meyer was unable to loosen up its style and adopt a new direction; as a result, it was forced into the ultimate loosening breakpoint, the dissolution of its manufacturing operation.

Exhibit 1–5 **Organizational Shifts (Simplified View)**

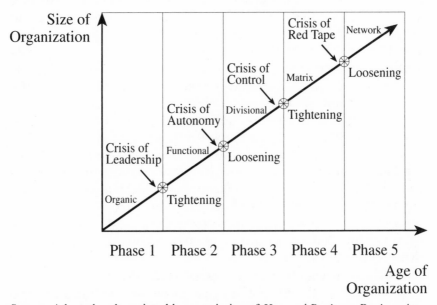

Source: Adapted and reprinted by permission of *Harvard Business Review.* An exhibit from Larry E. Greiner, "Evolution and Revolution as Organizations Grow," *Harvard Business Review* (July/August 1972), p. 41. Copyright © 1972 by the President and Fellows of Harvard College; all rights reserved.

BREAKPOINTS VERSUS TURNING POINTS

How sharp must the shifts be to qualify as discontinuous? To qualify as a breakpoint, the change should be sudden and radical, that is, rapid and fundamental in nature: it should create a noticeable break in the performance trend and break the rules of the competitive or organizational game, making recent experience useless.

However, radical change in a company's position may occur gradually over time. Change that is gradual and radical constitutes a turning point. For example, Asahi's market share dropped continually throughout the 1960s before stabilizing gradually in the 1970s (see Exhibit 1-3). The cumulative effect of such change can be quite radical, but Asahi's was not sudden enough to qualify as a discontinuity. Instead, it took the form of a turning point. In sum, turning points are gradual and incremental, whereas breakpoints are sudden and sharp. Both are forms of radical change.

To first movers, a change that they create in the competitive game seems gradual. It appears to be a turning point. To followers, those companies that only wake up later on in response to the cumulative effect, the same change looks sharp and discontinuous, more like a breakpoint. When one or more of the change characteristics described in this chapter occur within a period of one year, or possibly two, casual observation suggests that most followers regard these transitions as breakpoints.

In lower-tech industries like beer and cosmetics, breakpoints may be relatively few and far between. In these industries, product and brand life cycles may be quite long, supporting long periods of continuity. Shiseido's first cosmetic product, Eudermine, a skin lotion with a distinctive wine-red color and bottle design, is still on sale ninety years after its introduction. In high-tech industries like consumer electronics and computers, technological change is more rapid, product life cycles are much shorter, and breakpoints are correspondingly more frequent.

Performance shifts and behavioral shifts usually do not occur at the same time. Breakpoints caused by outside factors affect the performance of an industry or a company before its behavior changes. Thus, the plunging sales in the straw braid industry preceded the shifts in competitive strategy and behavior. Conversely, breakpoints that are initiated by players within the system will show up in behavioral shifts first, before performance shifts. The introduction of dry beer by Asahi was a change in competitive behavior which preceded the shifts in market share and other performance measures.

The important point is to identify potentially discontinuous change as early as possible. But because the features of a breakpoint, shifts in performance, for example, are only apparent after the breakpoint has occurred, one must be sensitive to the underlying forces, forces that have been gathering momentum, often, as we shall see, over a long period.

KEYS TO PRACTICE: DESCRIBING BREAKPOINTS

1. Describe the change in the industry or company performance. Select key measures of performance and find a way of graphing the performance that most simply reflects what is happening.
2. When you see a shift in performance, the way to tell if it is a random fluctuation or a genuine breakpoint is to look for an

accompanying shift in the rules of the competitive or organizational game. For example, is the industry experiencing rejuvenation with a competitive shift toward improving the value
of the product offering, or standardization with a competitive
shift toward rationalization and cost reduction? (The former
often shows up in the increasing problems that firms have
keeping up with the market, whereas the latter is associated
with problems of cost control.)

3. Monitor the behavior of the key players in the system with
special attention to whether they are initiating or reacting to
change. Behavior changes lead performance shifts when the
breakpoint is being driven by internal forces, whereas behavior lags behind performance when the breakpoint is driven by
external forces.

CHAPTER 2

Identifying Forces
of Change

D OLLAR SHIPMENTS in the U.S. construction
machinery industry had been growing,
albeit with two minor interruptions, for more than a decade. Major
players predicted ongoing growth. Then, in 1982, oil prices broke
and the Saudi market for construction equipment collapsed. U.S.
shipments in dollars dropped by more than 35 percent.[1] Among
others, Caterpillar, the largest competitor with more than 50 percent of the U.S. market, reported its first loss in half a century.

Despite the predictions of ongoing growth, there had been
signs of excess capacity in the industry for some time. The retail
sales index for construction machinery, adjusted for seasonality
and inflation, had been declining steadily since mid-1979. Following the completion of the interstate highway program and most
major airports, heavy construction spending in the United States
had been dropping since 1970. Housing starts had also been dropping since 1979 under the impact of rising inflation and interest
rates. The prime interest rate after a low of 3.5 percent in 1973 was
at 21 percent in the autumn of 1981.

Construction machinery sales were being sustained by spending on mining plant/equipment and exports to the Middle East,
both of which had been growing without major interruption since
the early 1970s. The oil countries were importing some 6,000
machines annually. However, many of them were lying idle. When
the U.S. Federal Reserve applied a monetary squeeze to control
inflation, the American economy went into recession. Instead of

counterbalancing the drop in American demand, the Middle East bubble burst as well, throwing many competitors into disarray.

Yet, with the assistance of rapid-falling interest rates and oil prices, the U.S. economy quickly turned around. By 1984, shipments of construction machinery were again expanding. In addition, the yen began to rise against the dollar. Komatsu was forced to increase its North American prices by 40 percent. Caterpillar, which had begun to sell into Japan at lower prices, recovered both financially and in terms of market share. Komatsu replaced its chief executive.

As the decade ended, the economic cycle began to repeat itself. The U.S. economy, especially housing and construction, was weakening again. In a replay of the early 1980s, Caterpillar and the other smaller U.S. manufacturers were under pricing pressure from a rejuvenated Komatsu in the early 1990s. Instead of having learned from their experience, the U.S. competitors were now under even more intense cost pressure.

Yet, both the unexpected collapse of construction machinery sales in 1982 and the repeating economic cycle in 1990 were sufficiently common patterns of change for an alert management to have identified them far sooner. Not in a complex statistical or econometric fashion, but in a common-sense way that incorporates both numerical and qualitative data. Notwithstanding the dubious merit of commentary after the event, it is clear that there were qualitative and numerical signs that should have raised a red flag about the cyclical weakening of support for construction machinery sales, as well as the rebound later on.

What should be done is to identify the telltale signs associated with the forces of change in the business environment. The strength of a change force shows up in the rate of change it creates in the environment. Even though history never repeats itself exactly, forces of change are associated with recurring patterns that reflect different rates of change.

This chapter describes the features of the more common patterns:

- Trends and trajectories
- Turning points, stimuli, and limits
- Cycles and recurring turning points

These are listed according to the strength of the related force of change. Trends represent forces of change to the extent that they change the business environment. Emerging or declining trends are typically weak, whereas growing or mature trends are strong. A turning point (or breakpoint) shows up as a shift in the direction of a trend, up or down, which corresponds to a strong force of change. Cycles comprise major turning points, at irregular intervals, that involve reversals in the direction of trends, which makes the force of change even greater. Fortunately, as we shall see, there is a basic pattern in cyclical phenomena which can be used to anticipate cyclical turning points.

TRENDS AND TRAJECTORIES

Existing trends are important, because playing out their implications is one of the best guides to the future. Peter Drucker, for one, says that he does not try to forecast the future, but he does take the consequences of existing trends very seriously. The increasing strain on the natural environment is a trend that cannot be reversed overnight, so its implications will be with us for many years to come. Similarly, ever wider diffusion of microprocessor technology has implications for innovation in many industries. Or, on a shorter time scale within one industry, a declining cost curve has pricing implications for all competitors.

Unfortunately, executives, caught up in the maelstrom of daily events, often have difficulty responding to the potential impact of otherwise obvious trends. In the construction machinery industry, the falling heavy construction and housing markets were a fact well before the Saudi market collapsed. Even if the latter hadn't occurred, existing trends indicated that business could not continue as usual.

To internalize the potential impact of trends, it is vital that top management in particular become actively involved in continually scanning the environment. In most cases, it is not enough to read reports from the planning department. Rarely do critical reports get the attention they deserve, and even if they do, important reports are difficult to recognize as such if one hasn't been monitoring continually the development of critical factors in the environment. As Fred Gluck, a McKinsey director, put it: "Decision making based on somebody else's analysis of the situation is simply too risky and can't lead to bold initiative." The place to start scanning is with the drivers of demand in the main segments of the business,[2] and with the factors affecting behavior on the supply side among the competitors, in the resource supply chain and distribution channels, and among the company's stakeholders.

In the construction machinery business, for example, the main segments are heavy construction, housing, and mining. Among the main drivers are GNP growth, both domestic and international, interest rates, government spending on infrastructure, and mineral commodity prices. On the supply side, critical factors include technological developments, new entrants often encouraged by foreign exchange fluctuations and local conditions overseas, the impact of a shifting demand mix on distribution channels, the attitude of labor unions, the investment community, and the quality of R&D, engineering, and other key human resources.

Technology trends are often difficult to describe for the uninitiated and need extra attention. Richard Nelson and Sidney Winter suggest the use of "natural trajectories" as a guide.[3] Natural trajectories and their implications are especially relevant in high-tech industries such as telecommunications. For forty years after their invention in 1880 telephone switches were operated by human operators. Then in 1920 mechanical switches were introduced which reduced the labor content to 50 percent; in 1940, electromechanical switches reduced the labor content to 25 percent; in the 1960s, with analog switches the labor content dropped further; until the 1980s when with integrated circuit switching the labor content was 5 percent. Meanwhile the development cost rose from $10 million for electromechanical switches in the 1940s to $1 billion for digital switches in the 1980s. If this trend continues, only larger and larger industrial groupings will be able to compete in the industry during the 1990s.[4]

When incorporated into a package of benefits for the customer, the overall trajectory of technology and product development is always toward more benefits and value for the customer at lower real cost, "more bang for the buck." This is quite apparent when successive technologies are viewed from a distance. The long-term effect is that the speed and comfort of transportation have increased both qualitatively and quantitatively with the successive arrival of the railroad, automobile, and aircraft, whereas the real cost has declined significantly. On a shorter time scale, in the PC market, successive rounds of product development and cost reduction have provided increasing value at lower cost to the customer (see Exhibit 1-2).

For the future of construction machinery, an ad hoc survey of one company's middle managers suggested that the following, already existing trends would have an impact on the industry in the 1990s:

On the demand side:

Declining raw material and energy content of industrial output in the developed countries;

Increasing economic weakness of third world countries;

Gradual conversion of Eastern Europe into viable market economies;

Continuing growth in Southeast Asia;

Reconstruction after the Persian Gulf War; and

Globalization and trading blocs.

On the supply side:

More customized, computer-assisted equipment;

Increasing flexibility, speed, and reliability of production methods;

Continual cost reduction;

New entrants from Southeast Asia;

Declining relative quality of U.S. labor force;

Volatility of oil and foreign exchange markets; and

Organizational subcontracting and alliances.

The question was which of these trends would dominate. Much of the answer depends on how long they persist and whether they increase or decrease in intensity.

TURNING POINTS, STIMULI, AND LIMITS

Changes in the direction of a trend can be either up, corresponding to increasing intensity or growth of the trend, or down, corresponding to less intensity or growth. The leading indicators of a potential upturn typically include new stimuli that replace or augment the basic drivers behind the trend. The indicators of a potential downturn include limits that inhibit or dampen the trend drivers.

Stimuli

The stimuli of an upturn take many different forms:

• Innovation in all its guises, but especially in new technology or products, is the most frequent and powerful stimulator of output trends.

- Emergence of a dominant design or standard product offering makes it possible to shift to much larger output.
- Specialization/customization opens up new and different market segments.
- Deregulation unleashes the stimulus of free competition.
- New management or a new approach may usher in a more dynamic organization.

Often more than one stimulus is involved at a time. New technology, or products, provide the stimulus for many upturns in tandem with evolving market needs. In the computer industry, new products have been introduced repeatedly against a background of increasing customer dissatisfaction with the real benefits provided by existing systems and an inclination to experiment rather than accept the industry's party line. It is worth recalling the number of discontinuities that IBM stimulated with successive generations of mainframe computers, reflecting the transitions from the vacuum tube to the transistor, and improvements in integrated circuits, each of which responded to growing client needs. DEC's minicomputer stimulated a breakpoint by allowing users to do most of their data processing in their own departments. Apple created the personal computer breakpoint by tapping independent software development to fill the latent need for customized data processing on the end-user's desk. In the 1980s, DEC and others tried to capitalize on their experience in distributed data processing to introduce networking that met the desire to link disparate systems together. And, in an otherwise depressed computer industry during the early 1990s, Toshiba and Compaq kept the trend toward individual computing afloat with their laptops and portables.

Limits

The limits that presage a downturn also come in a variety of forms:

- Natural laws of the sciences that put a physical limit on a trend.[5]
- Carrying capacity/resource exhaustion.
- Saturation of markets.
- Negative feedback effects that undermine growth.

- Underinvestment that cuts off growth.
- Fragmentation and chaos in markets.

In the construction equipment industry several change forces limiting sales growth reinforced one another in 1981: the excess industry capacity, the decline in heavy construction and housing, the rising interest rates, the onset of a domestic recession. Yet, imports by oil countries and the lack of a domestic U.S. recession were keeping demand up. The ultimate limit was the finite size of the Middle Eastern market. When it was reached, industry sales collapsed.

Combined Limits and Stimuli

The presence of stimuli and limits pointing in the same direction sometimes makes it easier to identify a potential turning point or breakpoint, especially when new stimuli replace old limits. The most common example is the transition from one technology development curve to another.

The limits to a technology flatten its growth curve out at the top. The resulting slower growth and lower returns make investment in alternative technologies attractive. The higher potential return on alternative technologies increases the chances of a jump to a new generation of technology. Gerhard Mensch studied the times when 112 major technological innovations were commercialized. He found that many were bunched in the middle of major world depressions. The findings confirm the notion that major technology shifts often have their origin in the years of weak returns, years that reflect both the end of the existing generation of technology and the higher potential returns associated with new technology.[6]

Competitive behavior during an industry life cycle also provides examples of how limits and stimuli may combine to create a turning point. The limits become increasingly apparent, for example, before competitive behavior shifts away from value competition. The return to product enhancement and customization declines. The offerings of competitors in the marketplace begin to look alike. Customers are less and less willing to pay for purely perceived value. At the same time, the stimuli for a shift toward more cost-based competition begin to make themselves felt. The convergence of the products favors the development of a dominant design which can be used to standardize the production delivery and service process. A broad potential market emerges sharing an implicit consensus about the basic features of a standard product offering.

The development of the generic drugs business in the pharmaceutical industry of the 1980s illustrates this interplay between limits and stimuli. For some time fewer and fewer new products were being launched, despite higher R&D spending. The cost of bringing a new product to the market increased, up to $100 million, while the process itself slowed to an average of ten years. Average volume growth for pharmaceuticals decreased from 15 percent in the 1970s to about 5 percent in the 1980s. In terms of stimuli for generics, there was growing worldwide political pressure for lower drug prices: in the United Kingdom, for example, profit ceilings had been set; in Japan, prices had already been submitted to an average 50 percent decrease. Moreover, the upcoming expiration of many major patents was opening the door for generics. In the United States, FDA approval had been greatly facilitated by the Waxman bill, while the increasing older population created more demand for cheaper medicine. The limits on the existing business and the stimuli in the direction of generics provided a strong signal about a possible major turning point in the pharmaceutical industry.[7]

CYCLES AND RECURRING TURNING POINTS

A cyclical perspective on human affairs can be very useful for identifying the patterns that link turning points together. Yet, a cyclical view comes more naturally to executives in the East. Sony, for example, talks about a twenty-five-year cycle in audio technology, beginning with the phonograph in 1875, followed by the gramophone in 1900, the electrophone in 1924, the LP stereo in the early 1950s, and the CD player in the late 1970s. As Heitaro Nakajima, a former managing director of Sony, put it: "This leads us to suspect that the next major revolution will take place in the beginning of the 21st century. And what will that be? My personal guess is that it will probably be an all solid state recorder using semiconductor memories. It might be called a 'Silicon Recorder.'"

Managers in the East often interpret cycles as part of Tao, a process of continual flow and change. Its principal characteristic is ceaseless cyclical motion, the ultimate essence of reality in Chinese philosophy. The yin and the yang are two phases or states that set the limits for the cycles of change in the Tao: "The yang having reached its climax retreats in favor of the yin; the yin having reached its climax retreats in favor of the yang." Although there are many interpretations, the yin can be seen as cooperative, supportive, partial to collective effort. The yang is competitive, aggressive, more individualistic. According to the ancient *Book of Changes,* all of reality including business is in a constant state of tension, reflecting a dynamic interplay between these polar opposites.[8]

In the language we have been using, cyclical change involves repeated turning points between opposing poles of behavior. The limits inherent in too much of one behavior create the opening for stimuli supporting the opposite type of behavior. Cycles incorporating the tension between opposing behaviors crop up everywhere, on the socio-political level, and the economic, industry, corporate, and business unit levels. Sensitivity to the characteristics of typical cycles, like the sensitivity to stimuli and limits, is key to identifying the forces of change as early as possible.

Militating against the notion of cycles, however, is a deeply ingrained Western belief in some form of continuing progress. This belief has a long pedigree going back to Jacob's dream of a ladder that reaches up to the heavens. The theme was picked up by the Christian philosophers such as Augustine who used examples from the Old Testament. And in the Greek and Roman Empires good was shown to triumph over evil.[9] The philosophers of the eighteenth-century Enlightenment went further and fashioned the concept of freedom, a belief in progress, and above all a commitment to the scientific method. Indeed, the accomplishments of science, and especially its technological and economic spin-offs, are visible signs of continuing progress. Western economists, moreover, emphasize the notion of market equilibrium, the idea that deviations will be cut short by competitive forces which drive everything back to equilibrium. Nothing could be more foreign to the ideology of progressive equilibrium than the notion of repetitive turning points and cycles.

The importance of cycles for identifying the evolution of change forces over time, in the face of the widespread belief in continuing progress, makes it worthwhile to consider the features that are common to some typical cycles so that they can be recognized more quickly. Analogues to Darwin's evolutionary cycle of random mutation and natural selection are especially interesting.

In human organizations (markets and hierarchies) the evolutionary cycle corresponds to variety creation on the one hand, and efficient use of scarce resources on the other. This cycle provides a simple framework for identifying patterns of change in several arenas. We begin with examples in the socio-political arena and gradually narrow in to the organization of the firm.

Socio-political Cycles

The first step is to identify the opposing poles of behavior that make up the cycle. Applying the cyclical view to the socio-political sphere, numerous pairs of opposing behaviors come to mind:

Individualism versus group orientation

Progressive versus conservative

Democratic versus dictatorial

Left wing versus right wing

To illustrate the evolutionary tension between variety creation and efficient use of scarce resources, we shall use the tension between individualism and group orientation. On one side is the individualist approach to socio-political affairs. On the other is the group- or community-oriented approach. Both reflect the pursuit of freedom, albeit in different, yet complementary, ways. Individualism reflects the yang tendency, an emphasis on freedom of choice, competition, a decentralized governance structure. It generates the variety that is the basis of evolutionary mutation. The group orientation embodies the yin view, an emphasis on freedom from want, by minimizing threats to survival through group effort and the protective authority of the state. This behavior provides the cohesion needed to prevail in the face of societal problems. Many variants of the two exist in dynamic tension with one another, often masked by an ideology of the "right" or the "left." An extreme version of one often encourages an extreme version of the other.

Two famous revolutions, the French and the Russian, created violent rebellions against corrupt state control. These abrupt loosenings of authority heralded brief periods of anarchic individualism. Soon they were followed by sharp tightening and restoration of a new form of collectivism, with Napoleon and Lenin respectively at the helm. The twentieth century in particular has been marked by the abrupt rise and fall of dictators and generals, accompanied by sharp shifts between individualism and collectivism. In the late 1980s, the collectivism introduced by Lenin reached its economic limits, resulting in a sharp turning point back in the direction of socio-economic individualism throughout much of the Communist world, only to be followed in the early 1990s by signs of a conservative backlash. As a result, large corporations have been struggling to loosen up their organizations to take advantage of the emerging opportunities in Eastern Europe, while adapting their control systems to deal with the risk.

American political turning points have been milder than those of the Old World. Being relatively nonideological compared to their European counterparts, the changing of the guard between Democratic and Republican presidents in the United States has relatively little impact, because the Congress is not necessarily loyal to the president. American decentralization is led by the Republicans, who believe in a reassertion of competitive individualism and greater economic freedom. The restoration of a more Democratic view symbolizes a return to the cooperative power of the state as a vehicle for reform. Looking at the U.S. political scene, Paul Samuelson found six alternating periods of conservative individualism and reformist cooperation.[10] The conservative competitive periods correlate with higher economic growth and less social cohesion, the reformist cooperative periods with low growth and more social cohesion. The Reagan era, with higher growth, a fraying social fabric, and a return to conservative ideals, fits the pattern.

The deregulation of the U.S. airline industry is an example of how a socio-political turning point can trigger several industry discontinuities. The free-market ideology of Reagan led directly to the deregulation of the airline industry, which in turn spawned numerous new competitors and a growing variety of different flight offerings to the consumer. People's Express was one of the more flamboyant incarnations of the new competitive behavior. But the trend toward differentiation floundered on the limits imposed by a saturating market and rising costs. The demise of People's Express and then Pan American symbolized the turning point back toward competition based on disciplined efficiency and streamlined operations. This trend was stimulated in the early 1990s by a worldwide recession which forced airlines to search for economies of scale in alliances and mergers; for example, Swissair's links with Delta, SAS, and Singapore Airlines.

In all the socio-political examples, two complementary turning points stand out which represent the extremes of the political cycle; each signals a shift from one of the two basic socio-political tendencies to the other. They are

Divergence and loosening of authority, marking a turning point away from a group orientation toward more individualism; and

Convergence and tightening of authority, marking a turning point away from individualism toward more of a group orientation.

These shifts embrace a whole range from relatively smooth transitions that characterize turning points to the discontinuous change that epitomizes breakpoints. The lesson here is that the forces of political change are much easier to identify if they are stripped of their ideological content and interpreted in terms of an imperfect search for balance over time between the two opposing poles of a cyclical process.

Economic Cycles

Cyclical economic change is manifest all the time in the analysis of the business cycle. Alternating periods of expansion and contraction, higher and lower real-growth rates, can be clearly demarcated by business economists, albeit after the fact. Although these business cycles have been attributed to innumerable causes ranging from sunspots to psychology, mainstream economists point to two general explanations.

First, there are the unanticipated changes in the behavior of government, business, or consumers. Unexpected monetary and fiscal policy moves on the part of government cause fluctuations in business and consumer behavior. Businessmen commit forecasting errors and then over- or underinvest in the economy. Consumers shift their demand and tastes, causing periodic ripple effects in the economy.

Second, inflexible prices prevent the markets from replacing scarce resources or using surplus resources. When prices are sticky, temporary imbalances don't get smoothed out. Rather they accumulate, thereby aggravating the surplus or deficit. The most dramatic recent examples were triggered by commodity shocks like the oil crises which resulted when oil prices shifted in response to imbalances between demand and supply.

Whatever the particular cause, cyclical fluctuations between expansion and contraction are an accepted fact of economic life.

They can be characterized in terms of two related turning points:

Divergence away from existing economic activity toward greater expenditure, expansion, and new growth opportunities; and

Convergence around existing economic activity, toward less expenditure, contraction, and lower growth.

Divergence occurs in the trough of the business cycle, where the contraction has run its course. Managers, seeing the strengthening in demand relative to supply, begin to find opportunities for branching out. Convergence takes place at the peak of the cycle, when a perceived shortage of some input, for example, causes key economic actors to cut back their plans for expansion and, instead, consolidate existing activities.

A full economic cycle is apparent in the recent history of the U.S. construction machinery industry. Both the 1982 and 1990 downturns were preceded by rising interest rates and weakness in the construction and housing markets. Even though it is difficult to predict when an actual turning point will occur, the limits to the upswing were readily apparent in both cases. These red flags suggest that competitors should have been alert for a cyclical shift in the economic rules of the game. Yet, on both occasions, leading players were surprised by the downturn.

In addition to shorter-term economic cycles, some economists see much longer cycles of fifty to sixty years, associated with major depressions like that of the 1930s. Looking at commodity prices, bond prices, wages, and bank liabilities, the controversial Russian economist Nikolai Kondratiev identified three great depressions, in the 1820s, 1870s, and 1930s.[11] Stalin banished Kondratiev to Siberia because his theory did not fit the official Communist doctrine on the ultimate collapse of capitalism. But Kondratiev was more right than wrong, because the market economies recovered strongly after the Great Depression. He also would have anticipated the great commodity price decline in the early 1980s, not to mention the final collapse of the Communist command economies.

Apart from prices, Kondratiev associated "other empirical patterns" with his long waves: an increase in the number of technical inventions during the two decades before a long upswing; accentuated short-term cycles with longer upswings when the long cycle is rising; more social change during the "rising wave of a long cycle"; longer downswings when the long cycle is declining; and a long agricultural depression during the downswing. Although some of this theory may be no more than the output of a creative mind, it is remarkable how closely these patterns fit recent history.

The automobile industry, for example, was founded at the beginning of the Kondratiev cycle that began in the 1880s. The emergence of the industry saw the appearance of hundreds of small companies making automobiles—Switzerland alone had several of them. But few survived the major turning point toward efficiency which marked the top of the cycle, a turning point that gave birth to Ford's assembly line production of the Model T. The end of the Kondratiev cycle was marked by the Great Depression of the 1930s. It almost saw the end of Ford Motor Co. as well. Henry Ford I refused to believe the shift in competitive behavior that accompanied the emergence of a new Kondratiev cycle, the differentiation of styles and colors that led to the founding of General Motors. Ford had to be removed from the board before his company could belatedly adapt to the new conditions. The top of the Kondratiev cycle in the 1960s again saw a shift toward the streamlining of production with the emergence of Toyota, Nissan, and Honda, a shift that put the American and European industries into a defensive position which has continued to this day.

Mainstream economic theory has little to say about long waves. Systematic long-run fluctuations don't exist, and there is a deathly silence about the possibility of breakpoints in the market environment. In terms of classical economic theory, the sustained growth over the past sixty years is indeed miraculous. Only half of it can be explained by an increased supply of the traditional economic variables: capital, labor, and land, including the impact of education. The other half is attributed to technological innovation, about which classical economics has little, if anything, to say. Technology is a so-called exogenous factor, a "deus ex machina."

Technology Cycles

Those who believe in long economic waves attribute them to bursts of technological innovation. Long-run economic growth seems to follow periods of intense innovation. A group of new technologies gives rise to a cluster of new industries which provide the engine of long-term growth, until they run out of steam. Joseph Schumpeter, the Austrian economist who was eclipsed by John Maynard Keynes in the 1930s, regarded innovation, the commercialization

of inventions, as the basic force behind capitalist market economies:

> The fundamental impulse that sets and keeps the capitalist engine
> in motion comes from the new consumers' goods, the new meth-
> ods of production or transportation, the new markets, the new
> forms of industrial organization that capitalist enterprise creates.[12]

Innovation, according to Schumpeter, is discontinuous. "Innovations appear, if at all, discontinuously in groups or swarms."
He claimed that this periodic bunching of innovations is caused by
the scarcity of entrepreneurial talent and the need for innovations
to feed off one another. Long waves, according to Schumpeter, are
characterized by a whole set of industries that use the same basic
technological innovations on the supply side and possibly complement one another on the demand side. Thus, the microprocessor
couples computers and telecommunications with a host of industries like banking, consumer electronics, transportation, machine
tools, and robotics. To take advantage of the new technologies,
existing industries have to regroup. While this diffusion and
absorption process continues, a long upswing underpins the
shorter economic cycles.

As we have noted already, the pace of innovation is stimulated
by economic depression. Good and easy times reduce innovative
activity: the relative return on new ventures is too low and the risk
of loss too high. The economic success of the microprocessor takes
attention away from other basic innovations that may be waiting in
the wings; their time will come only when the microprocessor wave
runs out of growth possibilities. When times are bad, the pressure
of economic survival forces people to break out of old ways. The
risk is low and there is little to lose.

The agricultural depression before the first industrial revolution stimulated the commercialization of textiles, iron, and steam
power in England and Scotland. The depression of 1815–1825, in
turn, saw the emergence of steel and the railroads which opened
up continental Europe and North America. During the depression
from 1870 to 1885, electricity, the automobile, and chemicals got
their start with the birth of such famous names as Daimler and
Benz, Hoechst, and Philips Gloeilampenfabriken. During the Great
Depression of the 1930s, aircraft, electronics, and petrochemicals
began to take off. The stagflation of the 1970s spawned the prolific
microprocessor, the beginning of a genetic engineering revolu-

tion, the commercialization of the laser, and new materials like ceramics.

Although the exact timing of these innovations is controversial, the important point is that depression-driven innovation provides the beginning of long-run, technology-driven industry cycles. The entrepreneurial phase is followed by the diffusion of the innovations throughout related industries. This stimulates growth in many other existing industries. Eventually, the diffusion process runs out of steam and the long-run industry growth rate peaks. Competition increases in the decades ahead and the growth rate slows. Ultimately, the leading industries slide into a long stagflation, or depression, during which a new wave of innovations is born.

The turning points that make up a technology cycle can be characterized in the following way:

Divergence of competitive behavior stimulated by the emergence of a new technology, based on widespread commercialization of an invention, or cluster of inventions, often accompanied by a swarm of entrepreneurs; and

Convergence around the existing technology that reflects the exhaustion and drying up of potential improvements to the technology, accompanied by the saturation of possible end-uses, marking the high point in the development of the technology.

From an executive point of view, these technology-related turning points are critical. Well-managed companies can deal with most short-term economic cycles by adjusting their growth and output. Turning points in the basic use of technology, however, mark the need for sharp changes in competitive behavior.

Competitive Cycles

It is in individual markets that the attributes of the product offerings supplied by competitors meet customer demands. Supply and demand evolve together in symbiosis, first one and then the other driving the process. The interplay between supply and demand creates competitive turning points and breakpoints. Although the government, the economy, or technology may play a role, competitive turning points are driven primarily by the behavior of competitors. This shows up most clearly in the service sector, where technology is less intrusive.

In the 1950s, the U.S. fast-food industry was made up exclusively of drive-in restaurants. Curb service was slow and the food was expensive. The industry was dominated by small players with no more than a few restaurants. The McDonald brothers had a single hamburger stand in San Bernadino, California. Then, in 1961, Ray Kroc, with a license to run a clone of the McDonalds' operation in Chicago, had the insight to buy them out and standardize the operation. The standardization of the hamburger stand triggered the turning point that led to the modern fast-food industry.

Standardized fast hamburger outlets sprouted up all over the country, aided by the stimulus of the population drift toward outlying metropolitan areas. Many competitors entered the market. The growth only subsided in the late 1970s, when other types of fast food began to capture a growing share of the fast-food dollar. The pressure on market share led to price wars. With the lowest-cost quality hamburgers, McDonald's usually emerged as the winner.

To break out of the cost competition, the large chains initiated a turning point in the direction of higher perceived value. New products were added and perceptions enhanced with strong advertising. To compete with other restaurants, the hamburger menu was expanded to include chicken, ham and cheese sandwiches, and so on, as well as breakfast and expanded dinner menus.

However, this enhancement move on the part of the hamburger chains soon ran into competition from the other fast-food restaurants (budget steakhouses, chicken, pizza, roast beef, seafood, Mexican). In addition, lower-price, full-service restaurants reduced their prices, forcing the fast-food chains to add service in the form of attractive dining facilities. As a result, the differentiation between the various restaurant types began to break down.[13] The increasing convergence in the low-price restaurant industry has initiated another turning point back toward renewed price competition. Value pricing is hot. Although menus are growing ever more diverse, they are being delivered by streamlined business systems that, apart from the ambiance of the outlets, are beginning to look more and more alike.

This example and the discussion of competitive shifts in Chapter 1 suggest the two basic types of turning point that make up competitive cycles:

> Divergence away from an existing product or business system standard, corresponding to a shift in competitive emphasis from delivered cost to perceived value competition; and

Convergence around a product, or business system standard, corresponding to a shift in the opposite direction from perceived value to delivered cost competition.

Sensitivity to these turning points can go a long way toward facilitating the early identification of the forces for change implicit in the competitive cycle.

Organizational Cycles

The path traced out by a company during its life cycle depends heavily on its industry environment.[14] In highly complex environments with little scarcity of resources, where a lot of innovation is required, companies can play out their life cycle with a decentralized, organic structure. By contrast, regulated utilities, facing relatively simple environments with abundant resources, can survive with a bureaucratic organization. Mining companies, with scarce resources but relatively uncomplicated markets, can manage with a mechanistic approach. In most global industries today, however, companies striving for excellence have to obtain high levels of both innovation and efficiency. They want to be as professionally managed as possible.

Unfortunately, reality mostly falls far short of the ideal. Over time, business organizations embody varying combinations of different behaviors and structures:

Authoritarian versus participative

Centralized versus decentralized

Concentrated versus diversified

Integrated versus differentiated

For survival and progress, however, two overall behaviors are essential: innovation and efficiency. Innovation is needed to cope with value competition in the environment. It creates the variety of possibilities and choices for adaptation to a shifting environment. Efficiency cuts total resource costs and enhances competitive position.

Whatever the industry, organizations oscillate between centralization and decentralization as they alternately pursue efficiency and innovation. When the emphasis is on enhancing adaptability through innovation, the company needs looser decision making and delegation of authority and responsibility to those on the front line, as in the organic, divisional, and network models. When the emphasis is on efficiency, as in the functional and strong headquarters models, the idea is to tighten decision making in order to enhance coordination. Business organizations also cycle between product line diversification and consolidation as they adapt to the expansion and contraction phases of the economic cycle. The competitive and economic cycles are reflected often in organizational cycles.

Each of the typical organizational turning points between innovation and efficiency, or between expansion and contraction, can be classified as either a divergent loosening or convergent tightening move:

> Divergence from structured, centralized, or coordinated organization and decision making toward a more unstructured, decentralized approach, designed to deal with environmental change and complexity by enhancing innovativeness; and

> Convergence from unstructured, decentralized, or autonomous organization and decision making toward a more centralized or coordinated approach, designed to economize on scarce resources by improving efficiency.

To anticipate organizational discontinuities requires sensitivity to the particular balance between convergence and divergence needed for adaptation to the outside world. Too much of one often provokes an overreaction in the opposite direction. Such overshooting may result in an alternating sequence of convergent and divergent organizational moves.

Basic Pattern in Cyclical Phenomena

The key to isolating strong forces of change is clearly the ability to anticipate cyclical turning points. Anticipating a turning point requires seeing the limits and stimuli that provoke it. Here the recognition of cyclical patterns is central, because cycles suggest the kinds of limits and stimuli to watch out for.

The behaviors of the main players can be used as leading indicators of cycles.[15] The evolutionary logic of the cycles described in this chapter suggests an underlying pattern of cyclical behavior: the turning points of the three market-related cycles (the economic, technology, and competitive cycles) are similar. All involve either convergence or divergence. The turning points of the hierarchy-related cycles (the socio-political and organizational cycles) also involve organizational convergence or divergence.

The basic pattern involved in all of these cycles is summarized in Exhibit 2-1.

EXHIBIT 2–1 **Basic Pattern in Cyclical Phenomena**

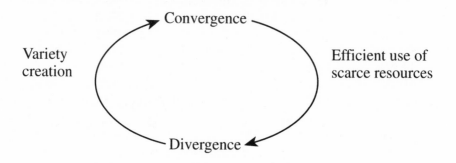

The key to identifying the turning points is to realize that if the industry or firm is presently in a period of divergence, the next turn of the cycle will bring convergence and vice versa. Thus, if you are in a divergent mode, focus on the indicators of emerging convergent forces and vice versa, since the next turn of the cycle will bring on the other type of change, supplanting the one prevailing now.

Experienced players normally have little difficulty describing the behavior that precedes common turning points: the behavior reflects an improved ability to manage scarce resources on the one hand (efficiency, price competition, technology diffusion, economic consolidation, socio-political cooperation), and on the other hand, the creation of greater variety (innovation, value competition, technology development, economic expansion, socio-political individualism). As an illustration, the typical behavior of industry change agents prior to competitive convergence (that often results in a price war) and competitive divergence (that often leads to a new product breakthrough) is outlined below.

Leading indicators of convergence
- Customers: the segmentation between customer groups looks increasingly artificial and starts to break down.
- Competitors: convergence is visible in increasingly similar products, service, and image.
- Potential competitors: very few, if any, new entrants on the horizon.
- Supply chain: suppliers and resources cannot easily be used as a source of competitive advantage.

- Channels: the bargaining power in the industry typically shifts downstream to the distribution channels.

Today these behavior patterns often span the globe. A classic vignette of competitors crowding one another is provided by the global market for incandescent light tubes. With 35 percent of world market share and the number-one position in Europe and the Far East, the Philips Lighting Division turned its sights on the Americas, where in the mid-1980s it was second in market share behind General Electric. Philips decided to attack by lowering the price umbrella on standard, commodity incandescent light tubes in the United States. Jack Welch, the CEO of General Electric, immediately flew in his private jet to Eindhoven in the Netherlands. There he told Van der Klugt, the Philips chief executive, that "market share is not negotiable."

Philips continued its American campaign. Soon after, the first signals of GE's counterattack were picked up by Philips Lighting's central information unit, which had sent out an alert for possible General Electric activity to the whole field sales force. General Electric Lighting, which had no presence in Europe, began advertising in Dublin for salespeople. Then the top Philips sales representative in Portugal received an offer to head up the new General Electric Lighting Division in that country. Meanwhile in Athens, Philips learned from one of its hotel clients that General Electric Lighting was organizing its first European Division meeting. With little to differentiate the products of the two companies, the increasing convergence of the General Electric and Philips product markets indicated that a price war was imminent in the European theater of the global incandescent market. For European competitors with high cost structures, the battle between GE and Philips was virtually certain to become a strong force of change.

Leading indicators of divergence
- Customers: an increasingly saturated market for the standardized commodity product reflects itself in declining growth rates.
- Competitors: declining returns because of cost reduction and rationalization force competitors to look elsewhere.
- Potential competitors: restless customers attract new entrants.
- Supply chain: new sources of supply and new resources, espe-

cially new technology, are frequently the source of new product development.

- Channels: change in the distribution channels is mostly a lagging, rather than leading indicator of competitive product divergence.

A new product or service rarely takes over a market immediately. The concept and creation of a new product is often spontaneous, unstructured, and unpredictable. But the commercialization of the product and penetration of the market require very deliberate and visible action. Observing competitors that are experimenting is one of the important leading indicators.[16]

A good example is the Dow Jones Corporation. Dow launched its Electric Information Division to compete in-house with its Business Publications Division spearheaded by *The Wall Street Journal*:

> After propelling Dow Jones for a century, the Journal—long one of America's finest newspapers—is shrinking. Operating income from business publications had fallen 44 percent in 1987/1988 . . . Dow Jones' other major operation is growing like a Los Angeles suburb. Information Services has supercharged its operating profits 69 percent over the same two-year period.[17]

Revenues from electronic information were projected to pass publications revenue rapidly. This indicator of competitor experimentation marked the advent of a new product turning point in the business publications industry. For all competitors in the publication of business information it was clear that the coming of age of electronic information signaled the presence of a strong force of change.

Timing of Turning Points

Turning points vary in the timing of their potential impact. Because of longer-term trends and trajectories, turning points and cycles never repeat themselves in detail. Their timing may be irregular and their sequence cannot be taken for granted.

To pin down the timing of turning points, it is useful to look for a coincidence of forces. In the U.S. construction equipment industry, excess capacity, the decline in construction, rising interest rates, and the gradual saturation of the Middle Eastern market all pointed to a downturn in sales. The timing of the impact of these limits to growth, and hence the timing of the downturn, depended on how much additional demand was still left in the Middle East and in the overall U.S. economy. In general, the timing of a turning point depends on the strength of the existing trend relative to its limits and the stimuli promoting a new trend.

Identifying the forces of change in the environment is the critical first step in anticipating breakpoints. Sensitivity to the change forces and their timing is essential if they are not to be a threat, but rather an opportunity to be exploited. And yet many companies are not even aware of the established trends in their environment, not to mention the timing of potential turning points and cycles. The 1981 and 1991 history of the U.S. construction machinery industry shows that those companies that do not learn how to identify change patterns and deal with their timing are condemned to repeat them.

KEYS TO PRACTICE: IDENTIFYING FORCES OF CHANGE

1. Identify the established trends in the socio-political, economic, technological, and competitive environments. The rate of change in the environment created by a trend is an indication of its strength. Emerging or declining trends are typically weak, whereas growing or mature trends are strong.
2. Use the basic cyclical pattern and the leading indicators to identify the limits and stimuli pointing to the next turning point:

    • When in a phase of divergent behavior look for leading indicators of convergence; look for the limits to divergence and the stimuli of convergence.
    • When in a phase of convergent behavior look for leading indicators of divergence; look for the limits to convergence and the stimuli of divergence.

3. Assess the timing of the next turning point based on the relative strengths of the existing trend, its limits, and the stimuli of a new trend.

CHAPTER 3

Assessing Resistance

66I N JUNE 1988, the dust was finally settling after the largest cross-border takeover in European history."[1] After a fierce fight with the Italian-based Carlo de Benedetti, the Paris-based Compagnie Financiére de Suez had finally gained control of the Société Générale de Belgique. La Générale was Belgium's biggest company. The subsidiaries and companies held by SGB contributed almost a third of Belgium's GDP. At the end of 1986, the company had direct or indirect holdings in 1,261 other companies worldwide, ranging from a railroad in Angola to a film production company in Los Angeles.

David Hover and John Pringle point out in their case study that the vulnerability of La Générale to a takeover had not gone unnoticed by its management. Statements about the need to ensure the viability of the company had been made repeatedly in its annual reports. In 1981, a strategic management group was formed to "provide a coherent synthesis of individual corporate programs and exploit promising new areas of activity." And in 1985, a new organization was announced: "The grouping of available services [into 10 business sectors] is designed to meet the basic criterion of efficiency . . . to face up to international competition." However, the resistance of the subsidiaries, many of which were only partly held by SGB, was strong. Tradition and the old order of extensive decentralization were deeply entrenched. "The nick-name, *'la vieille dame,'* the old lady, had been well earned."

SGB was founded in 1822 as a development bank by the then Dutch king, William I. Its objective was to raise capital for new firms and industries from the large Belgian banking families and the king's own sources. When Belgium became independent in 1830, SGB was its central bank, until 1850 when this function was taken back by the government. Many of the company's investments were in the growth industries of the period—mining, minerals, railroads, and steel. The policy was to hold equity participation at "a significant level, seldom exceeding 50 percent," but enough to influence the activities of the subsidiary.

La Générale board members were almost exclusively SGB executives and subsidiary executives; it helped to be "Wallonian and blue-blooded." Embarrassing questions were avoided on all sides. The main change agent in this cozy club was René Lamy, who took over as directeur general in the late 1970s, determined to restore the luster of SGB. He got the board to accept a strategic management group, a new organization concept, a corporation-wide information system, and a human resource committee. Still, change was slow.

Poor financial performance in the 1980s increased the takeover threat. In 1987, a defense against a hostile takeover was put in place with the help of loyal shareholders, large French and Belgian corporations, many of which were partly owned by each other and the SGB itself. The defense consisted of a poison pill designed to place a large number of new shares in friendly hands at the first sign of a threat.

Unfortunately, there was a Trojan horse in the defense. Cerus, a French telecommunications company and a SGB shareholder, was 40 percent owned by Carlo de Benedetti. In January 1988, he used it to buy SGB shares on the open market. Then he made a tender offer for enough shares to gain control and challenged the poison pill in the courts. A lower court twice ruled in his favor, but the decision was overturned on appeal.

Meanwhile, other members of SGB's original group of loyal shareholders banded together under the leadership of Suez. In March, they claimed control of 52 percent of SGB's shares and called for an extraordinary shareholders' meeting in April to decide the outcome. At the last minute, a previous Générale supporter defected. But the de Benedetti camp still could only muster 48 percent of the votes and the pro-management Suez group was victorious.

The story of La Générale shows how resistance can prevent change from taking root, to the point where an externally imposed discontinuity becomes inevitable. The story also illustrates several types of resistance. When assessing resistance it is important to keep in mind that its strength is the extent to which it prevents the industry, company, or business unit from adapting to the forces of change. As we shall see, some forces of resistance can be more readily realigned with the forces of change once the latter build up; others yield less easily and can only be realigned gradually over time.

In this chapter, we consider the main types of resistance in rough order of increasing strength:

- Closed attitudes
- Entrenched culture
- Rigid structures and systems
- Counterproductive change dynamics

The overall strength of resistance depends on the mix and strength of the various forces of resistance involved in a specific situation. The overall strength of resistance can be summarized in terms of a threshold beyond which increasing force for change causes the resistance to break down. The final section of the chapter summarizes the more common indicators of the strength of resistance.

CLOSED ATTITUDES

Closed attitudes reflect rigidity of mind-set and/or culture. For our purposes, the mind-set is the corporate "super-ego," the philosophy, beliefs, and implicit strategies that shape the organization's view of its world. A closed mind-set is, unhappily, very easy to develop. It may be created by delusions of success, ingrained strategies, or buried assumptions. Although a closed mind-set may be blind to change forces initially, their strength can cause a rapid reversal, once realization dawns.

Delusions of Success

Success breeds resistance to change. The longer successful managers have been on the job, the more they are convinced that their approach to the world is the right one. An extreme was Henry

Ford's immutable conviction that auto manufacture meant making one kind of black car in large enough numbers to reach the economy of scale that would give consumers value for their money. Given his success, Ford had every right to be adamant about his view. The problem is that no industry or market is stationary; while managerial convictions strengthen, industries and markets move.

In its comment on the excellent companies identified by Thomas Peters and Robert Waterman, *Business Week* pointed out that more than a third were no longer excellent two years later, in most cases because they missed major shifts in their markets. In several cases, management had been blinded by success; for example:

> Delta Air Lines, which had flourished by maintaining a low debt and exploiting a close-knit culture to keep costs low, failed to see that deregulation had changed its world. The Atlanta-based carrier was slow in recognizing the importance of computers to keep tabs on ticket prices in different markets. Consequently, Delta first failed to meet competitors' lower prices.[2]

Closed attitudes to change based exclusively on delusions of success often weaken as the success evaporates: Delta recognized the need for change once its profits weakened.

Ingrained Strategies

Strategies, having to do with the definition and scope of the business, can become so ingrained that they block the response to important external discontinuities. Ingrained strategies are typically more resistant than delusions of success to news of change because they form a basis for rationalizing away the importance of the news: the change simply does not affect the business as defined.

A major company with a long tradition in the engineering industry built its reputation on premium-quality products. Engineering designed and manufacturing produced superior products, including railroad locomotives with the best engines, parquet wood flooring in the driver's cabin, and heavy brass lettering on the outside. In the early 1980s, an increasing gap opened up between its prices and those of the competition. High production costs made it virtually impossible to reduce prices and market share began to erode.

Management was aware that the market had shifted to new, specialized segments that combined technology and service, along with a more mature traditional market that was increasingly driven by the low delivered costs of standardized products. In trying to adapt, however, the executives refused to do anything that might compromise the company's image in the mature market. Several years followed with shrinking share, sales, and profits that turned into losses. Eventually the company realized that the narrow emphasis on quality had prevented it from responding to a broader view of quality required to reduce the delivery times of reliable, cost effective, standardized equipment. This realization opened the way for a long and gradual process of revitalization which allowed the company to catch up with the market.

Buried Assumptions ("Not-Invented-Here" Syndrome)

The "not-invented-here" syndrome is replete with buried assumptions about the importance of in-house thinking and the lack of appreciation about what is happening outside. It is most difficult to avoid in large companies located in large countries because the domestic information tends to swamp foreign information. Bad news is simply screened out; or if it does get through, the content and implications of the news are rejected because they are inconsistent with the ways things are believed to be.

To preserve the sedate, civilized tone of their meetings, the old directors of La Générale studiously avoided bringing up bad news, or asking questions that might put their colleagues in the embarrassing position of having to reveal bad news. When the need for change was raised by René Lamy or others, the traditional role of La Générale as a pillar of the Belgian economy was often invoked to explain why change would be impossible.

Creeping forces, those that build up gradually, are a common cause of little or no reaction: crying wolf when there's no wolf yet. Managers get used to the problem, either by adapting slightly, or by learning to ignore it. Disdain for new competing products that don't make it right away is typical. After one or two new competitors fail, the established players become even more indifferent to other new entrants. Many a major player has failed to respond in time to creeping forces of change. IBM downplayed the importance of decentralized data processing and networking for years, until it was undeniably clear that the market's growth had moved toward networks.

The importance of SGB to Belgium's economy was such that the directors could not believe the government and the courts would allow a foreigner, even another European, to take it over.

As a result, they never took the takeover threat seriously enough to fundamentally change their ways, until it was too late. When the lower court twice ruled in favor of Carlo de Benedetti, the directors were sufficiently alarmed to find the least threatening foreigner available, another French-speaking company. According to an SGB executive, "SGB's former managers saw themselves as more important than the Belgian government did. Evidently, they didn't read the cards right."

Ignoring bad news may occur by default, through the lack of a sufficiently sensitive information-gathering system. SGB did not even have a corporatewide information system: "Reports to the board were frequently based only on annual reports with almost no supporting documentation. Auditors working on behalf of SGB were known to have been denied access to subsidiaries. 'Pas de chiffre' [no numbers] was the response." This may be a particularly extreme example; however, it all depends on one's point of view. Many Japanese executives would consider the way Western companies tap employees' views as hopelessly under-developed.

The ease with which Japanese and other Southeast Asian companies first penetrated the U.S. market had much to do with buried assumptions and the absence of a system for monitoring foreign competitors. Americans and Europeans had little information, and no reason to believe the low-price product copies coming from the East could possibly be a threat. The experience of the three decades since then has had little effect; there is still a strong tendency to underestimate the competitive challenge from Japan. For example, in a recent discussion at a leading business school it was concluded that Japan had serious problems stemming from an aging population, restless youth, the challenge of internationalization, and so on which would undermine that country's competitiveness.

Japanese executives, by contrast, make few assumptions. They continue to look, listen, and learn. When Masaharu Matsushita first visited the United States in 1951, he said that "of the 100 most important things his company had to learn, 70 of them would come from the U.S. and 30 from Japan." Forty years later, Mr. Sakuma, deputy president of Matsushita, followed up with the comment that "of the 100 most important things his company had to learn, 30 would still come from the U.S., 30 from Japan, and 40 were as yet unknown, to be researched and discovered."[3]

ENTRENCHED CULTURE

Culture is the corporate "id"; the values, emotions, behavior, and skills that drive the informal processes and politics of the organization. Well-developed corporate cultures turn out to be extremely resistant to change. Behavior and feelings are hard to stir with appeals to the intellect. People don't like changing their values under pressure, because change is often perceived to be tantamount to defeat, even surrender. The comments of the historian Carlo Cipolla on the cultural barriers to reversing economic decline are particularly insightful:

> It is remarkable to see how relatively numerous in declining empires are the people capable of making the right diagnosis and preaching some sensible cure. It is no less remarkable, however, that wise utterances remain generally sterile, because, as Gonzales de Cellorigo forcefully put it while watching impotently the decline of Spain, "those who can will not and those who will cannot."[4]

Behaviors and skills cannot simply be changed overnight. First they have to be unlearned, in the sense of breaking out of old habits. Then new behaviors and skills have to be acquired. The older managers and employees get, the more difficult such learning becomes. From an organizational point of view it means either allowing a lot of time for the learning process, or replacing significant numbers of people. The latter is certainly quicker, but it may destroy other desirable parts of the organization in the process.

The Ford Motor Company benefited, then suffered, from the culture of financial control imposed by Robert McNamara. In the early 1980s, one out of every six employees at Ford of Europe was a controller, auditor, or financial person of some kind.[5] Among other things, finance made the decisions about pricing and production scheduling. The operating line managers depended on finance to provide them with the numbers needed for their decisions. In addition, there were monitors to monitor the monitors. Despite or perhaps because of all the control, Ford's production costs remained well above those of its Japanese competitors.

About ten years had elapsed after the problem was first perceived before Ford was able to replace the finance culture with a more participative, line decision-making approach. It took several years to even recognize and then develop sufficient consensus that something fundamental had to be done. Innumerable study trips were made to Mazda, Ford's Japanese partner, before all functions started looking for ways to close the cost gap. The manufacturing study group blamed the problem on finance. The finance group responded that manufacturing didn't know how to count; the Japanese, it was said, had disguised their controllers as line people. In the end, finance recognized that change was a matter of survival.

After the first wave of cost cutting had run out of steam, task forces, meetings, seminars, and consultants were used to raise awareness of the underlying problem and shift decision-making responsibility back to the line managers. All these efforts eventually worked, at least temporarily, so that in 1987 Ford had record profits and was, in fact, the most profitable car manufacturer worldwide.

The unfortunate irony is that in 1991 Ford was again in difficulty. After twenty years, at least, of innumerable articles, books, and conferences on the topic, the *New York Times* reported that Honda's Marysville plant was not only the largest, but the most productive automobile plant in North America, producing about 50 percent more cars per head than the typical U.S. plant.[6] In this context, the only advantages the Japanese can possibly have are a younger, nonunionized work force and better management. Since there is nothing to prevent U.S. manufacturers from challenging the unions with new nonunionized subsidiaries, the sole remaining difference is cultural rigidity. Despite twenty years of trying, the U.S. auto industry has yet to learn fully how to learn from the competition.

RIGID STRUCTURES AND SYSTEMS

The word "structures" is used here in the large sense and refers to the organization, the business system, the stakeholder resource base, and the industry. The degree of resistance in any of these depends on switching costs, the costs of exiting from one type of organizational setup, business system, stakeholder resource base, or industry market and entering another. Entry barriers involve, for example, the acquisition of new technology, or scarce resources, as well as intangibles like image and relationships. Exit barriers are created, for example, by contracts and other binding relationships, or by organizational limits to the speed of change. In many circumstances, when they are under the control of management, structure and systems can be changed quite quickly. In other cases, when the structure is beyond the control of management, it may be an intractable obstacle to change.

Organizational Rigidity

Organizational structure and systems encompass not only the organizational units and reporting hierarchy but also the planning, control, compensation, communication, and information systems. These create large obstacles to change inside companies. In contrast to markets, where many players are continually searching for ways around structures and systems, in companies, some structure and systems are essential for their very existence. Although adaptable to some extent, there are obviously limits to how far a particular structure can go in accommodating to the changes in the environment. One needs to be on the lookout, therefore, for looming mismatches between existing structures and the trend in the environment. What may be perfectly adapted in one context could become a huge obstacle to change as the environment shifts.

Many multinationals preparing for the integration of Europe have found themselves boxed in by structure and systems reflecting the Old Europe. A petroleum company had administration costs in Europe double those in the United States. The national subsidiaries within the company embodied the national laws, the local currencies, and the distorted logistics created by national borders and the gray markets that span them. Similarly, a large food company came face to face with the historical strengths of national companies catering to different tastes, as well as dispersed and fragmented manufacturing.

The contrast between the original American (A/firm) and Japanese (J/firm) stereotypes is instructive.[7] The J/firm is characterized by direction through a shared vision and culture. Know-how is developed by teams learning by doing. Knowledge is less codified and is spread through the company by job rotation and horizontal coordination. Control is exercised through shared norms based more on the performance of the team and the business as a whole.

The A/firm is characterized by top-management direction through systems. Know-how is obtained from specialists who are highly mobile. Formal knowledge is embodied in manuals. A/firms are especially prone to tight financial controls and rate of return targets that can stifle innovative change. Control is exercised through variance from budgets.

The multilayered divisional groups and corporate management systems of the A/firm type are fine for planning growth, but hopelessly top-heavy relative to the value that management can add in the lean years. And positively stifling for entrepreneurial spirit, as many American conglomerates and others discovered when the growth of the 1960s gave way to the lean 1970s and the entrepreneurial 1980s. Xerox is reputed to have turned down prototypes of the personal computer because the proposed projects did not meet the required hurdle rate. Later on, a laser printer proposal was rejected for the same reason. Fortunately for the company, the product champion believed in the idea so much that it was developed by bootstrapping outside the tightly controlled organizational mainstream.

However, too loose an organization can also create resistance to change. A loose organization with little management control may be ideal for encouraging entrepreneurial innovative management, but a large obstacle if the market shifts to cost competition. A major European white-goods company that grew rapidly with loose controls during the boom years after the war was unable to manage the shift to cost competition because it couldn't figure out which product lines were making profits. At La Générale, hands-off, decentralized management of the earlier years left top management with virtually no systems whatsoever with which to deal with the lean years that followed.

Business System Rigidity

The existing business system, the transformation process comprising R&D, design, engineering, sourcing production, marketing, distribution, selling, and service, can be a major constraint on change. The continual fine-tuning needed to get maximum competitive advantage out of a business system makes it difficult to modify. Business systems can be very inflexible with respect to downturns in demand. This is a matter of fixed costs, both operating and financial, the bane of all capital-intensive and image-focused industries during a recession; one of the reasons for the pioneering Japanese push toward greater subcontracting, flexible systems, and variable employee compensation.

In the razor market, for example, Gillette committed its manufacturing, marketing, and manpower to make the TracII and Atra razors into industry standards. When Bic introduced its cheap disposable plastic razors, Gillette was slow to respond. Gillette's managers couldn't see what consumers found attractive in the Bic product. More important, there was no way they could switch their dedicated business system over to cheap disposables.

For seventy years, as David Mehegan reported in the *Boston Globe,* Gillette had adapted and fine-tuned its business to deliver shaving systems, "two-piece metal devices with replaceable, non-sharpenable blades."[8] Preceding the twin-blade TracII and the hinged-cartridge Atra were the one-piece razor, the super blue blade, the stainless steel blade, and the Techmatic with razor band. However, there was much more to a system than one set of hardware. Once they had razors, the idea was that customers would continue to buy blades. With this in mind, Gillette carefully cultivated a strong he-man image with an aura of special emotion about shaving. Gillette sponsored major sporting events around the world: "look sharp, feel sharp, be sharp" was the slogan during the baseball world series in the 1950s. Gillette became "a household name as sponsor of the Gillette Cavalcade of Sports and the Friday Night Fights."

Bic's disposable plastic razors changed the business system completely. Disposables turned razors into a commodity; the competing brands all looked very similar. Gillette responded with its own disposable, Good News, which captured a major share of the disposables market. But it was difficult to differentiate, so Gillette's potential in the market was limited. As disposables gained ground, Gillette's dominance of the total wet-shaving market eroded. On top of this, the low margin on disposables dragged down Gillette's profit margin. Even worse, they took advertising dollars away from Gillette's up-market, strong masculine identity.

In effect, Gillette was torn between two quite different business systems. The shaving systems business made it impossible to embrace disposables wholeheartedly. The divisions began to show up inside the company. John Symons, the head of the European group, led the fight for a return to quality shaving systems, while others felt disposables were "the wave of the future." Symons used market research to show that "men over 40 years old associated the Gillette name with warm memories of shaving as a rite of passage into manhood . . . and with top quality." He scored crucial points when advertising dollars taken from the disposables generated a big increase in sales of TracII and Atra.

As the pressure on profits mounted, the debate in Gillette grew until Colman Mockler, Jr., the CEO, decided in favor of tradition, in favor of an attempt to come up with a completely new shaving system that could beat back the disposables.

Seven years and $200 million of research later, Gillette unveiled its new high-tech Sensor, "the best a man can get," with three advertising spots during the 1990 Super Bowl: "Father to son, it's what we've always done." As Gillette's sales and profits began to soar, the tables began to turn. Now Bic was sitting with a rigid business system.

Stakeholder Rigidity

Stakeholders may obstruct change by limiting the access to necessary resources: men, money, material, machines, markets, and information. A labor union may resist modernizing its practices to allow the company to compete with nonunionized international competitors. Or government policy may make foreign material and technology expensive to obtain. Or the educational system may not be producing the right mix of graduates for the high-growth sectors of the economy. Or family members may prevent a private company from going to the market to get the financing and management skills needed to support its growth. In an historical comparison of the American, German, and British economies, Alfred Chandler argues that one of the main reasons why the British fell behind was their predilection for tightly held family ownership structures which prevented U.K. companies from getting the financing needed to support growth.[9]

Customers may become comfortable with certain product features and resist attempts to substitute them with something else. A major exporter of premium beer found that when the price was allowed to float downward with the exchange rate in one market, sales were lost to lower-price competitors. Unfortunately, when the exchange rates turned around, it was unable to recoup the sales by increasing the price because the up-market image was gone. Learning a lesson, it has maintained share in the face of strong competition in other markets by ensuring that prices are systematically higher than those of the closest competition. Consumers of premium beer are evidently buying more than a lightly alcoholic, malt-based beverage. The tastes and thirst-quenching attributes of the beer account for only part of its value. They are buying a relaxant for socialization, in addition to image and life-style. The demand for such intangible product features is especially resistant to change.

Large players in the supply chain can also impede change. In a famous case, when tin can manufacturers were being threatened by aluminum and paper composite substitutes as a force of change in the 1960s, the steel companies supplying tin plate rolled back price increases, engaged in research to produce thinner tin plate, and otherwise enhanced the attraction of the tin can for various end-users. More recently, European TV producers tried to counter the Japanese access to large distributors by combining the loyal, less accessible, smaller dealers into purchasing groups capable of offering consumers a better deal. Whereas these efforts did not eliminate the basic force for change, they certainly delayed and altered the impact.

Industry Rigidity

Industries are made up of a set of competitors serving overlapping markets. The drive for free markets notwithstanding, most markets are still subject to some form of rigidity. According to the spokesman for the German Federation of Industries, for example, at least 50 percent of the markets in West Germany were subject to some form of government intervention in 1989. Even when government is not involved directly, there are self-imposed standards and codes of conduct, if not regulations dictated by supervisory bodies, not to mention tariffs, subsidies, distribution systems, and local practice, all of which can be used by existing players to try and resist change. Cartels are a common feature of the German-speaking business landscape. The big German banks for many years were able to deny foreign institutions' access to the large pool of domestic deutsche mark savings by imposing prohibitive transaction and commission costs. In the consumer electronics industry existing television equipment is obstructing the introduction of high-definition TV. In many service industries, like accounting and law, long-term contractual arrangements create patterns of obligation, image, and behavior that impede change.

The Swiss watch industry shows how industry structure can create resistance to change.[10] Throughout its history, the industry has had hundreds of subcontractors supplying hundreds of "etablisseurs" (assemblers) who put the watches together. In the mid-1970s, the Swiss watch industry was hit by two discontinuities, the economic recession created by the oil crisis and the sudden arrival of large quantities of mid- and low-priced watches from Japan and Hong Kong. Each of the sectors in the industry reacted in its own way. But there was no coordination. In particular, it was impossible to achieve production runs large enough to compete with the cheap electronic watches from the Far East, or to justify the invest-ment in new electronic technology. Swiss watch production declined sharply from 96 million units in 1974 to 75 million in 1975.

One response to the Asian market was a wave of mergers. More frequently than not, for reasons of organizational pride, the mergers did not result in a proper rationalization of operations, but rather in a "federation-type affiliation." Instead of many small companies making small losses, larger companies were making larger losses. With each technological advance the Swiss lost more market share. By 1983, they were producing only 45 million units. In 1984, there were still about 260 assemblers of all sizes with their own designs and brand names covering all types of watches. They were supplied by 50 companies making movements or components, 130 making casings, dials, and so on, and 190 miscellaneous sub-contractors. Included among the assemblers were about a dozen vertically integrated watch manufacturers making either expensive products in small quantities, or large volumes by mass production.

The industry was saved by its financiers, the major Swiss national and cantonal banks. With exports declining, the industry's debt-to-export ratio rose to record heights. The situation would have been a complete debacle had it not been for the high-priced luxury segments, which were protected from the onslaught. The banks finally stepped in to break the barrier to change implicit in the industry's fragmentation. They forced a major reorganization, especially of the integrated manufacturers. Operations were ration-alized and bank debt was written off and converted to equity. The rationalization, coupled with an increase in global demand, restored overall profitability. In 1985, the banks were able to sell part of their equity in the major company that had been formed, Société Suisse de Microéléctronique et Horlogèrie (SMH), to a group of private investors. If there hadn't been a close relationship with the banks, fragmentation would have destroyed the Swiss watch industry.

COUNTERPRODUCTIVE CHANGE DYNAMICS

Change is a function of its history. The investments made ear-lier shape the capabilities available to support change later on. The learning accomplished during one phase of an industry, or product life cycle, is often a prerequisite for moving on to the next phase. The confusion stirred up by one reorganization can complicate a later reorganization, especially if the second follows rapidly on the heels of the first. Once change veers off in the wrong direction, away from adaptation to the environment, it thwarts change in the right direction.

The evolution of the banking industry in recent decades illustrates how the choices made to cope with change in one period constrain the alternatives available in the next period. In the good old days of the 1960s, when inflation and interest rates were relatively stable, banks earned healthy profit margins and returns on equity. Banks borrowed at floating rates and lent at fixed rates, absorbing the risk associated with the varying difference between long- and short-term rates.

In the 1970s, inflation increased, interest rates became more volatile, and the average cost of bank funds increased faster than inflation. Profit margins declined. To maintain the return on equity, despite lower profit margins, many banks chose a growth strategy, increasing the volume of business. As they took on more deposits, the banks increased their financial leverage, and lent to clients with lower credit worthiness. This was the era of recycled OPEC oil money. Many observers marvelled at the ability of the banking system to absorb and place billions of dollars. Not too many noted the way in which these choices were reducing the room for future maneuver.

In the 1980s, interest and foreign exchange rates became even more volatile. Third world countries had difficulty servicing their debt. The quality of the banks' loan portfolios deteriorated and their bond ratings started falling. Bank equity capital was not adequate to support further growth; there was not enough of it to satisfy regulatory requirements. Latin American debt, for example, was 120 percent of Citibank's equity in 1988 and 110 percent of the equity of Lloyds Bank. In addition, floating interest rate deposits made it very difficult to provide fixed-rate loans. As a result, banks that had chosen a growth strategy in the 1970s could no longer compete as suppliers of funds to prime corporate borrowers.

An alternative was to develop fee and service income. The banks began to offer new financial services and instruments, and charged commissions to trade the instruments in new markets that brought borrowers and lenders together directly. The commercial paper and swap markets began to satisfy much of the short- and long-term borrowing needs of prime corporate clients. Mergers and acquisitions advice facilitated a de facto market for the control of even the largest companies. Junk bonds and leveraged buyouts opened up new markets for the financing and control of lower-grade clients. To deal with the volatility in the markets, a whole panoply of derivative instruments was created, based on forward contracts, futures, and options. This was the era of Wall Street whiz kids, during which much of the banks' risk "disappeared" off their balance sheets. Those who asked where it had gone were drowned out by the euphoria of the moment.

Huge investments in personnel and information technology (IT) were made to support the search for fee and service income in both corporate and retail markets.[11] NatWest in the United Kingdom planned to spend $5 billion and Lloyds $1 billion on IT in the early 1990s. Citibank, one of the leaders in bank IT, had been investing continually throughout the 1980s: in 1984 alone, for example, it invested $100 million, and hired 250 telecommunication specialists and 1,250 systems analysts to connect 17,000 customers. These investments were not only strategically important, they increased fixed costs enormously. When the markets dropped dramatically, first in 1987 and then in 1990, these fixed costs, plus the weakness of the asset portfolios, made it virtually impossible for many banks, including some of the biggest, to scale back their activities without losing money.

Banks that made different choices traced out different change paths and were not nearly as constrained in many cases. German and Swiss banks, for example, did not pursue growth as vigorously as many of the American and U.K. banks in the 1970s. Their balance sheets did not deteriorate as much, so these banks had less need to pursue new instruments and did not get caught out on a limb when the markets softened.

When the junk bond market collapsed in 1990, the U.S. savings and loan industry found itself with diminished assets (it had bought junk bonds to boost its return on assets) and liabilities made up of high-interest-rate deposits. With interest costs greater than interest income, profits disappeared. The ensuing bankruptcies probably will go down as one of the greatest financial debacles in history. The moral of the banking story is that when change gets pushed too far in one direction, it often becomes dysfunctional. The momentum in one direction creates enormous resistance in the opposite direction. As the cycle of change develops, the old forces of change become the new forces of resistance: yesterday's choices become today's chains.

INDICATORS AND STRENGTH OF RESISTANCE

The strength of resistance shows up in the difficulty of adaptation to the forces of change. The industry, company, or business unit can be monitored for indicators of difficult adaptation in the categories of resistance discussed above.

Closed attitudes show up in an unwillingness to accept bad news, in the form of emerging forces that may be relevant but are not regarded as such. Other signs of an unwillingness to face reality include satisfaction with the status quo, avoidance of embarrassment and conflict, and lack of clear strategies and milestones.

Entrenched culture is reflected in values, behavior, and skills that are not adapted to the forces of change. The less the adaptation, the more resistant the culture. This often manifests itself in apparent indifference to the new rules of the game.

The rigidity of structures and systems can be seen in top-heavy organizations with inflexible management systems, an overly focused business system, squeezed stakeholders, and in industry regulations and conventions.

Counterproductive change shows up in the conflicting needs of different phases of a cycle, as previously successful strategies are overtaken by shifts in the environment and yesterday's change agents become today's status quo agents. Other signs include interest groups with narrow agendas, and politics and incompetence taking precedence over efficacy and efficiency.

Closed attitudes alone, or rigid structures by themselves, are unlikely to be a strong force of resistance. Attitudes reflecting delusions of success or incorrect strategies will change if the structure, systems, and culture are flexible and the forces of change gain momentum and their direction can be clearly seen. Similarly, rigid structures and systems within the organization will not be tolerated if attitudes and the culture are open to change and the inconsistency between the structures and the forces of change becomes apparent.

On the other hand, closed attitudes in the form of a not-invented-here syndrome embedded in an entrenched culture will be more resistant to change. Closed attitudes in such cases reflect behavior and skills that are not adapted to change. Even if the strength of the change forces is appreciated, the attitudes of the status quo agents will not change quickly because they would be worse off. A change in attitudes and culture will only come gradually if the old behaviors and skills can be cast off and new ones learned. The same applies to rigid structures and systems that are buttressed by an entrenched culture.

Counterproductive change dynamics on the part of status quo and/or change agents, whose evolving behavior runs counter to the forces of change, often constitutes the strongest force of resistance because it encompasses the other forms. To get rid of the resistance, the change agents have to be convinced they are on the wrong track, the supporting structure and systems must be altered, and new behaviors and skills have to be learned.

The overall strength of the resistance to change in a particular situation depends on the correlation between the different forces of resistance. The greater the correlation, the greater will be the overall resistance, especially when an entrenched culture is involved. The strength of the resistance can be summarized in terms of a threshold beyond which increasing force causes the resistance to break down. The height of the threshold reflects the power and resources that would be needed to realign the industry, company, or business unit, and its status quo agents, with the forces of change. For example, the more the behavior and skills of the status quo agents deviate from the direction of the change forces, the more they have to lose from the change; hence, the greater the resources needed to realign their interests and the higher the threshold of their resistance.

The various forms of resistance were highly correlated in the case of Société Générale de Belgique. Many of the resistance indicators were flashing prior to the takeover. Unwillingness to accept bad news, avoidance of embarrassment, lack of clear strategies, and indifference to new rules of the game all pointed to an especially acute case of closed attitudes. On the structural side, the company's problem was more a lack of control than too much of it. Most damaging of all, however, were the counterproductive change dynamics. Politics had taken increasing precedence over efficiency at headquarters. More important, subsidiary-centered interest groups claimed an increasing part of the change process. Although not bad in itself, the growing fragmentation made it virtually impossible for the parent to get agreement, not to mention implement, a coordinated approach to change. To reverse these change dynamics, to reduce the politics at headquarters, to get the subsidiaries to accept enough control to facilitate coordination of overlapping activities, and to open management's attitudes to the forces of change in the environment would have required more power and resources than the chief executive had at his disposal. At the time of the takeover, La Générale was a classic example of a company exhibiting a very high threshold of resistance to change. When the forces of change strengthened, a breakpoint became inevitable.

KEYS TO PRACTICE: ASSESSING RESISTANCE

1. Look for closed attitudes by examining what processes are in place for bringing new ideas into the industry, company, or business unit, especially at the highest levels; and by probing whether management is aware of the change forces.
2. Look for an entrenched culture by examining what processes are in place for reflecting on values and improving behavior and skills; and by enquiring to what extent behavior and skills are adapted to the forces of change.
3. Look for rigid structures and systems, by examining when the organization, business system, the stakeholder resource base, and the industry last changed significantly; and by enquiring to what extent the structures and systems are capable of accommodating the forces of change.
4. Look for counterproductive change dynamics by examining whether historical forces of change are driving the business; and by enquiring to what extent the historical forces of change have become the new forces of resistance.
5. Assess the strength of the overall resistance to change by examining to what extent the various forces of resistance are correlated with one another; and by describing the resistance threshold in terms of the power and resources needed to deal with the resistance.

CHAPTER 4

Mapping Out Scenarios

THE GULF WAR in the Middle East knocked the bottom out of the European market for softwood during the first quarter of 1991, prices fell by 15 percent, and in some national markets demand dropped by 30 percent. Capacity utilization of the sawmills plummeted and operating margins disappeared. As the largest exporter in Europe, the Finnish softwood industry was especially hard-hit: profit margins dropped by 10 percent, from 5 percent of sales in 1990 to −5 percent in 1991. Some of the biggest European sawmills in Finland were forced to throw out their budgets and rethink their situation from scratch.[1]

The largest market segments serving the construction and packaging industries were most affected. The drop in demand triggered by the Gulf War exacerbated an already difficult situation. Demand in these segments had been weak and the purchase criteria had been dominated by price for some time. The products in these segments were close to being commodities and hard to differentiate. By contrast, the furniture and joinery (renovation) segments were less affected because quality and brand image were the critical purchase criteria. The growth rate in demand was fundamentally more stable and value-added features were more important.

Important longer-term trends in the industry were increasing forward integration and concentration. Both trends were furthest advanced in the United Kingdom. Sawmills in Britain had already integrated forward to incorporate transportation logistics and the sales agents in their activities. Downstream in the United Kingdom, the importers were already doing secondary processing and merchandising. Moreover, the top five importers/merchants in Britain controlled 80 percent of the market. Profits and bargaining power were moving away from the more fragmented sawmills upstream to the more concentrated importer/merchants downstream.

Unfortunately, the industry was not as flexible as it might have been. According to one observer, "the number one obstacle to progress in the industry is the large number of small players." The largest producer in the European sawmill industry supplied less than 2 percent of the market. There were many small, family-owned companies with limited economies of scale. Because of weak marketing, their sales were erratic and inventory costs were high. In addition, many of the sawmills suffered from high transportation costs.

Traditionally, the strategies of competitors had been shaped by the country context. Geography conditioned the type of wood that could be supplied. Sorting standards and hence the consistency of the quality of the wood differed across countries. Exchange rates favored some countries over others.

The Russians supplied the bulk market with low-price low-quality timber. They had cheap labor and vast forests in Siberia. But they suffered from socio-political instability, old production technology, a lack of flexibility, large transportation distances, and different grading standards. As a result, Russia could not supply service, specific dimensions, or consistent quality.

The Canadians exported low-price medium-quality timber to Europe, targeted mainly at the construction market. They were aggressive exporters with integrated downstream facilities, including their own European terminal, warehouses, and inventory. Although the Canadians often benefited from the exchange rate, they faced rising production costs, increasing criticism from ecologists, and highly variable demand from the United States.

The Swedes occupied the top end of the market with a high-perceived-value product range aimed mainly at the furniture and joinery segments. Being well integrated downstream, they were close to the market. The Swedes offered customized shipments of consistently high quality, efficient sorting, and the latest production technology. Their main weaknesses were high operating costs, many small and medium-sized players, and an uneven spread of forest maturities.

The Finns, being the largest suppliers in Europe, offered a wide product range. They were perceived to dominate the middle of the market, between the Russians and Canadians on the lower end and the Swedes on the upper end. Their sawmills' operations had been partially restructured and were more concentrated than in Sweden. They benefited financially from being associated with larger pulp and paper operations, and they had efficient upstream production, but relatively little downstream integration. Moreover, because of strongly independent forest owners' associations supported by legislation, raw timber was 15 percent more expensive in Finland than in Sweden, and labor and energy costs were also high. As they surveyed the scene, the managers of one of Finland's larger sawmilling operations wondered what might happen to the industry and how they could best position their company to deal with the changes.

The situation in the industry could be described in terms of the three basic variables discussed in previous chapters: shifting rules of the game reflected in rapidly changing performance, increasing forces of change, and resistance to change, all subject to the impact of chance. Depending on the balance of power between the forces and resistance, between change and status quo agents, quite different patterns of change could emerge.

To clarify the possibilities and develop a view of the future, this chapter develops

- The change arena as the context for contrasting different types of change.
- Location in the change arena of the industry or business as a way of evaluating what type of change is occurring.
- Change scenarios that reflect the possible interplay between the forces of change and resistance over time as a way of describing what types of change may occur.

THE CHANGE ARENA

According to Joseph Schumpeter, "The success of everything depends upon intuition, the capacity of seeing things in a way which afterwards proves to be true." In dealing with radical change, it's important to extend one's view: to see the future, one has to stretch one's mind beyond day-to-day operating and strategic thinking toward a world that has yet to occur. Instead of extrapolating trends in a logical fashion, one has to sense how a discontinuity might develop and where it will lead. Instead of being approached piece by piece, the potential discontinuity must be looked at in the context of all possible scenarios that might occur.

As a first step, this can be done by mapping out a change arena, as shown in Exhibit 4-1, to get a sense of the possible range of change. In the change arena, neither the change forces nor the resistance can be precisely measured. The change arena does not provide an exact representation, but rather a perspective of the context in which change occurs. The force of change can be classified as weak or strong depending on the rate of change it generates in the environment (see Chapter 2). Resistance to change is characterized as weak or strong, corresponding to a low or high threshold, beyond which increasing force causes the resistance to break down (see Chapter 3). The rate of business change is captured by the entries in each of the corners of the arena. The change

EXHIBIT 4–1   **Change Arena**

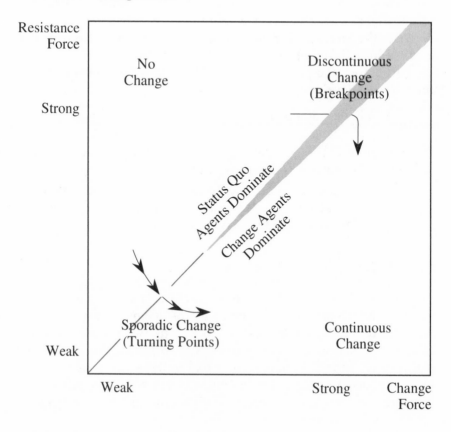

arena suggests four different types of change corresponding to strong/weak forces and strong/weak resistance to change.

In the top left-hand corner, weak change forces hardly affect an industry or company with strong resistance. Since the resistance threshold has not been reached, the status quo prevails and no change occurs. Status quo agents set the tone by emphasizing continuity based on old behavior.

This is typical of closed, inward-looking systems such as regulated markets and bureaucratic government organizations subject only to weak forces of change. Provided the force does not increase, the system may continue with this posture indefinitely.

American multinationals were in this position during the first decade after World War II. They dominated world markets and could shape the change forces in those markets rather than be shaped by them. Because they controlled their competitive environments they could maintain organizational stability by neutralizing external disturbances.[2]

In the opposite, bottom right-hand corner of the arena, the forces of change are strong and the resistance is weak. The forces of change exceed the resistance threshold, so there is little resistance. The system adapts continuously to the change forces. This represents a flexible industry or company, in which there is little resistance to change, responding to strong forces in the environment. All the participants perceive the forces for change. There are no status quo agents; everyone is a change agent. Whenever adaptation requires a change in the mix of activities, the full house of change agents ensures that the system responds accordingly. The industry or company adapts to the environment with continuous change.

Small new companies and independent business units facing strong forces, especially in high-tech industries, often come close to continuous adaptation. The closest are high-volume, competitive markets for commodities and financial instruments, in which there are no obstacles to change.

Continuous adaptation was also the situation faced by large companies during the 1960s. As Europe and Japan recovered after the war, a wave of growth unfurled across the developed economies. In the face of this strong force of change, the companies that did best were those flexible enough to adapt continuously to the developing growth opportunities.[3]

Bisecting the change arena is a diagonal which marks the boundary between the dominance of the status quo agents and the forces of resistance on the one side, and the dominance of the change agents and forces of change on the other side. Along the diagonal the forces of change and resistance are finely balanced. A slight alteration in the balance can shift the dominant influence in the system between the status quo and change agents.

In the bottom left-hand corner of the arena where the forces of change are weak and the resistance is weak, the boundary between old and new behavior is easily crossed. Neither the status quo nor the change agents are strongly entrenched; both are present with approximately equal influence on either side. The impact of the forces of change and resistance fluctuates because chance events can easily alter the balance between them. The alternating dominance of the forces of change and resistance results in sporadic change: change when the resistance threshold is breached from time to time and no change below it. However, if the change force continues to grow with low resistance, it causes the gradual conversion of status quo agents into change agents and results in a turning point.

Many intermediate-volume markets and medium-sized companies are flexible enough to adapt to weak change forces in a sporadic way. The absence of large stakes, locked into the prevailing status quo, makes it relatively easy for their participants to act as change agents. Moreover, frequent adaptation prevents them from becoming overly committed to the status quo. In these systems, a weak but emerging change force generates a turning point.

Sporadic change was common during the stagflation of the 1970s. During this period numerous industries were locked into a static economic environment. With the forces for change and the related resistance relatively weak, the change processes involved a lot of muddling through.[4]

In the top right-hand corner, where strong forces put pressure on systems with strong resistance, the change can be sharply discontinuous, forming a breakpoint. The transition between status quo and change agent behavior is characterized by a sudden sharp jump which is represented by the shaded part of the boundary line in the change arena. To the left of the boundary below the resistance threshold no change occurs, despite the fact that the change forces are strong; the status quo agents dominate largely. These are the markets and organizations where structure and stakes in the status quo initially neutralize the forces for change. Moderate pressure for change creates too few change agents to have a significant impact on the existing system. Strong pressure for change, of crisis proportions, is needed to shake up the status quo. Domination by the change agents occurs all of a sudden when the balance of power tips in their favor. Close to the threshold, chance events can make the difference in breaching the threshold. Once the change forces exceed the resistance threshold, on the right side of the boundary the resistance breaks down. Because of the strength of the change forces, the collapse of the resistance is sudden and rapid. A massive shift takes place from status quo to change agent behavior, thereby triggering a breakpoint.

Breakpoints in rigid systems are the stuff that revolutions, market crashes, and radical corporate reorganizations are made of. The abandonment of the Bretton Woods agreement and the oil price shocks of the 1970s, for example, introduced an era of sharply fluctuating exchange and interest rates, which completely changed competitive conditions in many industries from one moment to the next. The breakpoints in the financial markets in the late 1980s and the collapse of the command economies in the early 1990s have reinforced the trend toward more frequent radical shifts in the competitive environment and in organizations.[5] As long as strong forces continue to confront strong resistance, breakpoints will be frequent.

However, the change arena suggests that all four change types are relevant. The continuing and varying tension between the forces of resistance and change, between the status quo and a new order, determines the type of change that occurs. Even if one change type is in the limelight because of overall economic conditions, the position of individual industries, companies, and business units differs and evolves over time. The location of a business in the change arena during a particular period determines the kind of change that the business is likely to experience.

LOCATION IN CHANGE ARENA

Judgment and history are key factors in locating an industry, company, or business in the change arena. The nature and history of the forces of change and resistance can be used to assess whether a particular force is weak or strong as described in Chapters 2 and 3.

The Finnish sawmilling industry can be used to illustrate how a judgment can be formed about the location of a system in the change arena (see Exhibit 4-2). The change forces on the Finnish sawmill operators were strong. The industry was being torn between two forces: growing forces of divergence on the upper end of the market and mature forces of convergence on the lower end. The growing competitive trend to downstream integration and customized value-added products was putting pressure on the Finns to compete head-on with the Swedes on the upper end of the market. On the other hand, the collapse of demand for commodity products put the whole industry under intense cost pressure on the lower end of the market.

The forces of resistance in the Finnish sawmilling industry were also strong. The entrenched forest owners were able to maintain high prices and labor had high wages to compensate for the high Finnish cost of living. Neither of these could be changed eas-

EXHIBIT 4–2   **Location of Finnish Sawmilling Industry**

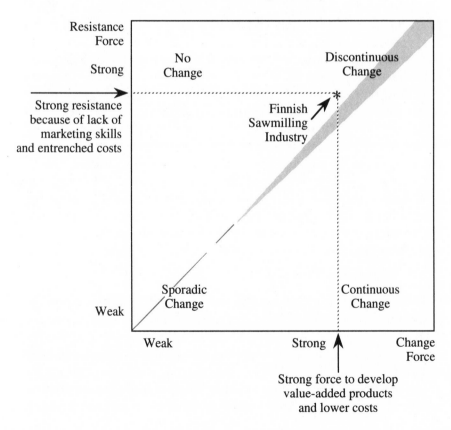

ily. The lack of downstream integration was compounded by weak marketing skills with correspondingly little sensitivity to evolving market needs. In addition, the Finns' product offering was perceived to have neither low cost nor very high value. Attitudes, the business system, and corporate culture would have to be modified to get around these problems. In brief, the Finnish industry was well up the resistance axis.

Combining the positions on the two axes, the Finnish industry was clearly in the top right-hand corner of the change arena facing a potential breakpoint. Although better off than the Russians who were in the midst of a major discontinuity caused by politico-economic change, the Finns were not as flexible as their more direct competitors, the Swedes, in the less cost sensitive furniture and joinery segments, or as well adapted to the low-cost forces as the Canadians who continued to benefit from the exchange rate. If demand did not improve, the Finnish players would be forced to make major adjustments in order to survive.

However, strong pressure and resistance by no means make a breakpoint inevitable. Chance events may intervene to alter the balance of power between change and status quo agents. More important, one or more of the players concerned may take action that alters the balance between the forces of change and resistance. Any action or event, even a small one, that alters the balance can either precipitate or postpone a breakpoint.

CHANGE SCENARIOS

Although breakpoints cannot be predicted with precision, when change forces are building in the face of strong resistance, one is asking for trouble if no preparation is made for the possibility of a discontinuity. The uncertainty surrounding a potential breakpoint demands consideration of scenarios to explore how the situation may develop.

Change scenarios involve movement from one location in the change arena to another caused by changes in the strength of the forces of change and resistance.[6] The range of possible scenarios depends on the initial location of the industry or business in the change arena. Here we shall look at the scenarios that might develop from a location on the edge of a potential breakpoint, as in the case of the Finnish sawmilling industry. From this position the system either migrates toward one of the other change types (there are three possible migration scenarios), or it goes through a discontinuity, or it collapses. Each of these possibilities is considered in turn below.

No-Change Scenario

In this scenario (see Exhibit 4-3) increasing resistance and confrontation contain and weaken the forces of change. Over time, the industry moves away from a potential breakpoint toward the no-change region in the change arena. Apart from confronting the change force, the competitive behavior of the industry remains more or less the same.

In most industry scenarios, resistance to change is built around nonmarket structures. Despite spreading communications technology and accompanying globalization, nonmarket structures

EXHIBIT 4–3   **No-Change Scenario**

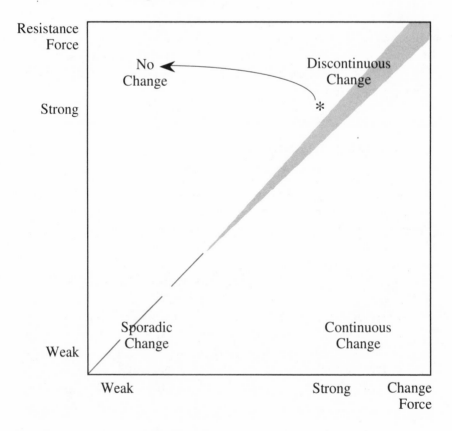

are still very much alive. Witness the difficulties during the negotiation of the General Agreement on Trade and Tariffs in the early 1990s, which were sacrificed on the altar erected by the European farm lobbies. In these cases of resistance, the nonmarket structures protect the industry players from the forces of change, allowing them to preserve their existing attitudes and structures more or less intact.

In Finland, the sawmill operators could have sought government help to offset their high costs and help them to increase market share by competing on price. The labor unions and forest owners already were benefiting from government intervention. If such government support were forthcoming, it would blunt the impact of the drop in demand and reduce the pressure to change, thereby permitting a migration of the industry away from the breakpoint boundary to the region of no change.

Continuous Change Scenario

In this scenario (see Exhibit 4-4), initial protection from the forces of change is needed to buy the time for a gradual conversion of status quo agents into change agents. The conversion of status quo agents reduces the resistance and makes the system more adaptable to the forces of change. The system moves away from a potential breakpoint and, once the protection is removed, goes through a turning point and migrates further toward the zone of continuous change. The continuous change scenario requires a progressively more open, responsive attitude to the change forces on the part of the players. This often occurs when the forces of change are on the supply side; the more competitors become change agents, the more the resistance declines and the forces of change gather momentum.

The gradual integration of the softwood industry in some countries and the development of value-added products by some players provided a good example of continuous change in the 1980s. The increasing use of integration to get closer to the end-users and segment their needs, together with better logistics and automation of production, allowed players like the Swedes to supply a continually more customized product offering.

The Finns could follow the same route by capitalizing on their existing large customer base. They would develop closer ties with importers and merchandisers through alliances and/or selected takeovers. Then better information on end-user needs would be used to drive the production process and develop a continually more responsive, market-driven approach. The shift from a pro-

EXHIBIT 4–4   **Continuous Change Scenario**

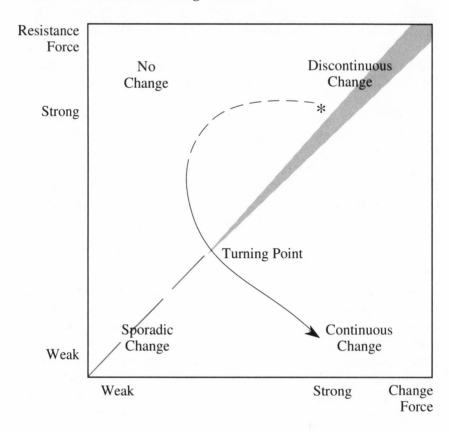

duction to a market-driven culture would be accompanied by the development of value-added products for different market segments. Such a move by the Finns would almost certainly stimulate further moves by the Swedes, thereby strengthening the dominant force of competitive change in the direction of value-added products.

Sporadic Change Scenario

Groups of status quo agents decide to become change agents from time to time and/or the structural impediments to change are removed in a stepwise fashion. Some initial protection may be necessary to give the declining resistance time to take the heat out of the forces of change. The sporadic change scenario (see Exhibit 4-5) often occurs when the forces of change are on the demand side; the more competitors satisfy the demand, the weaker the

Exhibit 4–5 **Sporadic Change Scenario**

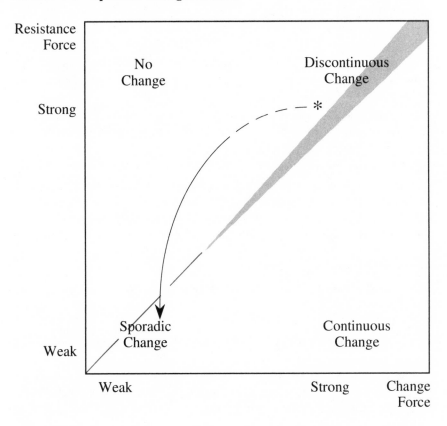

demand force becomes. Since the force of change declines with the declining resistance, there is no need for the industry to go through a turning point. The industry moves away from a potential break-point in the direction of sporadic change, in the lower left region in the change arena.

The sporadic change scenario often occurs during the final phase of the life cycle of a change force when it is weakening. For example, during the final phase of product divergence, a better price-benefit package is periodically tailor-made for a different market segment. Examples have been observed in a wide range of industries: car servicing, watches, sailboats, printing and writing paper, and computer workstations.[7] In all cases, small periodic improvements targeted at particular market segments were made in the original product or service. The impact of each adaptation taken alone was not especially impressive, but taken together, these adaptations added up to a significant response to the final phases of product divergence.

In the sawmilling industry, the drop in demand might be signaling the onset of the final phase in the life cycle of the existing commodity products. The decline in demand would trigger further periodic attempts to reduce the cost of the existing commodity products. The Finnish would first combine forces with the pulp and paper business to campaign for better terms from the forest owners and labor unions. Then they would aggressively pursue greater productivity through further rationalization of facilities and improvement in work processes. In so doing, the Finnish players would become the low-cost leaders in Europe, capable of beating the Canadians for the business vacated by the Russians. In Europe, the Finns would effectively dominate the final cost-driven phase of the old commodity product life cycle.

Discontinuous Change Scenario

Resistance delays change until increasing force suddenly overwhelms both the status quo agents and the existing structure, causing a breakpoint in behavior. This change scenario (see Exhibit 4-6) plays itself out in the top right-hand region of the arena, where the rules of competitive behavior in the industry change sharply. When force and resistance are finely balanced, even relatively minor chance occurrences can trigger a breakpoint. All that's needed is for one competitor or one player to switch sides, and suddenly the entire industry or market changes its sentiment and behavior.

According to one account, the U.S. stock market, in the late summer of 1987, was finely balanced between change agents following the deteriorating fundamentals and status quo agents with expectations adapted to recent price trends. The mere hint of waning support for the dollar from the U.S. Treasury was enough to tilt the balance in the direction of the change agents. The result was Black Monday, a day that upended the financial services industry.[8]

New products can generate an industry breakpoint. A new product may emerge through unrelated trial-and-error attempts by different competitors. Frustrated with the low returns from the status quo, change agent competitors begin to experiment. Status quo competitors mock the results of the abortive experiments. Nothing is really visible in the marketplace until the new product makes its mark in the market. Even then, established status agents may try

EXHIBIT 4–6   **Discontinuous Change Scenario**

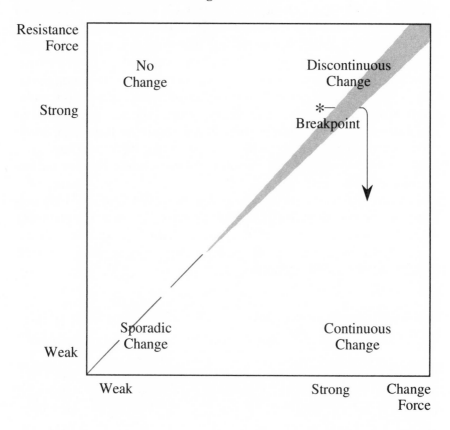

to ignore the new product as irrelevant to the main competitive game. When sales reach a certain level, however, one of the established players jumps in, the others are forced to follow suit, and the industry goes through a sharp shift in competitive behavior.

Price wars can also trigger industry breakpoints. To survive the drop in demand, the Finns and other competitors might be forced into a further round of radical consolidation designed to bring the supply of softwood in Europe down into line with the lower demand. Such restructuring could suddenly transform the competitive structure of the industry, resulting in fewer, bigger, but leaner players better adapted to the low-cost force of change.

Collapse Scenario

Increasing resistance is met by increasing force and that eventually causes a fatal breakpoint in the form of a structural collapse of the system. In the change arena (see Exhibit 4-7), the system moves to the upper right-hand corner and then falls off the chart. The final downward direction of the arrow reflects the collapse of resistance once the structure gives way and the system drops out of the domain of stable behavior.

Markets rarely collapse in the sense that they suddenly go out of existence. Most price collapses fall into the category of a discontinuous change scenario, during which the market may stop functioning, at most temporarily. In the rare case that markets do disappear suddenly, it is usually the result of government intervention, as in the new Commonwealth of Independent States that has replaced the Soviet Union.

Companies and other institutions, however, frequently do collapse at the end of their life cycles. Some do so more dramatically than others as in the case of Drexel Burnham Lambert. Industries, made up of a set of competitors, may also collapse when they are overtaken by a new technology, or new rules of the competitive

EXHIBIT 4–7   **Collapse Scenario**

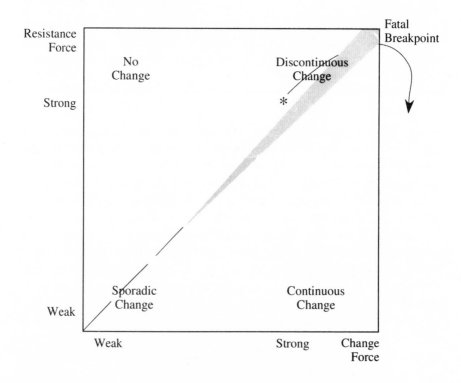

game. In the softwood industry, if demand were to drop further, accompanied by persistently higher Finnish raw material and labor costs, and no change in strategy, the Finnish industry could collapse. The Finnish players would be priced out of the market.

Probability of Scenarios

The closer a system is to the edge of a breakpoint the less room it has for maneuver. On the very edge of the breakpoint it is difficult to avoid getting pushed over the edge by a small fluctuation in the forces of change or resistance. In this situation collapse is often the most likely scenario. A little further back from the edge, there is more chance that a discontinuous change scenario can be initiated in a controlled way, or, alternatively, that the resistance can be strengthened to contain the force of change. Still further from the edge, the resistance is strong enough to protect the system from the forces of change while any of the scenarios, including sporadic or continuous change, play themselves out. The probability of the various scenarios depends on how the forces of change and resistance evolve, taking into account the possible moves of the various players.

The Finnish sawmilling industry was still far enough from the edge of the discontinuity (with sufficient financial reserves to give the activist tradition of Finnish management and the government enough time) to make the no-change and collapse scenarios unlikely. A breakpoint in the form of radical restructuring would be defeatist and was only likely as a last resort, but nevertheless could be precipitated by chance events. Assessing the relative probability of the sporadic change scenario and the continuous change scenario was more difficult. The former required government intervention to deal with the unions and forest owners, whereas the latter required substantial reserves to support the slow process of continuous change.

However, the purpose of developing scenarios is not primarily to assess their probability. The uncertainty surrounding them makes this a hazardous exercise. Rather it is to stretch the mind of management so that it can put together a course of action for dealing with the possible outcomes. Looking at the sawmilling industry, the management of a major Finnish player concluded that the best way of exploiting the situation was not sporadic change aimed at cutting costs to the bone, as some of their competitors were doing, because this would have meant adapting to a potentially declining force of change. Rather they drew on the financial strength of their parent company for protection while initiating continuous adaptation to the growing force of change favoring value-added products.

KEYS TO PRACTICE: MAPPING OUT SCENARIOS

1. Locate industry in the change arena using an assessment of the strength of the forces of change and resistance. The history of the forces provides a useful check on their strength. Compare predicted behavior with the observed state of the system; if inconsistent, re-examine forces of change and resistance.
2. When the forces of change are weak but growing with relatively low resistance, look for a turning point in the industry; when the forces of change are strong and growing against strong resistance, look for a breakpoint.
3. Use the five standard scenarios (no change, continuous change, sporadic change, discontinuous change, and collapse) to map out different ways in which the forces of change and resistance might evolve, allowing for possible moves of the various players.

CHAPTER 5

Developing Strategic Change Scenarios

H ANS WINZENRIED APPARENTLY had a golden opportunity when he took over as managing director of Securiton AG. One of two leading companies in the Swiss alarm systems industry, Securiton had a large installed base of systems, with an enviable reputation for up-to-date quality, reliability, and service. Securiton also benefited from being part of Securitas, the financially strong, family-run group that dominated the provision of guard services throughout the country.[1]

In the two years that followed Winzenried's appointment, sales increased, but a fierce competitive price war squeezed profit margins. Under the influence of the government's safety regulations, competitors' products had converged toward a high-quality standard. Growth had slowed to 5 percent per year and price became the main competitive weapon, with a disastrous impact on margins.

At the same time, the technology of alarm systems began to change quickly. The major innovation was the introduction of software. In both the intrusion and fire alarm sectors, software was creating a shift from simple devices to "intelligent" systems, from signals to screening out false alarms, from recording events to dispatching assistance, from dispersed to centralized computer-controlled systems. Another visible trend was the emerging concept of integrated building management, the integration of air-conditioning, lighting, access control, fire detection, and protection systems, as well as maintenance, into a single system controlled by a central computer. In addition, cameras and videos were replacing human guards, while telecommunication was linking building systems into networks.

A wave of new entrants was threatening the established players. Companies active in computers, lighting, climate control, telecommunications, and electronics were looking at the growth opportunities offered by the European security industry. Multinationals with financial strength, economies of scale, and marketing capabilities were leading the way. IBM, Philips, and Siemens were active in access control. Honeywell was using its base in climate control to develop expertise in total building management. Even smaller companies like the Danish Group ISS, active in office cleaning and cafeteria services, were moving into security with alarm centers and well-trained intervention forces.

Insurance company and government regulators, however, were inhibiting change. In Europe, standards differed slightly from country to country. Some European standards applied in Germany, for example, but not yet in France. European Community norms were beginning to bite, even in the Swiss security industry. The development of standardized products at the European level would create a continental market, opening doors for the large, internationally active companies. Many feared that standardization within Europe would reduce requirements to the lowest common denominator and Swiss standards would sink as a result.

In the case of fire alarms, the Swiss closely followed the German norms. Government safety regulators set the standards for fire alarms in schools, hotels, hospitals, and public office buildings. The regulations combined minimum technical requirements with judgments on the reliability of the systems manufacturer and the adequacy of its service network. Important criteria for official approval of a specific security system included the size and reputation of the company, as well as the number of systems already installed. Insurance companies recorded the established prescriptions and made sure they were observed.

Inside Securiton, Winzenried was struggling to cope with the price war, not to mention the gathering forces of change. Although Securiton was a leader in the Swiss market, its earlier strengths were rapidly becoming obstacles to change.

The more aggressive style of Winzenried was tempered by continual interaction with the owner–manager family. Winzenried's office was next to Manuel Spreng's, the eldest brother and third generation of the family. The Spreng family ran the group paternalistically, looking after loyal employees in the tradition of a family firm solidly rooted in the Canton of Berne known for its deliberate response to events. The managers of administration, marketing, and production, for example, had been appointed years ago. Laying off employees was only to be done as a last resort. Centralization and tradition were hallmarks of Securiton's management style.

Securiton's mind-set had been shaped by the company's origin as a support for the surveillance operations of the larger Security Services Division. Securiton began as a technical profit center, developing security products and acquiring know-how. Later it became a separate company with its own sales force and entered new areas. The managers took it for granted that good detectors and alarm systems would sell themselves.

The history of the company resulted in a functional, top-down structure that made the whole organization slow to respond to market pressure. Within Securiton's overall functional structure, each area—marketing, production, administration—had its own separate information and computer system. The weak communication among functions made planning and control difficult.

The nature of Securiton's production process in particular made change slow. The production process involved the customized design, assembly, and testing of alarm system control panels and certain specialized detectors. Job shop–type production with short runs made it difficult for the company to adapt to price competition. Most of the parts were bought outside. When Securiton lacked part of a new technology, such as the surface-mounted devices for new control panels, the know-how had to be acquired, which increased the time needed to get the product to the market.

As the technology moved further toward microprocessor-based systems, Securiton had less of the necessary know-how in-house. Product development was adapted to available software which came primarily from other industries. Although Securiton had a development department, it undertook no fundamental software research. Ideas for new technologies, products, or processes usually came from visits to exhibitions, or from joint projects with competitors and other industries such as telecommunications.

Recruitment was becoming more acute with the shortage of both software and electronic engineers in Europe. As Winzenried put it:

> The labor market has dried up. It is increasingly difficult to keep
> young people in the company. Our salaries within the industry are

comparable, but our young technicians get better job offers mainly from service industries that can afford higher salaries such as banks. So after two years of training, they leave. It is costing us a great deal.

In 1986, 22 percent of the employees left the company and at the end of 1986, 48 percent of Securiton's employees had been with the company less than two years.

As he surveyed the situation, Winzenried realized that he was at the helm of a leaking ship. The big question was whether he should fix the leaks by making Securiton more cost effective, or whether he should change the company's strategy.

However, the strategic alternatives that would emerge from the change under way in the industry were not immediately apparent. Because the change forces were still emerging, the change process was not as advanced as in other situations where the new competitive strategies are implicit in the behavior of competitors. Before mapping out the industry scenarios and deciding on a course of action for Securiton, Winzenried had to project the changes in the competitive game.

This chapter provides guidelines for projecting

- Changes in competitive behavior when the forces of change are still emerging and weak. The new competitive behavior shows up on the demand side in terms of new products and markets, and on the supply side in terms of new activities in the industry chain, accompanied by new competitive strategies.
- Strategic change scenarios that combine the new competitive strategies with the change scenarios discussed in Chapter 4. Since the change forces are weak, the industry is still far enough from the edge of a discontinuity to have access to the full range of change scenarios.

CHANGES IN COMPETITIVE BEHAVIOR

The forces of change provide the key to the new competitive behavior that is likely to be successful beyond radical industry change. The trends and trajectories, turning points and cycles, identified as forces of change can be used to inform the intuitive process in projecting the strategic alternatives that will be available in terms of products and markets, supply chain and distribution channels, and competitive strategies.

Implications of Trends and Trajectories

In a competitive market, the value/price offer can only improve over time. Breakthroughs in new products, services, and intangibles like image offer more perceived value at a similar price, while process breakthroughs lead to price battles that offer the same value at a lower price. (Monopoly situations and scarce resources are the main exceptions: if a price war leads to a concentration of market power, the value/price offer may deteriorate when prices stabilize.)

In the alarm systems industry the natural trajectory was toward more intelligent and integrated systems. The spread of the microprocessor made it only a matter of time before more intelligent, automated systems began to dominate the market. At the same time, integration was being shaped by the progressive development of software capable of managing the interface between the different technologies that go into a building.

Implications of Turning Points and Cyclical Change

The basic cyclical pattern of alternation between divergence and convergence is central to projecting new strategies. If competition has been around product differentiation and perceived value, for example, the new competitive strategies will probably emphasize process and cost control. The sequence during an idealized industry life cycle is a useful reminder of what might happen:

Turning point	Next phase of cycle	Basis of new competitive strategies
New product breakthrough	Diverging new products	Product technology and perceived product value
Price drop	Converging growth	Market share and product cost
Product differentiation	Diverging differentiation	Market share and perceived value
Price drop	Converging maturity	Process technology and cost reduction

Competitive disequilibrium is common after a turning point. The sharper the turning point, the more the transition is like a breakpoint, and the more the overshooting in the opposite direction. The pendulum analogy is appropriate: the farther the pendulum is pulled out on one side, the farther it swings to the other side. Especially when information is scarce, change agents will push the system farther than necessary before the uncertainty is reduced and it becomes clear that the correction has gone too far. The other side of a discontinuity is invariably a disequilibrium that is the very opposite of the competitive equilibrium that neoclassical economics talks about so much. It is an environment in which big names with outdated strategies become obsolete and new stars with new strategies emerge overnight.

The new strategies are often characterized by high return and low risk. Normally, high returns are only available at high risk. But on the other side of a breakpoint, those who make the first good move to exploit the new situation have an excellent chance of success at low risk because there is little competition. Apple created a breakpoint by opening up the huge market for individual, decentralized computing and launching itself as a major new player. After Apple, the best response was IBM's full jump into the new market. The conservatism of the other big computer companies left them either on the other side, or in the middle of the discontinuity, in both cases an expensive mistake. The highest-risk strategy is yesterday's conservatism.

Product/Market Changes

The market segments beyond an industry turning point may be simple to project because they are typically the outcome of external trends, like demographics or the economic cycle. If there is a breakpoint in the external trends, however, then the anticipation of future demand segments becomes as creative as guessing the technological side of the product.

The market segments in the Swiss alarm systems industry showed no signs of significant discontinuity. The major segments in the large building market, defined by slightly different buying criteria across the main industry groupings, were unlikely to change their basic preferences. Intrusion alarm systems would remain somewhat more important to the banking industry, while fire alarm systems would continue to interest the hotel and chemical industries. All big building owners would still look for a security partner that could provide the image and service necessary for a long-term relationship. The renovation business was likely to rival the new systems market. The technical performance necessary to satisfy the insurance and government regulators would be taken more or less for granted. However, as the systems became more complex, the big clients would inevitably rely more and more on consultants to make the necessary price/performance comparisons.

In the small-owner and household market, the price performance relationship would continue to dominate. The main channels of distribution would be the electrofitters for more complex systems and mass merchandising outlets for simple, self-contained systems. Because of the low penetration so far, the new systems market would dominate the renovation market. In brief, the market segments would be an important element of continuity in the industry.

To estimate what the successful new product will be is often at the heart of a strategic change scenario. As failure rates consistently demonstrate, "seeing" the new product is by no means self-evident. The 1973 oil crisis produced an interesting example in the market for car radios. The sudden jump in the oil price was accompanied by a vertiginous drop in the demand for car radios, making it very difficult to see future demand segments. The solution in this case was to suspend judgment and fall back on the core product. While other competitors were cutting back production, one company augmented its market share dramatically by heavily promoting its core product.

In other situations product development trends and especially the technology trajectory can be important. These can be summarized with a mapping of the product history.[2] On the dimensions of perceived value and delivered cost, previous products can be either positioned as customized products or reduced in cost relative to the core. New core products develop as hybrids of previous core products or, alternatively if the breakpoint is sharp enough, out of an altogether new technology. The advantage of the product history mapping is that it highlights the underlying technology trajectories and the recent product development and therefore where the development after the breakpoint is likely to be.

The product offering of the Swiss alarm systems industry was expected to change fundamentally over the next few years in the big building segment. The performance/price curve was shifting rapidly. Today's offerings in the broadest definition included safes, workplace protection, fire protection, guard service, fire and intrusion alarm systems, and access control. Tomorrow's product, in the big building market at least, would be part of a highly customized, integrated building management system: fire and intrusion alarms; access control; technical (camera and other) surveillance, not only for fire and intrusion but also for inside climate control, lighting, and maintenance; information processing from the alarm and control devices; and communication of relevant information to intervention and maintenance services. One of the roles in the new competitive game would be the design and supply of integrated building management systems for industry, banks, hotels, and public sector projects.

In the household and small-owner market, the change in the product offering was likely to be much less pronounced. The advantages of integrated systems were known to decline with decreasing size. Operating costs, especially in terms of personnel, decreased much less than proportionately in smaller buildings. In this segment, the rules of the game would remain centered around the supply of a range of standardized devices and self-contained systems to mass merchandisers with the possibility of integration into home computer systems and neighborhood guard services on the upper end of the range.

Industry Chain Changes

Supply and distribution channels can be as central a part of the changing rules of the competitive game as the products themselves. The more radical the product discontinuity, the more likely it will be accompanied by a major discontinuity in the industry chain made up of suppliers, manufacturers, and distributors. But the relationship is not one to one. Even if the product does not change dramatically, the industry chain may be at the center of a shift in the rules of the game.

A useful internal clue to the new industry chain configuration is the locus of profitability. Early on in an industry cycle, most value is added upstream, in R&D and design. This is also where the most profits are made, until the competition builds up. Once that happens, a competitor may create a breakpoint by shifting the locus of profitability farther downstream through cost reduction. As the industry cycle evolves, either smoothly or discontinuously, the locus of profitability in the supply chain often shifts closer to the customer.

The product change in the alarm systems industry inevitably would create a dramatic shift in the industry chain. The locus of value-added and profitability in the large building market segment would shift down the industry chain, toward systems consulting which could integrate the disparate building system technologies into a coherent, customized approach. The systems consultants might master one or more of the basic building system technologies in-house. Alternatively, they could concentrate on systems integration while subcontracting out the system building blocks.

Specialized original equipment manufacturers would fill out the upstream part of the supply chain. One of the new roles would involve specialized security system producers making a range of standardized systems that could be plugged into an integrated building management system. Very little in the big building supply chain would remain continuous. The role of every player would be redefined and most alarm systems manufacturers would not survive in their present form.

In the household market industry chain by contrast, manufacturers would continue to sell their products through mass merchandisers on the low-price end of the market and possibly through electrofitters or other building subcontractors on the high end. The role of electrofitters per se would diminish, however, as radio and other signals become more widely used to communicate between detectors, alarms, and control panels. In brief, the industry chain in the household segment would show relatively little change over time.

New Competitive Strategies

The new competitive strategies (see Exhibit 5-1) embody the response of competitors to the developments in the product markets and the industry chain caused by the forces of change. This response is shaped by the resistance, especially that associated with the competitors' existing business system. As a result, four different types of strategy can be identified in most change processes. These correspond to the different combinations of forces of change and resistance in the change arena.

Old game strategies. These are the strategies associated with old rules of the game still operative in those market segments that will be characterized by strong forces of resistance and weak forces of change.

An example in the alarm systems industry would be the sale of customized alarm systems to smaller building owners and larger home owners. This would be the closest thing to a niche formula

EXHIBIT 5-1   **New Competitive Strategies**

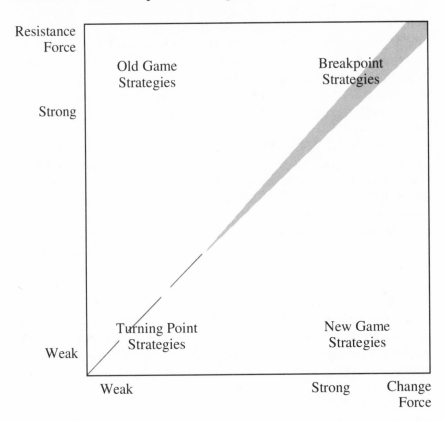

not affected by the forces of change. These buildings would be too small to make integrated building management economically attractive. However, the needs of the occupants would be too diverse to be adequately served by the standardized black boxes sold through the mass merchandisers. An integrated offer of guard services could be used to protect the niche from the security subsystems offered by other manufacturers in the large building segment. Apart from a good relationship with contractors, as well as project design and service skills, the key success factors would then include the telecommunication technology for tying in the guard service.

New game strategies.   These are the strategies associated with the change agents creating new rules of the game applicable in all segments that will experience strong forces of change. New game strategies are accessible to those competitors able to lower their resistance and make the full transition from the old status quo to the new change agent competitive behavior.

In the alarm systems industry an example would be the design and supply of integrated building management systems for the large building market segment. The key feature of this strategy would be the ability to integrate the various components of a building management system. Competitors would either make their mark here or fail, especially with respect to the software know-how needed for the interface between the technologies of the various building subsystems. In the portfolio of competencies, the key requirements would be software engineering skills, consulting ability combined with a flair for marketing, and project design and management. To nurture these competencies, the organizational mind-set and culture would have to be closer, not to those of a manufacturing but to a professional firm. Another example of a new game strategy in a different market segment would be the sale of small, self-contained systems through mass merchandisers to middle-income home owners. Apart from the critical initial design, the key feature of the strategy would be the combination of purchasing, assembly, and distribution to provide low delivered cost. However, the necessary economies of scale probably would require production volumes that exceeded the potential demand in the Swiss market. An international distribution network, therefore, would be essential. Consumer marketing and brand image would make all the difference. The organization culture best suited to this high-volume, low-cost strategy would be that of an international consumer-products company.

Turning point strategies. These are the strategies adopted by players making an incremental transition between the old and new competitive behavior. Alternatively, if these strategies are not developed further into one of the new game strategies, they may be adapted to market segments that will be protected from the full impact of the change forces.

In the alarm systems industry, a turning point strategy might involve the sale of partially integrated systems incorporating, for example, fire, intrusion, access, and voice communication control to small- and intermediate-sized building owners. Alarm systems manufacturers would use this as a first step toward the development of the systems know-how for integrated building management. Alternatively, they might be able to create a new longer-term niche market for dedicated systems that do not involve full integrated building management.

Breakpoint strategies.   In a reactive mode, these are the strategies adopted by players forced to make a discontinuous transition from the old to the new competitive behavior. They do not have time for a turning point strategy with continuous or stepwise acquisition of the competence needed to play the new game. Instead, they are constrained to quickly modify their old game strategies for the new game.

In the alarm systems industry, an example would be the sale of standardized alarm subsystems for integration into building management systems. The key would be to standardize the existing alarm systems and provide modular, adaptable, cost effective subsystems that could be easily integrated with other building technologies. The existing approach could be modified quite quickly because, apart from the design function, the other business system activities could be carried over with relatively little change.

STRATEGIC CHANGE SCENARIOS

Viable competitive strategies not only reflect the interplay between forces of change and resistance, but if adopted by enough competitors, they shape the interplay of forces. As a result, the choice of competitive strategy influences the probability of the industry change scenarios and conversely. This two-way link between the dominant strategies followed by most of the competitors and the likely scenario results in the strategic change scenarios listed below (see also Exhibit 5-2):

Strategic Change Scenarios

Dominant Strategies	*Likely Change Scenario*
Old game strategies	No change
New game strategies	Continuous change
Turning point strategies	Sporadic change
Breakpoint strategies	Discontinuous change

In the case of an industry that is well back from the edge of discontinuous change, all the change scenarios are feasible. The collapse scenario is not shown above because it does not constitute a viable basis for strategic change. Moreover, since the industry is

EXHIBIT 5–2   **Strategic Change Scenarios**

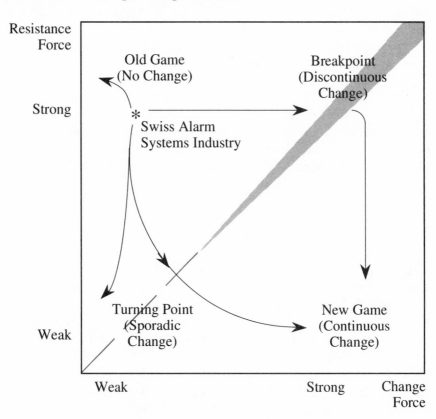

anticipating change the collapse scenario is much less likely than it would be if the industry were reacting from the edge of the discontinuity.

To get from the old game dominated by the status quo agents to the new game promoted by the change agents, there are two basic sequences of strategic change:

1. The resistance to change is lowered first and the industry moves through a turning point as the forces of change pick up in strength. The industry thereafter begins to adapt more continuously.
2. The change forces strengthen before the industry has had a chance to adapt. The industry is forced through a breakpoint to eliminate the resistance so that thereafter it can adapt more continuously.

Alternatively, if the forces of change do not prevail entirely, the balance between the forces of change and resistance will determine which of the four strategic change scenarios obtains. The industry either persists with the old game, moves to the new game, or gets stuck on the boundary between the two.

Old Game Strategies—No-Change Scenario

In the alarm systems industry, the difference in standards and regulations between Switzerland and the European Community might persist, which would protect the domestic competitors playing the old game. Alternatively, the old game might continue on a reduced scale with niche strategies designed to sell customized alarm systems to smaller building and large home owners.

New Game Strategies—Continuous Change Scenario

The nature of the forces of resistance both inside and outside the industry made an immediate continuous change–new game scenario unlikely. In the large building segment, administrative costs would preclude a gradual, smooth adaptation of local regulations to European norms. In the low end of the market, attempts to develop a black box mass merchandising strategy would stimulate price competition by encouraging continuous competition from Southeast Asia. Because of the high local production costs this scenario would be suicidal for the Swiss competitors. However, in the longer run, the technical and multinational competitive forces suggested that the new game strategies would dominate with integrated building management for the large building segment and black boxes for the consumer segment. The question was how the transition from the old to the new game might occur.

Turning Point Strategies—Sporadic Change Scenario

The sporadic change scenario was plausible, because it was compatible with the possible strategic moves of both local and international competitors. Not only could a stepwise harmonization of standards be envisaged sometime in the future, but even more probably, the larger local competitors would begin acquiring the competencies necessary for integrated building management. At the same time, new multinational entrants would presumably expand their local presence in integrated building management. The increase in supply would soon satisfy the local demand for integrated building management, thereby reducing the change force until other factors intervened to create a new increase in demand later on.

Breakpoint Strategies—Discontinuous Change Scenario

The breakpoint–discontinuous change scenario would bring the foreign multinationals into the Swiss market at one fell swoop as standards were harmonized in a single step. Unless they had prepared for this eventuality, the Swiss competitors would not have time to acquire the competence needed for integrated building management. The multinationals would dominate this key segment, forcing local competitors into the roles of either original alarm subsystems suppliers, or status quo small building niche players. Alternatively, the Swiss competitors might initiate the breakpoint by merging or otherwise aligning themselves as alarm subsystems suppliers with the foreign multinationals.

Considering these strategic change scenarios, Winzenried realized that Securiton was faced with a particularly complex situation. Some of his top managers were not convinced that radical change was necessary. Securiton had difficulty responding because of its traditional mind-set, inflexible organization, and lack of technicians and engineers. The forces of change plus the continued pursuit of traditional product improvement without concerted rationalization were pushing Securiton closer to a potential corporate breakpoint requiring a major streamlining of its organization.

At the same time, Securiton was under increasing pressure to follow its main competitor, Cerberus, in a radical redefinition of its product offering. Cerberus had already rationalized operations and was beginning to form international alliances to obtain economies of scope, as well as some of the technology necessary for integrated building management. In effect, Cerberus had initiated a turning point strategy.

Some of Securiton's managers had been consoling themselves with the observation that, despite the threat of new entrants, integrated building management had made little headway in the Swiss market. As one of the leaders in the market, the company merely had to hang on until the price competition ran out of steam. However, the strategic change scenarios highlighted its myopia. Precisely because no headway had been made, the change when it came could be especially abrupt and discontinuous. Traditional companies like Securiton were particularly vulnerable. The more the wave of change was held up by resistance, the more competitive turmoil would be unleashed when it broke.

When Hasler, the international Swiss telecommunications company, also active in security systems, approached Securiton about an alliance, Winzenried seized the opportunity. He decided that an alliance would be the best way of getting some of the necessary technology for integrated building management, while circumventing the resistance to change within Securiton. Hasler was especially interested in getting access to Securiton's new intrusion alarm control unit in exchange for cash and a joint marketing and service arrangement. After some typically discreet negotiations an agreement was signed.

Some commentators were quite skeptical about Securiton's long-term chances with a partner several times its size; they believed Securiton would soon be reduced to the role of a specialized subsystems supplier. Nevertheless, Winzenried, who personally managed the Securiton side of the alliances, increased Securiton's role. Taking advantage of the shake-up that the alliance created, he streamlined Securiton's management and administration, and tackled the high turnover of personnel with better salaries and longer training. In 1990, three years after the alliance was formed, Securiton was managing the joint security business of both partners, while benefiting from Hasler's technology and software know-how. Although it still suffered from employee turnover and a cost hangover, Securiton had become one of the change agents in the industry. Together with Cerberus, it was implementing a turning point toward an integrated building management approach to the market.

With the two leading domestic players moving in that direction, a turning point strategy with sporadic change was becoming the most likely scenario in the industry. The old game strategies with no change had been left behind by the two leading players. New game strategies with continuous change were still some way off because of the external government-related nature of some of the resistance to change. Breakpoint strategies with discontinuous change in the near future were still possible, but unlikely, given the reluctance of the Swiss authorities to lower their safety standards and regulations to allow pan-European players into the market. And the more local players began adapting to the forces of change, the less of a jump or collapse could occur in the future even if standards were harmonized.

Securiton, like other companies, found that forming a realistic view of the future is as much a struggle with the resistance to change as it is an effort to discern the forces of change. Hence, the importance of all executives being involved in a regular process of scenario development and testing. To anticipate breakpoints, it is crucial that the scenarios integrate the new competitive behavior into the change process.

The attitude of the Securiton executives illustrates how misleading projections of strategic behavior can be if they are not embedded in change scenarios. The existing cost reduction strategy with a no-change scenario had been favored by many executives until a closer examination of change and resistance forces suggested that if nothing was done, a corporate breakpoint was far more likely. But the Securiton story also shows how the development of strategic change scenarios can be used not only to anticipate breakpoints, but also to position the company for the future.

KEYS TO PRACTICE: DEVELOPING STRATEGIC CHANGE SCENARIOS

1. Describe the rate of business change.
2. Identify forces of change.
3. Assess resistance to change.
4. Locate the industry in the change arena.
5. Use forces of change to project the new competitive strategies. Distinguish between new game strategies that will be relevant if the forces of change prevail, and turning point and breakpoint strategies appropriate for the transition between the old and new games.
6. Sketch out strategic change scenarios based on the possible interplay between forces of change and resistance, including the moves and strategies of the various players.
7. Test resulting scenarios against the unfolding reality, repeat steps one through six, and update.

PART II

Exploiting Breakpoints

E VEN WITH THE BEST of attention, a company can be late anticipating a breakpoint. Shifts in the rules of the competitive game can be provoked by sudden events outside the industry, or by a sudden move by competitors. The shift may not be perceived as radical change until well after it begins. Whatever its origins, a fundamental shift in external conditions looks like a breakpoint to those who are late sensing it.

This part of the book contrasts the possible responses to an imminent breakpoint. The force of change is largely external, associated with an industry scenario that has already begun to unfold. Under these conditions, the intervention path chosen by management is crucial for success. Chapter 6 looks at the viable intervention paths corresponding to different combinations of the forces for change and resistance as experienced by the company or business unit. Chapter 7 contrasts organizing approaches appropriate for the intervention paths. Chapter 8 considers how the organizational energy for radical change can be mobilized with corresponding implementation styles. In Chapter 9, all of this is brought together to examine how a latecomer can come from behind to exploit the breakpoints and leapfrog the competition.

CHAPTER 6

Choosing an Intervention Path

THE AUTOMOTIVE MARKET for robots suddenly collapsed in the mid-1980s. Competitors were forced to restructure. Cincinnati Milacron announced a $52 million write-off in 1985. GE lost $200 million and later abandoned the business. Westinghouse stopped making naked robots and closed the industry's pioneering company, Unimation. General Motors Fanuc consolidated its six locations, centralized services, and targeted nonautomotive segments.

The market for stand-alone "naked" robots was saturated. For many production managers, robots were a disappointment: "Although robots are full of clever chips, they have to be programmed and configured for each task, which is a laborious business." Customers were unable to use many more naked robots without the potential for additional applications. The predominant form of stand-alone robots was often expensive, dedicated to one product and justified only for very large production volumes.

Jean-Pierre Jeannet and Robert Howard have described how ASEA Robotics, the largest European player, was considering its alternatives.[1] In the words of Nick Rizvi, one of the executives at ASEA Robotics,

> The rules of the robotics game appear to have changed; it is no
> longer clear what the future rules will be. Where we were once
> safe selling naked robots, we now need to take bigger risks and
> sell complete systems. To meet the growing systems demand, we

must find sufficient human resources with diverse engineering backgrounds. The financial risks associated with bidding in the systems area are not small.

The issue for ASEA was whether to follow its American competitors and cut back. Alternatively, three basic competitive strategies seemed to be available for staying in the game. The first was the naked robot strategy, where ASEA and its competitors had put most of their competitive effort up until 1985. The second was the robot package strategy, which equipped a naked robot to perform a given application such as welding or gluing. And the third was the systems strategy, which involved integrating one or more robots into a production process.

The first alternative, ASEA's existing naked robot strategy, was threatened not only by the demand shift, but also by Japanese competitors like Fanuc, Yaskawa, Kawasaki, and Matsushita Electric. These players were at the forefront of robotics hardware and were expected to remain there for the immediate future. Japanese robots had more flexible controls, which made them easier to adapt. Being quicker at new product introduction, the Japanese had a wider product range and were also very cost competitive. However, they were not as sophisticated in software development, or client problem solving.

Competing head-on with the Japanese was a challenge that Stelio Demark, the head of ASEA Robotics, and his team were not willing to ignore without some thought. The profit margin on basic robots was still 10–15 percent. Apart from moving to more flexible control panels, the product line concept and customer mix would not have to be changed much. But it would mean a transformation of the organization, making it more cost competitive, better at adapting naked robots to different end-uses, and quicker at new product introduction.

ASEA had already been drawn into the second strategic alternative, robot packaging. The robot centers in the national ASEA sales organizations often provided the application package. But this was done on an ad hoc basis, without any coordination with the experience elsewhere in the company. "In the process," said Demark, "we give our customers a considerable amount of applications knowledge free of charge because it is so difficult to sell engineering advice as a hardware supplier. However, if we already had tailor-made solutions for given applications, we could sell the robot as a package and get paid for it." An applications package typically added 30 to 75 percent to the value of the base robot, with a net margin after engineering and hardware of 10 to 15 percent.

Some 200 potential applications were identified in a preliminary review. Each corresponded to a standardized production task on the shop floor with a minimum of systems engineering. However, the robot packaging strategy would require a major, focused effort to develop the packages. On average, five to ten man/years would be required per package. Demark estimated that the subsidiaries were already devoting approximately fifty man/years to ad hoc applications, but he had only indirect control over the engineering resources at the robot center in the sales organizations abroad.

The attraction of the third alternative—the systems business—was high gross margins associated with high value-added. The systems integrator assumed the role of the general contractor and delivered the entire robot system at the prearranged price. "For a typical system of about $20 million, the robot content is about 10 percent, or $2 million, which is about the cost of 25 naked robots. The average net profitability of a systems integrator is 2 percent or $400,000."

Although gross margins were high, cost overruns, or unexpected events, could easily wipe out the entire profit on a systems project. A German company was rumored to have lost as much as DM100 million on one contract alone because of unanticipated cost overruns. ASEA already had systems orders at the subsidiary level, but Demark only considered the Swedish and U.S. subsidiaries to have real systems strengths. The main competitors from Germany—Kuka and Comau—had a competitive advantage because they were essentially production line builders. They could avoid the risk of working with unknown systems by specifying their robots for their production line systems. If ASEA were to make the systems business a major thrust, it would require a radical improvement in systems know-how to ensure profitability and the development of marketing to a new type of customer in the high-potential consumer electronics industry.

ASEA Robotics knew it was in the middle of a major industry breakpoint. The sharp competitive restructuring was characteristic of a discontinuous change scenario: the industry was changing rapidly and radically, forcing the company to deal with the breakpoint. Doing so required the choice of a viable path of management intervention, one that was consistent with the interplay between forces of change and resistance as experienced by the company or business unit.

This chapter looks at

- Management intervention paths of resistance, revitalization, renewal, and restructuring.
- Importance of consistency between the characteristics of the chosen path and the interplay between the forces of change and resistance.

MANAGEMENT INTERVENTION PATHS

When reacting as a latecomer to shifts in the industry environment, managers do not have much influence over the forces of change. The unfolding industry scenario is typically too far advanced and the forces of change too strong to be influenced by a latecomer. Managers are restricted to influencing the forces of resistance and through the interplay between the forces possibly having a small effect on the forces of change. The nature of the interplay between the forces shapes managerial choice by determining the most viable intervention path for the company or business unit. Successful leaders of change are those who are able to capitalize on this interplay between the forces.

There are four available intervention paths leading to the areas of the change arena (see Exhibit 6-1). Their main characteristics are contrasted in Exhibit 6-2.

When choosing an intervention path on the edge of a breakpoint, the key is a correct assessment of the forces of change and resistance. If the change force is strong and still growing, only the more radical change associated with restructuring and revitalization will be able to adapt the company to the change force and allow it to adopt the new game strategies. Restructuring will be needed to break the resistance, when the forces of resistance are entrenched and closed to change. In cases where the organization is open to change, the resistance can be reduced gradually to initiate a corporate turning point followed by all-encompassing revitalization.

If the change force is strong but declining, then the less radical change associated with renewal or resistance will be appropriate. Putting the company through more radical change would be counterproductive. In cases where the forces of resistance are strong

EXHIBIT 6–1   **Intervention Paths for Reacting to a Potential Breakpoint**

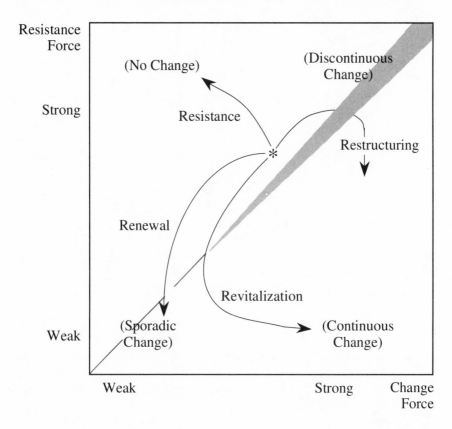

and closed to change, it may be possible to increase the resistance to contain the weakening change force. In cases where the organization is open to change, the resistance can be reduced gradually to initiate sporadic change in the form of a renewal path.

The main characteristics of a chosen intervention path are the scope and pace of change and the approach to closing the competence gap. The scope of change reflects how much of the organization is involved in the process of acquiring new competence. When broad organizational capabilities have to be acquired, for example, more of the organization will be involved than when a particular functional competence has to be developed.

The pace of change reflects the time needed to complete the intervention: whether it occurs in a sudden jump or via ongoing spontaneous adaptation. The type of resistance is crucial in determining the speed with which the change process can be accom-

EXHIBIT 6–2 **Intervention Path Characteristics**

Interplay between Forces of Change and Resistance	Management Intervention Path	Scope of Change	Pace of Change Process	Approach to Closing Competence Gap
Change force strong but declining; resistance closed to change	Resistance	No internal change	Depends on ability to contain change force	No competence gap
Change force strong and growing; resistance open to change	Revitalization	Ongoing change throughout the organization	Slow continuous adaptation	Long-term investment in organizational learning
Change force strong but declining; resistance open to change	Renewal	Change limited to parts of the organization	Periodic stepwise change	Incremental investment over intermediate period
Change force strong and growing; resistance closed to change	Restructuring	Intense change on a few dimensions	Sudden change jumps	Focused investment over a short period

plished. A dramatic restructuring of strategies, structures, and systems can be implemented rather quickly within a few months because it does not attempt to change behavior and skills, nor the organizational learning process. Whenever old habits have to be discarded and replaced by new skills and behavior to be learned, the change process can take years.

The competence gap refers to the deficit in functional skills and organizational behavior relative to what is needed for dealing successfully with the forces of change. The approach to closing the competence gap reflects the kind of investment that can be accomplished on the intervention path.

Resistance Path

This path is appropriate when strong resistance that is closed to change confronts a change force that is strong but declining. The resistance path presumes the firm can avoid a potential organizational breakpoint by working on its environment to create more stable conditions where the change force is weaker. What little change occurs internally is directed toward reducing the pressure exerted by the change force. The resistance path often involves interacting with government and public agencies, trade and industry associations, and other external groups that can channel and reduce the forces of change in the business environment.

MCI Communications Corp. has continually used the courts, regulatory agencies, and appeals to members of Congress to reduce the competitive pressure from AT&T.[2] The company was formed in 1971 when the Federal Communications Commission (FCC) began to allow increased competition in the long-distance telephone market. Lacking sufficient revenues, MCI had to suspend the construction of its communications network because AT&T refused to provide a full range of interconnection services. In March 1974, MCI filed a successful antitrust suit, forcing AT&T to provide the full range of connecting facilities. Over the following decade, MCI grew rapidly to $1 billion in revenues and $170 million in profits.

In 1982, settlement of the antitrust suit between AT&T and the Justice Department separated AT&T long (distance) lines from its regional operating subsidiaries. MCI and the other long-distance competitors like Sprint were guaranteed equal quality of access to the local telephone networks but had to give up their lower access charges. When AT&T forced customers to use extra digits, MCI lost money. MCI appealed to the FCC, and later did so again when

AT&T proposed to match MCI's lower prices with selective discounts to key customers. Once again, rulings in MCI's favor gave the company the room it needed to increase its sales, this time to $5.1 billion for a market share of 12 percent in 1988 and profits of $333 million.[3]

A resistance path alternatively might involve the pursuit of a niche formula, designed to avoid the need for sharp change by finding a corner of the market protected from the change force. This formula is generally more useful for smaller players. Rolex, Audimar Piguet, and the other up-market Swiss watch companies carved out a high-quality niche that shielded them from the massive breakpoint created by Seiko, Citizen, and other East Asian competitors. As one of their managers put it, "We have never heard of the Japanese."

Niche formulas are common in the German-speaking world. Specialized, high-quality products represent the strategy of thousands of medium-sized and small German companies, the so-called "Mittelstand." They have created highly profitable, well-protected niches in the world market. From their niches, the Mittelstand contribute a great deal to Germany's record exports, despite the discontinuities faced by the more exposed major players.

In the robotics industry, the German players, Kuko and Comau, avoided the breakpoint by pursuing their niche strategy of supplying specialized production systems which included robots. However, this was not attractive or really feasible for ASEA and the larger American players. Mounting a campaign to get government protection was also not appealing because of the relatively small size of the industry, not only on a national scale but also relative to the total sales of most of the parent companies involved.

Revitalization Path

Revitalization is appropriate when resistance that is open to change must be adapted to a strong and growing change force. Under these conditions, lowering the resistance usually stimulates the change forces; converting status quo agents into change agents results in a stronger force of change. The pace of change is slow, but continuous and all-encompassing. The company's internal organization is mainly involved. Strong external change forces drive the internal processes. Revitalization can only be implemented if the firm can protect itself from the force of change long enough to accomplish the necessary organizational changes.

On the macro level, if the company becomes more of a complete change agent in its own right, its revitalization may stimulate the change forces in the industry. This is often the case when the forces of change come from the competitors; the more change agents among them the stronger the force of change.

When Jan Carlzon took over as president, the Scandinavian Airlines System (SAS) was struggling with the impact of a worldwide recession and an accumulated two-year deficit of $30 million after seventeen consecutive years of profits.[4] Carlzon felt that SAS had not been putting enough emphasis on customer satisfaction:

> We used to think our biggest assets were aircraft, overhaul stations and technical resources. But we have only one real asset, and that is a satisfied customer prepared to come back to SAS and pay for our costs once more.

Together with a small team of hand-picked people, Carlzon decided to position SAS as the "Businessman's Airline."

While competitors cut back on new product development in the face of sagging demand, SAS invested heavily in its Businessman's Airline Program. Among many initiatives were a cost reduction drive, a new corporate identity, and new marketing projects. Carlzon also instituted a punctuality drive, which he supervised from his office with a viewing screen providing him with details of all flights, their departure and arrival times, and delays. Occasionally he even personally phoned the pilots.

The centerpiece of the change process, however, was a cultural revolution. Under Carlzon's influence, the resistance to change was relatively weak and SAS was open to a continuous change process. Responsibility for action was delegated downward to the front line, putting employees in charge. Management was asked to serve as consultants rather than as leaders of the organization. To implement the cultural revolution, Carlzon and his team personally visited the front line all over the company and established a training program on the new concept of service for 20,000 managers and employees.

According to Carlzon, "Giving a person freedom to take responsibility for his ideas, decisions and actions is to release hidden resources." This type of revitalization works best when the forces of change are strong. Within two years, the $10 million loss at SAS was turned into a $70 million profit. The number of full-fare passengers had increased by 8 percent in Europe and 16 percent in the zero-growth intercontinental market. Corporate overhead was reduced by 25 percent. *Fortune* rated SAS the best business-class airline, and a few months later it received the Airline of the Year Award for outstanding service to the traveling public. Unfortunately, dealing successfully with an imminent breakpoint does not guarantee success with the next turning point. By the early 1990s, SAS had fallen from grace again because it was unable to deal with the new forces of change created by the 1991–1992 recession and the gradual integration of the European aviation market.

Renewal Path

Renewal is appropriate when resistance that is open to change must be adapted to a strong but declining change force. Under these conditions, reducing the resistance usually dampens the change force; the change agents stop pressing for change once their demands are satisfied by the status quo agents. The scope of the change is limited to parts of the company and the pace is sporadic. Both internal and external organization with various stakeholders may be involved. When renewal is used to deal with demand side forces, its success often weakens the change force by satisfying the market demand.

In the 1980s, Procter & Gamble, the detergent giant, and Frito-Lay, the potato chip maker owned by Pepsi, invaded the $2.2 million cookie market that Nabisco had dominated for almost a century. First, Frito-Lay introduced Grandma's cookies that were "so fresh they taste suspiciously close to homemade." Procter & Gamble followed with its Duncan Hines new soft and chewy chocolate chip cookies. "The initial onslaught came in Kansas City, that slice of middle America where consumer-product makers like to test their wares. . . . Whipped into a cookie frenzy with coupons, special displays and advertising, Kansas City's cookie consumption rose 20 percent." Traditionally, very little money was spent to promote cookies. With a heavy barrage of advertising, Frito-Lay was said to have captured 20 percent of the Kansas City market in a few weeks. Procter & Gamble spent $20 million on advertising and promotion for a comfortable 25 percent share in six months.[5]

Nabisco could not help but notice the invasion by Frito-Lay and Procter & Gamble. Nabisco's initial reaction was to add more chocolate chips to its Chips Ahoy hard cookies. Stock analysts on Wall Street were not convinced by this lame response. The management decided to shake off its reputation as "a sleepy sales company that did little to push its products." It initiated a renewal of the product range with the company's biggest cookie development project in years.

Sixteen months after Frito-Lay's first attack, a new Nabisco line with fifteen varieties, called Almost Home, appeared on supermarket shelves. Presented as "the moistest, chewiest, most perfectly baked cookies the world has ever tasted . . . well, almost," the new line was supported by a $25 million advertising counterattack. When the dust finally settled, Frito-Lay's market share had fallen back to 8 percent, Procter & Gamble's to 20 percent. Nabisco with its established warehousing, distribution, and sales strengths had renewed its product line and captured 35 percent of the soft cookie segment.[6]

The renewal path was appropriate for Nabisco because to deal with the change force only part of the organization was involved, in this case, the product development and marketing departments. Moreover, the change force was limited to competition in the market segment for chewy cookies. Once this competition was dealt with and the demand for chewy cookies was satisfied, the change force was much weaker.

Restructuring Path

Restructuring is appropriate when a strong and growing change force confronts strong resistance that is closed to change. On this path the organization is given a sharp shock to adapt it to the environment. The scope of the change is highly focused, typically on organizational "hardware" such as strategy, structure, and systems. This facilitates control of the transition and avoids possible disintegration.

Because of the speed of the organizational leap, not enough time is available for a basic change in beliefs and behavior. Thus, if the leap is to succeed, either it will be the first stage in a multistage intervention process, or beliefs and behavior will have been changing before, in reaction to the crisis created by the resistance to the change force. If behaviors have not changed and appropriate skills have not been learned ahead of time, the reorganization will provide only temporary relief; later on, behavioral aftereffects may undermine the whole change process. In this case, being unable to keep up with the pace of change, the firm ultimately would be vulnerable to collapse.

Organizational restructuring via acquisition, divestment, reorganization, downsizing, and so on is a common way of trying to respond to an external breakpoint, especially in the Anglo-Saxon world. In continental Europe and Japan, the restructuring often takes place within a larger industrial group, where the parent company and related banks play a major role. For companies with strong forces of resistance, the shock created by a radical change imposed from the top down is often the only way of unfreezing and changing existing behavior before the forces of change overwhelm the company.

In the robotics industry, all the major players tried some form of restructuring. After losing $200 million, GE decided to enter a joint venture with Fanuc, based on the latter's strength in machine tool controls and GE's automated production systems know-how. After closing Unimation, Westinghouse began a factory automation joint venture with Matsushita. General Motors Fanuc and ASEA both consolidated their operations.

But for some of the players, restructuring alone was not enough to stay in the game. By the end of 1987, Westinghouse was unhappy with its joint venture and questioning the continuation of its robotics business. General Electric had decided that Fanuc would manufacture all robots in Japan, while GE would distribute Fanuc's products with GE software in the United States. The only way GE and Westinghouse could have remained in robot manufacturing was if these operations had been given the financial backing to implement more fundamental behavioral change.

IMPORTANCE OF CONSISTENCY

Picking an intervention path that is not consistent with the interplay between forces and resistance can lead to disaster. For example, attempting a resistance path in an environment where increased resistance results in stronger forces of change will put the company face to face with a breakpoint it cannot possibly manage. Campaigning for government protection from low-priced imports can lead to disaster later on, unless the time gained is put to good use trying to catch up with the foreign competitors.

Unfortunately, too many industries with protection sit back and reap the benefit of higher margins. If the protection is finally withdrawn, the foreign competition is invariably even further ahead and the domestic industry can no longer compete at all.

Similarly, the sporadic reduction of resistance on a path of renewal cannot be sustained in a disequilibrium setting, no matter whether the disequilibrium is on the industry, economy, or societal level. Anglo American, the dominant mining conglomerate in

South Africa, long prided itself on being a force for change supporting the removal of apartheid. Within the corporation's many subsidiaries, the change in the position of its black employees was one of sporadic evolution. However, when the walls of apartheid actually came tumbling down after the release of Nelson Mandela in February 1990, Anglo American found itself scrambling for protection from the fallout.[7] To deal with this socio-political breakpoint, Anglo American at a minimum should have put its whole management through a crash program to evaluate black–white relations in the company and give them a chance to acquire the skills and behavior needed to adapt to conditions in the "New South Africa."

Conversely, putting a company through a breakpoint when the forces of change are still weak and evolving can be very risky. Since the forces are changing rapidly, it is difficult to know exactly what kind of discontinuity is appropriate. When Texas Instruments introduced the electronic watch, it decided to move rapidly to mass production so as to be as far as possible down the learning curve before competitors followed. Big investments were made in new production technology for electronic watches. Unfortunately, the market did not accept the TI watch as a standard. Instead of following TI across the breakpoint, the industry continued with spontaneous product development. Seiko and others made improvements which soon put the TI watch out of date. Its huge investment in the related production technology was obsolete. In effect, TI tried to trigger a standardization breakpoint in the industry before the product's development had run its course.

In the robotics industry, the forces of change driving the industry breakpoint were in the direction of higher-value-added products in the form of packaged robots and integrated robotics systems. German competitors well positioned for this change were driving in the direction of integrated systems in the upper end of the market. In the lower end of the market, the Japanese were driving in the direction of individual robots with greater value-added. The collapse of the market highlighted the fragility of intervention paths that were not consistent with either of these two unfolding industry strategies. The Americans in particular were so late in reacting to the industry shift that they were heavily constrained in their ability to implement an appropriate intervention path.

Although the restructuring undertaken by the major American competitors was consistent with the initial configuration of financial change forces and internal resistance, little if any account was subsequently taken of the competence gaps they faced in dealing with the competitive change forces created by the Japanese and Germans. By the mid-1980s, the Americans had incurred large losses. They were unable to maintain the support of their parent companies long enough to get back into the game. Or, putting it another way, the parent companies lacked the insight or persistence needed to choose a time-consuming intervention path consistent with the forces of change and resistance.

At ASEA Robotics, the situation was not as desperate. Performance was weak but not yet a threat to survival. The division had the advantage of having a parent company that saw the business as sufficiently important for its core activity to warrant longer-run support.

On the lower end of the market, the performance standard established by the Japanese was high, both in terms of flexibility of the product and its production cost. To adapt to this strong force of change would require not only product redesign, but also the acquisition of the subtle and intangible organizational capability that makes a company more flexible, productive, and faster to respond to the market. Since there were no large, well-positioned takeover targets available, catching up with the Japanese could only be achieved via a long revitalization. However, ASEA was constrained by a lack of time and competence, forces of resistance that prevented it from implementing a revitalization path in the direction of robotic packages. While ASEA was trying to revitalize, the Japanese would be moving further ahead. It was not clear how ASEA could accelerate its learning process relative to the Japanese.

On the upper end of the market, ASEA's transformation toward more of a systems culture, to exploit the growing change force created by the German competitors, would require the acquisition of skills and behavior that could only be developed slowly over time. Fortunately, the division already had some of the competence needed to follow a revitalization path in the direction of robotic systems. ASEA had been pursuing change by integrating robot manufacturing with the sale of automated production systems for some time. Already in the late 1970s, ASEA had teamed up with the Swedish firm ESAB for welding applications, and SAAB for integrating spot welding into automotive production. When it saw the downturn in the automation market, ASEA reoriented toward the electronics and domestic appliance industries by acquiring VS Technology, a U.K. systems integrator. Two separate marketing divisions were created; one for automotive and one for industrial application, which facilitated ASEA's incremental moves into different market segments. The sale of integrated systems accelerated and by 1987 comprised 30 percent of total ASEA Robotics sales. By the end of the same year, ASEA had edged GM–Fanuc from its leadership position in terms of world market share. Adopting an intervention path of revitalization consistent with the forces of change and resistance, ASEA became the world's largest supplier of robots with sales of $190 million and a market share of 11.2 percent.

KEYS TO PRACTICE: CHOOSING AN INTERVENTION PATH

1. To deal with a breakpoint as a latecomer, select one of the four management intervention paths (resistance, revitalization, renewal, or restructuring) based on whether the change force is strong and growing, or strong and declining, and whether the resistance is closed to change, or open to change.
2. Although an initial intervention path may have to be chosen to deal with strong corporate-specific forces of change, thereafter the chosen path must be consistent with the forces of change implicit in the unfolding industry scenario.

CHAPTER 7

Organizing for Radical Change

"OLIVETTI'S FIRST TYPEWRITER, the M11, was displayed at the Turin Fair in 1911. The Italian Navy ordered 100 machines and from then on the company never ceased to expand." The expansion was driven by both geography and technology: key breakpoints were its first foreign subsidiary and its development of the M40 typewriter in 1930, its rapid geographic expansion after World War II, entry into the American market via the purchase of the Underwood Company in 1959, and the industry slowdown after the 1972 oil shock.

As Juliet Taylor and George Taucher point out in their case series, by 1978 Olivetti was in financial difficulty and undercapitalized because of the family's insistence on maintaining control.[1] "It looked as though the once so buoyant and stylish typewriter manufacturer would either go bankrupt or fall into the hands of the Italian Government." Olivetti's chairman turned to an outsider to find a new leader. He approached Carlo de Benedetti, who had a substantial fortune of his own, largely made when he sold his golden handshake (a 6 percent share of Fiat) back to the Agnellis. De Benedetti injected $17 million of his funds into Olivetti, making himself the majority shareholder, and took over as vice chairman and CEO.

De Benedetti wanted to move from mechanical to electronic typewriters as quickly as possible. However, Olivetti's Research Department believed that about five years would be needed to enter the market. Carlo de Benedetti had a much shorter horizon.

He set up a separate electronic typewriter task force with members from the key functional areas. Using an existing prototype, they reduced the development process to a few months and beat IBM to the market by several months. Olivetti's machine turned into a star product which made it the number-one typewriter company worldwide, ahead of IBM. On the way, Olivetti's revenues climbed from $1 billion in 1978 to $2 billion in 1983.

De Benedetti did not rest on his laurels. He initiated the re-tooling of Olivetti's plants to boost the production of electronic equipment. Costs were cut relentlessly: "New accounting systems were introduced, control tightened, low profit products discontin-ued and plants closed or revamped." After the unions were con-vinced that manpower reduction was essential for survival, the work force was reduced from 61,500 to 47,600 within a few years.

Instead of increasing the R&D budget as a percentage of sales, de Benedetti spent $60 million on minority interests in 22 small high-tech companies in the United States. A joint venture with Docutel, the maker of automatic bank teller machines, turned sour after one year because Docutel was in the red. However, Olivetti successfully acquired Hermes Precisa of Switzerland, Logabox of France, and Data Terminal Systems of West Germany.

As its best-kept secret, Olivetti had developed one of the first PC-like machines, known as the Programma 101, in the early 1960s. It had 500 different software programs from Underwood Oli-vetti. Although remarkable for its time, the machine was not very user-friendly. More important, the typewriter-oriented sales orga-nization was not keen to sell more complex equipment. To finally get a PC onto the market, de Benedetti set up a separate PC group with a research base in Silicon Valley. Olivetti's first personal computer, the M20, was launched in 1982, followed by the IBM-compatible M24 a year later. The machine had open architecture, superior graphics, and a competitive price. But Olivetti was unable to get significant sales worldwide and still less to penetrate the U.S. market. Only 42,000 units were sold in the first year from a capacity of 200,000.

Then Gianni Agnelli of Fiat called de Benedetti to suggest a meeting with Charles Brown, the chairman of AT&T, to which the Olivetti CEO responded eagerly. The strategic alliance which developed out of this contact looked excellent.[2] The fast, market-oriented, entrepreneurial Olivetti, with a strong distribution net-work in Europe, a good understanding of the office environment and substantial international experience, looked like the perfect complement to AT&T's Information Systems Division with its outstanding research capability, especially in networking, its massive financial resources and power, and its very strong distribution network in the United States. AT&T paid $260 million for a 25 percent stake in Olivetti. As a result of the alliance, Olivetti marketed and distributed AT&T's 3B minicomputer in Europe, while AT&T did the same for Olivetti's M24 PC in the United States.

Immediately after the alliance was set up, the dollar rose against the European currencies. The AT&T 3B computer became very expensive in Europe. The Olivetti M24 became cheap in the United States. The M24 offered "clone plus" advantages, whereas the 3B needed major modifications to meet European needs. The result was that Olivetti sales of PCs rose from 40,000 to over 300,000 units in the first full year of the alliance, and AT&T sold virtually no 3Bs in Europe. While the two parties argued over the best networking system for PCs, AT&T's Information Systems Division was making losses estimated at $1 billion per year. The head of the division was fired and replaced by Vittorio Cassoni of Olivetti. Unfortunately, the transplant did not work. In 1989, both sides began to withdraw from the alliance and Cassoni returned to a seat on the Olivetti board. By this time, Olivetti had revenues of $6 billion.

To deal with the shift in demand away from hardware toward systems and software in the late 1980s, Olivetti, on its own again, invested $400 million to set up a separate Information Systems Division. The company was effectively split into two pieces: a Black Box Division selling PCs and other office equipment on a stand-alone basis, and a Systems Division selling integrated solutions to information management problems. To demonstrate the systems, a prototype office was set up with idiot-proof equipment. However, notwithstanding some successes in the banking industry, the Systems Division recorded large losses in 1990. The head of the division was removed after six months and replaced by Elserino Piol, one of de Benedetti's right-hand men. In November 1990, however, facing a slump in computer demand, Olivetti announced that it was laying off 7,000 employees.

The ups and downs of the Olivetti story illustrate several different ways of organizing for radical change: foreign subsidiaries, acquisitions, venture capital participation, task forces, strategic alliances, and restructuring into separate divisions. The intriguing question is why the acquisitions and task forces methods worked so much better than venture capital participation, strategic alliance, or restructuring into separate divisions.

To explore the answer, this chapter looks at how the interplay between forces of change and resistance reflected in the choice of an intervention path dictates the approach to organizing for radical change. The change force creates the need for specific organizational capabilities to close the competence gap. With this in mind, we shall look at the

- Internal organization needed to provide a diverging innovation, or a converging cost reduction capability, while coping with the resistance on a given intervention path;
- External networks and alliances needed to complement the internal change organization; and
- Scope and pace of organizational change needed for consistency with the chosen intervention path.

ORGANIZING TO INNOVATE

The nature of a gap in innovation capability can be described in terms of the need created by change forces for innovation, and the organization's resistance to innovation. By innovation is meant the commercialization of an invention, taking an invention from the research lab to the marketplace. With respect to the change force, two broad types of innovation can be identified: fundamental and incremental. Fundamental innovation involves a major shift in the product offering and/or the business system. Incremental innovation, by contrast, involves stepwise improvement.

Similarly, with respect to the forces of resistance, the innovative disposition of the organization can be divided into two broad categories: open and closed. Organizations open to innovation are characterized by low resistance to new ideas and change, with correspondingly frequent innovative activity. Organizations closed to innovation are more rigid, resisting new ideas and change, with sparse innovative activity.

The combinations of forces of change and resistance dictate the need for four different organizing approaches to innovation which correspond to the intervention paths discussed in Chapter 6: incremental innovation in a closed environment for the resistance path; fundamental innovation in an open environment for revitalization; incremental innovation in an open environment for the renewal path; and fundamental innovation in a closed environment for restructuring.

Four corresponding approaches to the organization of innovation can be found in existing management practice (see Exhibit 7-1).[3] Examples of each will be discussed in turn below and related to the corresponding intervention paths.

Organizational Spin-Offs

Spin-offs operating outside the organizational mainstream provide an approach to innovation that does not upset the existing organization. Rather than attempt to integrate the innovating team into the corporate mainstream, this approach allows for virtually total autonomy on the outside. However, as the experience of companies like Xerox and Control Data suggests, spin-offs once developed are difficult to re-integrate into the corporate mainstream. As

EXHIBIT 7–1   **Organizing to Innovate**

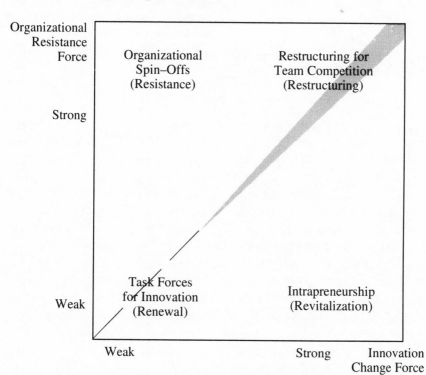

a result, spin-offs are suitable for companies with a small innovation capability gap and strong resistance to change within the mainstream organization.

Xerox, under the parent company's financial umbrella, has spun several internal innovators off into divisions or firms of their own, while maintaining rights to the resulting technology. Control Data has gone further; it is reputed to have generated spin-offs with a combined business activity rivaling that of the parent. Control Data used its Employee Entrepreneurial Advisory Office to assist employees in starting their own businesses, with advice in planning, marketing, production, finance, and so on. Outcomes of the program ranged from independent employee firms to licensing arrangements or new Control Data ventures.[4]

The extent to which these spin-offs have benefited either Xerox or Control Data, however, is not clear. Most reports indicate difficulty getting the benefit of new technology developed by spin-offs. Managers of spin-offs are reluctant to hand over the benefits of their work. And they have enough independence to frustrate systematic attempts to capitalize on their innovations. In Europe, mature corporations like Société Suisse de Microéléctronique et Horlogèrie and ABB have also experimented with highly independent entrepreneurs operating externally with very loose (but definite) ties to the main organization. Here, too, the benefit to the parent companies is not clear.

Intrapreneurship

Intrapreneurship involves the spontaneous emergence of self-motivated project champions and teams. The prototypes are the product champions at 3M Corporation, who drive continual innovation from the bottom up, within a well-defined corporate culture, or the Procter & Gamble brand managers, who compete for company accolades within a circumscribed but highly touted arena of marketing variables. In both settings, employees are given the autonomy and encouragement to be innovative with respect to those activities over which they have some control, but always in harmony with corporate strategy. The continual nature of the innovations mainly in the product, plus the spread of the innovating process throughout the organization, indicate that intrapreneurship is appropriate for companies with low resistance facing well-developed forces of change. A climate supporting intrapreneurs is the typical objective of an innovation-oriented revitalization path.

The better-known cases of intrapreneurship are associated primarily with companies having a high-tech and/or strong market orientation: Hewlett-Packard, Apple Computer, Texas Instruments, 3M, Procter & Gamble, Frito-Lay, United Airlines, Sears, Schlumberger, Dana, and Raychem. An extensively documented model is provided by Hewlett-Packard (HP). The original "HP-Way" encouraged product innovation throughout the company mainstream by autonomous teams, which split off from existing divisions once the latter became too large. These teams competed with one another to "sell it to the sales force." Divisions comprising collections of such teams were limited in size and quite independent, having separate responsibility for most of their own support functions.

Task Forces for Innovation

Task forces are given an often critical task to perform by top management, with maximum possible freedom of action. Although independent of the company's main control systems, the task forces have easy access to all needed resources, both human and financial. While not much flexibility is required of the organization when setting up the task forces, their re-integration into the mainstream is another matter. Re-integration is often managed by allowing the task force to evolve into an independent business unit. Whatever the approach, if the rest of the organization is to benefit, it must be reasonably open to the task force's output. Independent task forces are appropriate, therefore, for the stimulation of incremental innovation in a relatively open environment. As such, they fit intervention paths of renewal.

The reports of independent task forces come mainly from companies in the growth and maturity phases and involve relatively important product innovation: for example, the IBM PC, Lockheed's U2 aircraft, GE's first locomotive, and plastics. One of IBM's chief executive officers referred to his company's independent task forces as examples of the way in which new ideas are "incubated."

Task forces can be large. On September 1, 1989, Canon's president, Ryuzaburo Kaku, formally inaugurated a companywide task force for the development of the personal copier.[5] Task Force X, as it was known, the second largest horizontal development team in the history of Canon, had about 200 members. They were divided into three main groups: Group A with seven subgroups was responsible for technological development and design; Group B with ten subgroups was responsible for production engineering; and in a loose third group, staff functions were taken care of by six subgroups responsible for task force coordination, cost, quality, patents, marketing, and user applications. The role of coordinating the subgroups was critical not only in managing the effort, but also in ensuring the transfer of information and know-how among the subgroups.

Olivetti successfully used dedicated task forces to deal with two major innovation discontinuities: the electronic typewriter and the PC. The task forces were charged with converting existing R&D into a commercial prototype, debugging the prototype, and getting it onto the market as quickly as possible. In both cases, the need for innovation was incremental because Olivetti already had some of the necessary technology. The task forces included members from all areas of the business affected by the desired innovation. With the introduction of the product, the task forces then evolved into new business units.

Restructuring for Team Competition

In this approach, the company, or division, is decentralized into business units, or teams, each pursuing its own business or project as independently as possible. Control systems are reduced to a minimum. The need for restructuring implies that the company is relatively closed to change. Nevertheless, for the approach to succeed there must be enough entrepreneurial executives in the middle ranks ready to take up the challenge and opportunity presented by greater independence. In those cases where this strength is available, the restructuring can occur rather rapidly. The potential for originality in the products and business generated by team competition, plus the potential pace of restructuring, suggest that it is suitable as a response to strong forces of change.

When Percy Barnevik took over ASEA and later merged it with Brown Boveri, both organizations were struggling to react to the huge overcapacity in heavy electric equipment like turbines, generators, and transformers caused by the drop in electricity consumption: "Over eight years we were confronted with zero growth of world imports of electric goods. In Sweden, the home country of ASEA, the nuclear program came to a halt and demand declined in mines, steel and shipyards."[6] To deal with the breakpoint in demand, Barnevik successively decentralized first ASEA and then

Brown Boveri radically to encourage a more entrepreneurial spirit. In 1990, the new ABB Group included some 1,500 legally separate business units, all organizationally separate. Competition between the units and their rivals in the marketplace produced the entrepreneurial spirit and the financial performance which made ABB Group one of the most successful large corporate combinations of the late 1980s.

ORGANIZING TO CUT COSTS

The need for cost reduction, created by the forces of change, and the organization's resistance to change can be used to delineate four different approaches to cost reduction which parallel those just described for innovation (see Exhibit 7-2). The main difference is that organizing approaches to cost reduction may fit in more easily with the existing organization.

EXHIBIT 7–2   **Organizing to Cut Costs**

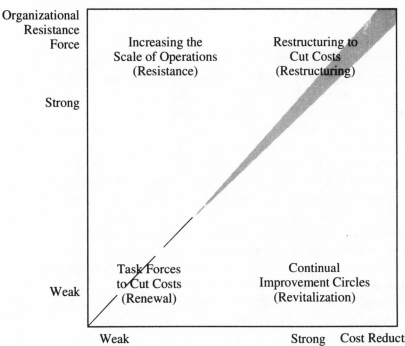

Increasing the Scale of Operations

Economies of scale and investment in new plant and equipment are examples of cost-reducing approaches which can be pursued within the existing organization structure.[7] Increasing the scale of operations makes the most sense in industries with a declining long-run cost curve, provided the benefit of the experience can be protected from the competition. In this case, higher market share leads to a further cost advantage. But over time most information gets out, so that the latest competitor to invest in capacity expansion undercuts those that invested earlier on. To stay ahead, the first movers have to lead not only in capacity expansion, but also in lowering the costs of existing capacity.

Hence the importance of new plant and equipment to reduce costs further. What is needed is an ongoing procedure for encouraging and evaluating proposals for improving plant and equipment performance. To the extent that this is done through the planning and budgeting cycle, the organization is merely extended rather than changed. Without more extensive cost reduction efforts, these approaches are consistent with an intervention path designed to avoid major organizational change in an environment with relatively weak forces of change.

Continual Improvement Circles

The ongoing quality circles, suggested by Deming and pioneered by leading Japanese companies in several industries, are now the classic example of how to organize for continuous cost improvement from the bottom up. Cost improvement teams apply the benefits of the learning implicit in the accumulated output and experience of the organization. Not often mentioned is the commitment to cost reduction at the very top of Japanese companies like Toyota, Honda, Sony, and Canon; a commitment essential for sustaining a cost-conscious culture. On several trips to Japan trying to understand the origins of Ford's cost disadvantage in the early 1980s, groups from Ford of Europe remarked on the presence of a cost reduction team at the executive-committee level in every one of the automobile companies that they visited.[8]

Aiming for a cost-conscious culture is consistent with a revitalization path. It takes time to open up the organization to the point where it can support strong pressure to lower costs from the bottom up spontaneously. Successful Japanese companies have demonstrated that this pressure must be built up and maintained over the years by top management. The repeatedly successful Japanese response to endaka would never have been possible without it.

Task Forces to Cut Costs

Cost reduction in bigger bites than improvement circles can provide requires the top-down organization of tasks. Task forces are appropriate for incremental cost-cutting which is concentrated over an intermediate time period. As such they are consistent with a renewal intervention path. The main difference between these task forces and those used for product innovation is their mission.

The objective of cost-cutting task forces might be to develop new cost-reducing processes and systems. Alternatively, the objective might be to simplify the business, its organization, products, and processes. Many corporations have used task forces to make suggestions and show how decision making might be simplified, most commonly by getting rid of excessive administration and control. Exposing and weeding out the hidden factor of unnecessary transactions is a major part of this effort.[9] The finance function in Ford of Europe set up 10 different task forces to streamline all its activities from capital appropriation to auditing, not to mention the organization of the function itself. The number of personnel was reduced by 30 percent. Northern Telecom re-engineered the standard telephone to perform the same function with fewer parts, thereby simplifying its products, operations, and control. Total unit costs were cut by half.[10]

Restructuring to Cut Costs

Eliminating marginal products, operations, and organization is the quickest way of cutting costs. This is the domain of the turnaround manager: first, identifying the potentially profitable parts of the business; second, pruning the deadwood; and third, giving the business a viable direction for the future. Organizing a turnaround is very much a top-down, authoritarian move which fits a restructuring path. Rapid, focused, specific change is the order of the day.

As always with discontinuous change, there are severe limits to the change in behavior and beliefs that can be accomplished in the time available. On the other hand, if a crisis has convinced everyone of the need for radical change, the turnaround manager can draw on the change agents in the firm to help execute the leap.

ORGANIZING TO COMPLEMENT INTERNAL CHANGE

Often the resources and competence needed on the other side of a breakpoint cannot be developed in-house, especially under time pressure. The resource commitment may also be too large or risky for one company alone. External organization is the key to the successful handling of a breakpoint in such circumstances. Olivetti did not have the time to establish a significant presence in the European PC market, nor the resources to crack the American market. The AT&T alliance was critical to the success of its strategy for exploiting the PC breakpoint.

Four basic types of external organization can be identified to complement the internal change process (see Exhibit 7-3). These correspond to a strong and weak change force represented by the strategic need for external organization and strong and weak resistance caused by lack of a cultural fit with potential outside partners. The strategic need for external organization depends on how much of the organizational capability gap can be closed in a cost-effective and timely manner with internal organization: the more provided internally, the less needed externally.

Arm's-Length Relationships

Licensing agreements, R&D-limited partnerships, and venture capital participation all provide the promise of bringing focused expertise into the business relatively quickly without altering the existing mainstream organization. The focus and specificity of licensing and R&D partnerships have produced a better track record than venture capital in actually transferring expertise. These relationships can be particularly useful in providing quick access to incremental competence and resources.

General Electric has regularly used arm's-length relationships to complement the expertise of internal task forces developing new business ventures.[11] For example, after deciding to forward integrate into compressors, the Turbine Division hired the Stanford Research Institute to analyze the industry and competitors and explore ways of entering the business. On the recommendation of the institute, the necessary technology was obtained through a licensing agreement with an Italian firm. In another division, the X-Ray Programs Department acquired some smaller companies to augment its skills in diagnostic imaging. In addition, the depart-

EXHIBIT 7–3   **Organizing to Complement Internal Change**

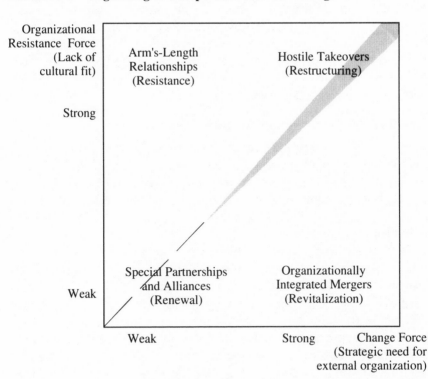

ment developed digital X-ray equipment with a clinical research team at the Stanford University Medical Center.

To hedge their development bets, some large corporations have set up corporate venture capital funds, designed to act as screens and save valuable management time which otherwise would have been needed to evaluate small-scale equity participation. Unfortunately, most of the venture capital funds have had difficulty delivering on their promise. The cultural gap makes the transfer of technology from venture subsidiary to the parent very tricky. The problems encountered by Exxon Enterprises, General Electric's Gevenco, and Genstar's Sutter Hill Ventures in the mid-1980s are documented examples of the general failure of corporate venture capital to perform as hoped.[12]

Olivetti's minority stakes in 22 small U.S. high-tech companies were venture capital participations. The idea was to give Olivetti early access to new developments and keep it abreast of trends in the United States, the leading market in the office equipment industry. Tracking progress in the United States was meant to enhance Olivetti's marketing in Europe and help speed up bringing product developments to the market. Olivetti's experience was the same as that of other large corporations. The transfer of technology was minimal. However, Olivetti made money when it later sold its shares in these companies.

Organizationally Integrated Mergers

The successful integration of two existing organizations is possible only on the basis of a good strategic and cultural fit. Merging two organizations is a notoriously lengthy and difficult process which affects both profoundly, even when the cultural gap is small. Hence the need for an important long-term strategic payoff, like that provided by revitalization.

Nestlé's acquisition of Rowntree is part of the former's response to the sudden spate of consolidation in the European food industry, prior to the disappearance of trade barriers in the Common Market after 1992. The integration of Rowntree, as a product division reporting directly to Nestlé's Management Committee, marks a sharp break with Nestlé's deeply entrenched geographic organization based on five regional zones. Indeed, the takeover negotiations almost collapsed at one point with Kenneth Dixon, the CEO of Rowntree, insisting on a separate confectionery division. Ramon Masip, the head of Nestlé's European zone, insisted as strongly that Rowntree would just have to fit into Nestlé's geographical structure. Only the intervention of Helmut Maucher, the head of Nestlé, saved the day. He had his reasons for agreeing to the Rowntree request: since taking over the helm of Nestlé, he had been gradually revitalizing the food giant by delegating power downward into the markets to encourage more intrapreneurship. Rowntree was the first major step toward a more product line–oriented organization better able to meet the challenge of greater Pan-European and global food marketing.

Yet organizational mergers have to be used with care as an external complement to internal change. When the cultural fit is poor, organizational mergers have a very low rate of success. Numerous studies have documented the importance of cultural fit on the postacquisition process of integration, which is crucial if the benefits of the merger are to be realized. The bottom line is that organizational mergers make the most sense when the strategic need is high and the cultural fit is good.

Special Partnerships and Alliances

Supplier and customer alliances and networks, union partnerships, and government-supported projects provide an intensive basis for exchanging know-how and building new internal competence. In addition to know-how, specific resources can be traded or pooled to deal with a breakpoint. But the development of a fruitful relationship takes time and presupposes that the cultural gap between the partners can be closed. Relative to an acquisition, the range of resources traded or pooled can be limited to complement the internal change process. This opportunity for concentrating the interaction makes special partnerships useful on a renewal path; for example, as a way of out-sourcing and subcontracting parts of the business system.

In response to the low cost and increasing quality of competition from the Far East, Xerox was forced to lower its high product cost while enhancing quality. The internal task forces charged with raising manufacturing performance found that this was critically dependent on the quality and reliability of Xerox's suppliers. But the existing base of 5,000 suppliers could not possibly be managed in a cost effective way. Xerox decided to move toward sourcing alliances with single suppliers on a global basis. Over five years, from 1981 to 1986, the number of suppliers was reduced 16 times from 5,000 to just over 300. The alliances led to completely different supplier quality and reliability, thereby facilitating just-in-time manufacturing with large savings in inventories, control expenses, and other hidden factory costs.[13]

Hostile Takeovers

When the strategic fit is there but the cultural fit is not, common sense suggests an acquisition that avoids organizational integration. In an organizationally separate takeover, the resources of the acquiror and acquiree may be shared. Because of the poor cultural fit no attempt is made to integrate the two organizations and share activities. Nevertheless, to get the full benefits of the synergy implied by a good strategic fit, some integration and sharing of activities are called for. This contradiction is one of the main reasons why such acquisitions have so high a failure rate: those that attempt integration flounder on the cultural gap; those that avoid integration forego important synergy.

A hostile takeover seems to be one of the few ways in which the acquisition of a disparate organization can succeed. In one classic scenario, the two senior layers of the target management are removed; managers from the acquiror take over the top of the acquired company; at the same time, third-level managers in the acquired company are promoted to the second level. Since the target management can usually sense what is going to happen, it will rarely recommend this kind of takeover to its board. As a result, the takeover becomes hostile both in financial and organizational terms.

Yet, hostile takeovers can be very successful. A leading company in the consumer credit card industry with keen operators, high profits, and excellent management used hostile tactics to acquire a "me-too" company with a poor credit card portfolio, losses, and mediocre management.[14] After a thorough examination of the target, the latter was taken over, cleaned up, and turned around in one month. Apart from top management, the main transfer to the new subsidiary was in-depth industry know-how. The acquiree was remodeled as a separate duplicate of the parent, its name kept alive as foil against the competition. In the years that followed, the new combined company was a great success, with growing market share and soaring profits.

Although not hostile at the board level, the successful combination of Swedish ASEA and Swiss Brown Boveri followed a similar approach. As a quid pro quo for placing the headquarters of the new ABB group in Zurich, Percy Barnevik of ASEA was made CEO. He wisely didn't attempt to merge the two culturally disparate organizations. Rather where local ASEA and BBC units overlapped, he quickly appointed one person as the head of the combined operation. In many regions where BBC dominated, he promoted tens of managers into the corresponding new managing director positions. The restructured BBC could then be managed in the same decentralized way as the previously restructured ASEA, albeit in the new ABB group. Fortunately for ABB, the heavy electrical engineering industry is still sufficiently fragmented by national contracts and standards that an entrepreneurial decentralized company still has some advantages over more organizationally integrated companies.

When Olivetti launched its PC, it had to get a significant market presence rapidly. AT&T with its size and U.S. market reach was the ideal partner. Merging the two organizations would have had little likelihood of success, given the time constraint and the cultural gap. The strategic partnership that was tried created too many complex problems to be decided within the fragile context of an alliance. The ideal solution would have been a takeover of AT&T's Information Systems by Olivetti, keeping the organizations separate, except for tight coordination of marketing and distribution. But Olivetti did not have the capital for a takeover. Instead, Olivetti approached the ideal solution implicitly by taking maximum advantage of AT&T's distribution in the United States with little overt concern for the alliance itself.

SCOPE AND PACE OF ORGANIZATIONAL CHANGE

The scope and pace of change implicit in an organizing approach must be consistent with the intervention path chosen and the type of resistance to be overcome. Ideally the whole organization would change at the same pace. However, a business facing radical change is typically full of different kinds of resistance characterized by different rates at which the resistance can be overcome. Guiding an organization through radical change with as little trauma as possible requires understanding of the different rates at which change can occur on different dimensions.

Organic-type organizations require more careful change management than mechanistic organizations. With a lot of shared intangible knowledge, performance norms, culture, and often vision, the teams within organic organizations are difficult to change quickly from the top down. They tend to adapt more spontaneously on their own. If this incremental flexibility is to be maintained, the integrity of the teams has to be respected. Although the portfolio of teams can be restructured, intervention in organic organizations should be restricted to the hardware in the business system and resource network. By contrast, more mechanic systems and culture can be altered rapidly with less damage to overall cohesion.

The difference in scope and pace of organizational change varies with the type of intervention path: the more rapid the intervention, the greater the variation in the rates of change in different parts of the organization.

On a successful resistance path, very little changes. Apart from the strategy, most of the structure and behavior of the organization, including the culture, can be maintained, which, of course, makes resistance the favorite path for those with a low propensity to change. The use of organizing approaches that create more change than is needed can create friction with the status quo agents and jeopardize the success of the resistance.

The revitalization path unfolds slowly, allowing a lot of time for the gradual alteration of values and behavior, as well as goals and beliefs, strategy, structure, and systems. Since the change is gradual, it can occur more uniformly across the different dimensions of the organization. Indeed, the ultimate objective is gradual and fundamental change throughout the organization. As a result, very little of the original organization remains at the end of the intervention path. Organizing approaches with more restricted scope and greater pace will create an organization that is in part unchanged and in other parts changed incompletely.

Being sporadic, the renewal path provides less time for change, not only in the business and organization hardware, but also in goals and beliefs. Task forces are well suited to this sporadic change because their composition and mandate can be tailored over time to the specific kind of change needed. Other organizing approaches are more difficult to turn on and off.

A discontinuous restructuring has to be implemented with speed in one jump. In the words of a Polish diplomat, "You cannot cross a chasm slowly in two steps." The speed of change inevitably means that deeply ingrained beliefs and behavior will lag behind during the discontinuity. If the transition is to succeed, allowance must be made for the much slower change in beliefs and behavior after the strategy, structure, business systems, and resources have been reorganized. At the time of the breakpoint, however, only rapid restructuring approaches to organization will be adequate. Other slower organizing approaches will subvert the intervention path owing to lack of time.

The most natural fits between intervention paths and the various forms of internal organization are summarized in Exhibit 7-4. The appropriate external organization is less tightly limited to the chosen intervention path because it depends on the extent to which the internal organization by itself is adequate for dealing with the interplay between forces of change and resistance.

The Olivetti story highlights the importance of selecting an organizing approach for radical change with a scope and pace that is consistent with the intervention path. Whenever Olivetti violated this rule, its efforts at change failed. A task force producing prototypes was hopelessly inadequate for moving from black boxes to information systems (divisionwide systems intrapreneurship would have been more suited to this revitalization effort). The arm's-length interests in small high-tech companies were not appropriate for the renewal that Olivetti had in mind (alliances with culturally

EXHIBIT 7–4 **Summary of Links between Intervention Paths and Organizing Approaches**

| Intervention Path | Typical Internal Organization for | | External Organization |
	Innovation	*Cost Reduction*	*Organization*
Resistance	Organizational spin-offs	Increasing the scale of operations	Arm's-length relationships
Revitalization	Intrapreneurship	Continual improvement teams	Organizationally integrated mergers
Renewal	Task forces for innovation	Task forces for cutting costs	Special partnerships and alliances
Restructuring	Restructuring for team competition	Restructuring to cut costs	Hostile takeovers

compatible partners would have been appropriate). The existing conservative, typewriter-oriented sales organization did not have the skills to sell Olivetti's Programma 101 (restructuring of the sales force is what finally got an Olivetti PC onto the market). The strategic alliance with AT&T was inadequate for sharing activities with a culturally incompatible partner (a hostile takeover would have been required). In brief, if radical change is to succeed, the organizing approach must be consistent with the configuration of change forces and resistance implicit in the intervention path.

KEYS TO PRACTICE: ORGANIZING FOR RADICAL CHANGE

1. Use interplay between forces and resistance implicit in the chosen intervention path to determine the appropriate kind of internal organization.
2. Use the strategic need for additional capabilities and the degree of cultural fit with potential partners to determine the approach to external organization.
3. Fine-tune the organizing approaches in terms of the variation in scope and pace across the organization to avoid more change than needed to deal with the forces of change and resistance.

CHAPTER 8

Mobilizing the Organization

J ORMA JERKKU was the new chief executive of Oy Sisu Auto Ab, the Finnish manufacturer of heavy trucks and other vehicles, when the world market demand for heavy-duty trucks dropped by 35 percent because of the oil crises of the 1970s. Pierre Casse and Suzanne de Treville report in their case study how Jerkku summarized the crisis facing Sisu:

> Sisu has just had its third straight year of making losses. Productivity in our manufacturing operations is terrible. Inventories are high. We are getting constant complaints from customers. Our toughest sales job will be to convince the Advisory Board that a company manufacturing four trucks a day can compete effectively against competitors like Volvo and Mercedes Benz.

Although it benefited from neither subsidies nor protective trade legislation, Sisu's losses had made the Finnish government the largest shareholder. And now the government wanted out.[1]

Although not charismatic, Jerkku naturally adopted the commander approach as a result of his strong personality, as well as his appointment, to make Sisu react to the new market conditions. He was the definite leader of the management team. As one senior manager commented: "Although everyone in the company knew his door was open, he was definitely a directive and 'top-down' leader. He did not want you to question what he told you to do—he just wanted action."

The crisis situation called for either liquidation or a completely new strategy. Jerkku and his management team opted for the latter. They decided to concentrate on the core business of heavy-duty trucks, eliminating all other products including buses, tractors, military vehicles, and passenger cars. First, they obtained assurance that the government would support a change process. Then they planned a restructuring of the plants and manufacturing technology to give the company a competitively viable base from which to launch a focused product concept. It was decided that the changes would involve both physical restructuring and two project task forces, each with its own manager. Third, the mission of the company was redefined from the marketing of trucks to the marketing of "solutions to transportation problems." Ideally the customer and salesperson would custom-design the truck on the spot, using a computer simulation model which helped the customer choose the best combination of features for his needs.

Tough objectives were set for cost reduction: to improve direct labor productivity by 100 percent, indirect labor by 50 percent, inventory turns from 2.8 to 7.8 times per year, and the cost of purchases by 6 percent, all within three years. Employees who could not accept the new situation did not stay. This set the pattern. Having acquired the support of the unions and management, Jerkku used implicit coercion on resisters: "If things did not go the way he expected, he could get extremely angry. Many people in the company were afraid of him. People who did not agree with his decisions soon left the company."

Once the new assembly operation was in place, Jerkku moved on to the marketing part of the new strategy. This involved adding expertise for "transportation problem-solving" onto the streamlined business system. During this renewal process, the implementation style was a collaborative one between top marketing management and the frontline salespeople. The heart of the solutions expertise was a portable computer simulation model which allowed the salespeople to custom-design trucks on the spot with their customers. The model selected the best combination of available features for the customers' needs. This added-value put Sisu out in front of other specialized truck manufacturers. All the quantitative objectives were achieved within the three-year target. Sisu went from strength to strength and in 1989 opened an office in the United States.

The Sisu story illustrates how a company can be mobilized for radical change, including the need for different implementation styles which are consistent with the various intervention paths used for different combinations of the forces for change and resistance. This chapter looks at the main steps involved in mobilizing for radical change:

- Selecting an implementation style from the following: committee, cultural, collaborative, or commander.
- Motivating the change for key stakeholders.
- Triggering the organizational leap.
- Dealing with status quo agents.
- Dealing with multiple change forces.

SELECTING AN IMPLEMENTATION STYLE

At least four different styles of implementing radical change can be distinguished in existing management practice.[2] As shown in Exhibit 8-1 and described below, these can be classified in terms of their consistency with the intervention paths.

The forces of resistance determine to what extent middle and lower management, and even the employees, can be involved in deciding on the change agenda. When the organization is closed to change (strong resistance), top management has to make the decisions for everyone else about the needed change; when the organization is open to change (weak resistance), the change decisions can be pushed down the organizational hierarchy. On the horizontal axis, the change force determines how much executive involvement is needed during the implementation process. When the forces of change are strong, they influence the implementation program and process; when they are weak, more top-management input is required to keep the implementation process on track.

The implementation styles also differ in the pace of the overall change and hence the intervention path for which they are most appropriate. The rapid, decisive style of the commander is needed to implement restructuring. By contrast, the all-encompassing, delegating, cultural style fits revitalization. Any attempt to use the commander style on a revitalization path, or the cultural style for restructuring will doom the intervention before it starts. The committee and collaborative styles are more versatile and more frequently found in a variety of settings. Ideally, the committee style is more suited to a path of resistance, whereas the collaborative style is more suited to renewal. The examples that follow are

EXHIBIT 8–1   **Implementation Styles**

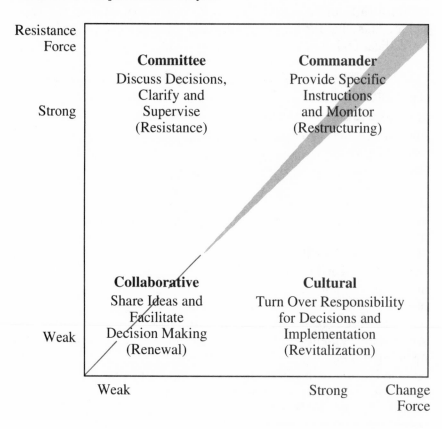

fleshed out to reveal some of the details associated with the various styles.

Committee Style

A team comprising the chief executive and key division and staff executives hammers out the intervention path and competitive formula with appropriate organization and systems. Each executive provides input about where the company should go. Intensive discussions follow until a consensus is reached. The number of people involved outside the committee is limited. The committee executives have to sell their decisions to the rest of the organization and then implement them in their respective business areas.

The committee style is well suited to an intervention path of either resistance or focused renewal because the pace and scope of change are limited. The committee style is not appropriate to crisis situations where strong forces demand that the organization be overhauled despite heavy resistance. The recommendations of a committee typically are not radical enough nor can it summon the collective power to overcome heavy resistance.

A well-known example is provided by the response of IBM's Central Management Committee (CMC) to the emergence of the Apple computer. Task forces with free access to all necessary resources and reporting directly to the CMC were set up to develop and put an IBM personal computer onto the market as soon as possible. Within 18 months, the IBM PC was launched and, shortly thereafter, it became the new market standard.

But IBM as a company did not really change. The PC was developed and launched outside the corporate mainstream. The company as a whole remained committed mainly to large stand-alone computers. Its powerful marketing was driven more by what IBM believed its customers needed, rather than a real understanding of what they wanted. As a result, the company did not fully appreciate the strength of the move toward distributed computer networking in the mid-1980s, nor was it able to follow up adequately on the success of the first PCs. In the early 1990s, John Akers, the IBM president, in an unprecedented attempt to shake up the organization, went public with his frustration over the slow response of the companywide committee structure to the forces of change. As the industry went into a slump and profits dropped sharply for the first time in many years, IBM was no longer in the steady state environment of continuing large computer growth that had been so well managed by the committee system.

Cultural Style

Here, the CEO and senior managers develop the guidelines on how the company is going to deal with the discontinuity. The guidelines include the new mission of the company, its values and acceptable behavior, and concrete objectives like catching up with the number-one competitor. Supporting systems and processes are then developed to encourage each individual to adopt his or her activities to the mission and objectives. Implementation is delegated to the frontline executives, who can best adapt the company's response to the environment, in harmony with the corporate vision. The cultural style involves the delegation of both decision making and implementation to frontline executives.

The strengths of the cultural approach are also its weaknesses. After beliefs and behaviors have adapted, the implementation of decisions is rapid and effective. Once developed, shared values embedded in a strong culture can hold an organization together during times of adversity. But the change in beliefs and behavior can take an enormous amount of time. Moreover, a strong culture can make the organization vulnerable to the not-invented-here syndrome.

The cultural approach is highly appropriate for an intervention path of revitalization. Early revitalization avoids the later need for a sudden radical restructuring to deal with radical change. The cultural approach cannot be used successfully, however, in crisis situations. By the time action plans are formulated in the cultural model, the business will be overwhelmed by the discontinuity. Nor is the cultural approach appropriate for the partial renewal of an organization. The all-encompassing reach of cultural change typically goes beyond the more focused change expected of task forces charged with renewal.

Pilkington Brothers is an example of a company that responded to a breakpoint with a cultural approach to revitalization of the operations. Pilkington dominated its core markets in glass and insulation in the United Kingdom, prior to the sharp growth decline in the early 1980s. The two main markets for Pilkington's products, the U.K. automobile industry and insulation market, both dropped sharply. The situation was aggravated by the presence of new entrants from the previous upswing. Although Pilkington was not as cost competitive as some of the new entrants, it had resources for the change process.

Top management decided to revitalize the company with a radical but gradual decentralization of all decision making designed to change the culture.[3] The objective was to make the whole company more market-sensitive by widening the responsibility of both divisional and operating management, and to raise productivity by increasing the responsibility of the employees and workers. At the management level, the new approach was introduced through the planning process. Entrepreneurial, cost-cutting, and action-oriented projects were encouraged. In particular, local management was given responsibility for plant-level finance and marketing. In a classic reflection of the cultural style, most of the decision making and implementation were delegated to the frontline executives.

To demonstrate how high-value-added products could be introduced while productivity was being improved, a new plant was opened at Greengate. This plant turned out to be four times more efficient than any of the other plants. The main reason was fewer, more flexible job descriptions, fewer technical specialists, fewer layers of accountability, and much greater worker responsibility, especially for quality and efficiency.

However, when Pilkington's management tried to transfer the Greengate approach to the rest of the company, it was blocked by the unions. To deal with the resistance, management by-passed the blocked central negotiations and appealed directly to the shop stewards for cooperation in new local bargaining processes. The shop stewards agreed. "Divisional management could now bargain as stand-alone units, freed from corporate direction." Small joint teams from management and the unions analyzed jobs and the work group division of labor. This negotiation process led to practical proposals and committed employees. "A highly differentiated work force was replaced by multidisciplinary craftsmen." The net result was a profound and pervasive revitalization of the whole corporate approach, stimulated by the decline in the shop floor force of resistance and the strong productivity-driven force of change.

Collaborative Style

The chief executive and his team share ideas and facilitate decision making throughout the organization. Their subordinates are typically able and open to change but unwilling or insecure. The forces of change are weak, so it is not clear in which direction the company should change. However, the organization being open to change, top management can involve the frontline managers in deciding what and how to change. Top management encourages them to flush out what the need for change means on their level, or for their activity. Since the pace of change is intermediate and the scope is limited to certain organizational dimensions, this participatory approach is best suited for renewal.

A nice example of collaboration is provided by Seiko. When Ichiro Hattori announced the ambitious diversification goal to reduce the dependency on watches from 90 percent to 50 percent, endless heated debates occurred with the managers concerned, corporate staff, and union leaders. To bring everyone on board, Hattori used what was later called a "cascade approach."[4]

He started at the top by raising a series of strategic questions at every board of directors meeting. For example, "What should Daini Seikosha's strategy be in the watch business to generate enough cash for investment in the diversification program?" When Hattori was satisfied with the answers, he moved to the second stage, a companywide conference for approximately 50 senior managers. Each was asked to "propose a three-year strategic plan at the divisional and departmental levels relating to the corporate survival scenario for 1990." In early 1982, once these plans had been accepted by the board, the third stage began with a three-day seminar for 250 junior managers who were asked to develop the implications of the plan at their level. Finally, a Total Quality Control program was initiated to "ensure the highest level of corporatewide implementation." And at the time of the centenary celebrations in 1982, the corporate identity and name was changed to the Seiko Instruments and Electronics Co. Ltd.

It took longer than expected to get corporatewide consensus, and to develop the necessary new manufacturing and engineering expertise. Moreover, the diversification cost more than anticipated and the customers wanted a wider product range. Yet Seiko easily achieved its diversification target in 1986, four years ahead of schedule. Seiko had developed a new line of sophisticated graphics devices that accounted for 50 percent of sales. The collaborative cascade approach clearly had been appropriate for the prevailing weak forces of change and resistance.

Commander Style

The chief executive plays a dominant and often charismatic role in determining the intervention path and competitive formula, as well as the main organizational and support systems. Being unable, unwilling, or insecure, other executives and employees play only a secondary role in the decision-making process. On the implementation side, the chief executive's personality and organizational power are central to the implementation process, but his or her involvement is limited. Once the CEO has told everyone what to do, a lot of employee effort is still needed to translate the decisions into action. This approach is the quickest and therefore makes the most sense in crisis situations which demand discontinuous change when the forces are strong and time is short.

At Sisu, the Finnish truck company, Jerkku was in full command of the change process. As the undisputed head of the management team, he was in charge of obtaining government support, of managing the restructuring, and initiating the marketing renewal. In a typical pattern for commanders, he set specific and ambitious cost reduction targets, for example, with respect to productivity improvement and asset management. Under financial pressure and in pursuit of results, the emphasis in the early phases was on speed. He broke the resistance and was willing to use implicit coercion when necessary. As in the case of other applications of the commander style, in a crisis created by strong forces of change and resistance it produces results. All the ambitious cost reduction targets at Sisu were met within the target period.

MOTIVATING THE CHANGE

The first test of implementation style is building the organizational energy needed to implement radical change, especially later on in the change process when the initial motivation may have dissipated. Two aspects shape the creation of organizational energy.[5]

Getting People to Recognize the Need to Change

Communication and education can be used to make an analytical appeal for recognition of the strength of the change forces and the threat of a breakpoint. This is especially important in organizations with closed attitudes to change. The intervention paths for dealing with strong resistance call for variations in this motivating theme; more communication when the forces of change are strong and more education about the need to change when the forces of change are weak.

Developing the Emotional Motivation to Change

Facilitation, participation, and delegation encourage a response to the tension between where the company is and where it should be to deal with the discontinuity. Emotional ownership of the response generates commitment to its implementation. This comes most naturally in organizations with low resistance, where the collaborative and cultural styles can be used. In cases calling for the commander or committee style, the threat of sanctions often has to be used to galvanize change.

According to Percy Barnevik, CEO of ABB, radical change management consists of "5 percent analysis—finding out what has to be done—and 95 percent creating a demand for and executing change."[6] For Barnevik, analysis of competitive position is one of the best ways of creating the need for change. He advocates participation and delegation, giving line managers the tools of competitive analysis such as product portfolio diagrams, product life cycles, and SWOT analysis to analyze their own situation.

In ASEA prior to the merger with Brown Boveri, Barnevik used 10 internal consultants as his personal emissaries in the restructuring process. They assisted the line managers in analyzing their business units and reported directly to the chief executive. "It is necessary to go several layers down to really speed up the process of change." These consultants acted as facilitators. They came from various functional areas, were recognized within the company as competent, and were highly analytical. External consultants were perceived as having too little credibility.

In Barnevik's combined commander and collaborative style,

> High speed is of utmost importance. It is better to be quick and approximate than slow and precise. Don't be too fast in deciding but once you have made the decision, you have to move very fast. It is ten times more common that you wait too long and try too many things than doing it the other way around; that you throw the baby out with the bath water.

Over a two-year period, ASEA got rid of a lot of plants and products and some 4,000 people. In the second phase of the change process, however, 6,000 new jobs were created in growing business units. The number of engineers increased while blue-collar work became redundant. Sales increased from 12.5 billion krona in 1980 to 30.2 billion in 1983, while profits went up almost 10 times from 273 million krona to 2.1 billion.

At Sisu, survival of a competitive Finnish truck company was the motivating theme. Nevertheless, despite the disastrous financial results, the employees did not see the urgency of the situation. Since the state had saved the company in the past, they believed that "Sisu existed to give them employment, rather than to make money." To convince them otherwise, a heavy investment in education and communication was made at all levels. Articles appeared in Finnish newspapers about Sisu's problems. The Advisory Board, including the worker representatives, began to actively discuss the problems and the initial legal steps required for closing plants were taken.

Then, Jerkku sent a letter to all employees outlining the situation. The action plan was presented to the workers in the form of a choice between a focused manufacturing operation and a reassembly operation requiring fewer workers. Jerkku visited the manufacturing sites to explain the manufacturing proposal, what would be entailed, and what the workers would have to do. He was very blunt about the bad news. Management had little doubt that the workers would choose the manufacturing option, which they did by an overwhelming majority.

TRIGGERING THE ORGANIZATIONAL LEAP

The acid test of motivation is the move into action. This is especially so in organizations with strong forces of resistance. For companies coming from behind their competitors to deal with radical change in their environment, the move into action is critical.

The activation process is especially important in organizations having little experience with real change. For example, companies facing a breakpoint are often in that situation because they were unable to respond early when the forces of change were weaker. For such companies, even with widespread recognition of the need to change, the prospect of the quantum leap may be so foreign to current practice that nothing happens. The emotional commitment is not sufficient to overcome the resistance to change. To make things happen, to trigger the organizational breakpoint, the change organization requires objectives with deadlines, responsibilities allocated, and a feedback process with milestones for tracking progress.

During the 1980s, two successive CEOs at Philips tried to initiate fundamental change to deal with new market and competitive developments, but nothing much happened. When the magnitude of the 1990 loss became apparent, the Philips Supervisory Board had little choice other than to select someone like Jan Timmer, known for his commander style, as the new CEO. Timmer had demonstrated his ability to manage restructuring when he turned around the ailing Philips Consumer Electronics Division.

When Timmer took over the whole company in late 1990, as the electronics market began to slump and a corporate crisis was breaking, he initiated "Operation Centurion." Apart from intensive communication and training to ensure that everyone was motivated to change, he triggered the actual process by bringing his top 90 managers together in De Ruvenberg Training Center and agreed with them on a profit-improvement program, including a 40,000-person headcount reduction to be achieved by the end of 1991. For

Philips with its tradition of life-long employment, this was the unfortunate shock that was needed to convince both the internal and external stockholders that, this time, meaningful change was actually going to occur.

The heart of Operation Centurion was the personal contract covering action for the year ahead, which each manager agreed to with his superior. As Timmer put it in announcing the operation, "Centurion was the rank given to an officer in the Roman Army who received his assignment in the form of a personal contract. Philips managers, too, will have to handle their personal assignment, i.e., their budget, as a personal contract. It will mean keeping your word by following through on your promises."[7]

The budget reviews started the day after Timmer's kick-off speech, when instructions were sent to the Product Division and business unit managers (the business units constituted the core of the change organization). "The budget review should reflect a searching, thorough process on the fundamentals of the business. To be effective, a profits improvement plan begins by facing the facts. Because until you do, there will be no progress." Budget review meetings between the management board, the product divisions, and the business units took place in autumn 1990 to evaluate feedback and progress. In addition, "listen to" sessions and progress report sessions were planned whenever a member of the General Management Committee paid a visit to a business unit. Once Operation Centurion had been launched, even its opponents knew that this time the change would be real.

At Sisu, physical relocation and project group assignments were used to trigger the organizational discontinuity. All production-related activities were moved to a single site, starting with product design, process engineering, and frame manufacturing. The production process was split in two: a regular flow line and a specialized job shop line for highly customized products. The central warehouse was replaced by a two-week supply of domestic components and a four-week supply of imported components on the shop floor parallel to the assembly operation.

The two project groups—one for cabin and frame manufacturing, the other for final assembly—were instructed to implement a new technology strategy aimed at continual improvement of the weakest part of Sisu's technology relative to the competition. "If you visit our plant," said the technical director, "you will not see any sophisticated equipment moving trucks through the plant. In fact, our technology on average is pretty simple. However, when a new technology can buy us both efficiency and flexibility, we are now ready to use it."[8] By the time this comment was made, the organizational leap had been well and truly initiated.

DEALING WITH STATUS QUO AGENTS

No matter how well motivated and activated, radical change exposes status quo agents who cannot be converted. Their interests are directly threatened. For them, yielding to the change pressure is much less attractive than resisting. The wave of motivation and excitement created by successful change during the initial phases of the change process can be dashed on the rocks of this submerged resistance.

In May 1982, Reiner Gohlke took over as chairman of the Deutsche Bundesbahn (DB) in a flurry of excitement and anticipation. Gohlke had been nominated to the Vorstand (Management Committee) by the federal minister of transport in January. In selecting an outsider, the minister dramatized the need for a response to the recent rapid growth in DB debt. The economic downturn of the early 1980s sharply accentuated the weakness in DB's competitive and financial position. During the 30 years since 1950, DB's share of goods transport had dropped by half. It only retained one-fifth of its postwar share of personal transport. The year prior to Gohlke's appointment, DB reported a 1981 loss of DM4.04 billion, with total debt outstanding of DM34.4 billion.[9]

From the government's point of view, the rapidly rising subsidies needed to finance DB's losses were an unacceptable burden on the federal budget, especially since rising unemployment had dramatically increased the budget deficit. Management, on the other hand, believed that the performance of DB was obscured relative to other forms of transport, not only because DB had to finance its own infrastructure, but also because it had to subsidize public service transport within urban areas.

In terms of their attitude toward change, the middle management civil servants fell into two groups. A small minority, perhaps 5 percent, could be labeled as "young Turks" who were enthusiastic about the possibility of some movement within the organization. The vast majority, however, were more interested in preserving their position within the status quo. Many had built long careers with DB. They were known as "Eisenbahners" (railroaders), especially when their association with the railroad went back one or more generations. All DB personnel—workers, employees, and civil servants—were represented in the public arena by the German Railroad Union. The three groups were also represented internally by the Workers' Council, which played an important participative role in management.

As a first step, Gohlke established a task force of senior managers around himself to develop a plan of action. The four main elements of their plan were: a much stronger market orientation; decentralization; management by objectives; and open decision making through creative conflict.

To implement these ideas, Gohlke began at the top. Each senior member of the management board was given direct responsibility for a business function and the number of management layers was reduced from five to three, essentially a single operating headquarters and a two-level field organization with 10 regional offices. To signal a change in style, Gohlke introduced an "open-door" policy whereby he undertook to meet with as many DB personnel of all levels as possible. He had numerous meetings with both the Railroad Union and the Workers' Council to explain the new plan. He also introduced informal breakfast meetings with management and employees, where he could gain better understanding of the style and culture of DB.

To prevent the budget deficit from exploding, Gohlke ordered a freeze on all new hiring and investment. To improve revenues, individuals in the Marketing Department were given responsibility for product and market performance. New marketing ideas included the conversion of railroad stations into public centers of attention through art exhibits and other events.

Gohlke also began a low-key campaign to get the government to take direct responsibility for the development of railroad infrastructure. In addition, he began to sound out the possibility of eventually privatizing DB's commercial business. Transport Minister Werner Dollinger was reported in the press as saying that he did not rule out the possibility of converting the railroad's passenger and freight handling divisions into stock companies.

Between 1982 and 1985, the Bundesbahn recorded strong improvement in its position. Productivity increased by 10 percentage points in real terms, with a sharp drop in the number of personnel. Instead of increasing, as initially projected, the total loss dropped. In 1984, DM80 million of debt was actually refunded. As a result, the total debt increased by only DM0.7 billion over the period.

But in 1985, the government announced that an extra annual contribution of DM2 billion to finance the expansion of the rail network would not be forthcoming. The sentiment in the Bundestag among the governing Christian Democrats was that things were improving at the Bundesbahn, as shown by the declining losses. Hence, a change in the legal status of the Bundesbahn, or an increase in the federal subsidy, was unnecessary. For their part, the opposition Social Democrats preferred a change in the composition and role of the Bundesbahn Supervisory Board rather than additional subsidies.

Apart from the refusal of the government to take over rail infrastructure development, the Bundesbahn employees were resisting some of the changes, commuter revenues were declining, interest expense rising, and increased deregulation of road trucking throughout the European Common Market was approaching. The 1981 Federal Railroad law still required that substantial organizational changes be accepted first by the DB Supervisory Board comprising federal and state politicians and union leaders, as well as representatives of industry, and then be approved by the federal minister of transport.

Early in 1990, Gohlke left the Bundesbahn to become director of Treuhandanstalt, the trust agency responsible for privatizing East Germany's economy. The change process clearly had not taken root at the Bundesbahn. What went wrong?

The DB environment, with strong forces of change and high resistance, had been crying out for a commander who could implement a quantum leap. Gohlke, despite his forceful personality, was forced into a committee style. His lack of railroad know-how, plus the nature of his appointment at the same time as others on the Vorstand (Management Committee), was such that he had little choice other than to pursue the committee approach. Not surprisingly, the committee came up with a program of gradual renewal which it then proceeded to sell to the various stakeholder groups. Yet this phase of the change process worked well: after three years, DB was much more market-oriented, decentralized, managed by objectives, and open in its decision making.

But the necessary leverage had not been established for catching up with the competition from other forms of transportation. The new management of the Bundesbahn should have started its campaign immediately to have the government take over responsibility for the railroad infrastructure while performance was at its worst. Instead it first chose to stop the hemorrhage of cash flow and improve performance.

What followed was one of the classic ironies in the possible interplay between forces of change and resistance. Whereas an improvement in performance might have impressed bankers, it completely undercut the Bundesbahn's case with the politicians. Rather than being impressed with Gohlke and his team, halting and then reversing the Bundesbahn slide toward larger and larger deficits, the politicians used this progress as an excuse for not correcting the economic fundamentals which distorted the competitiveness of the Bundesbahn. As the chances for change in the status of the Bundesbahn dried up, the employees also began to dig in their heels. Coming from the private sector, Gohlke and his team had completely misjudged the kind of pressure required to motivate change among the stakeholders. The approaches adopted by Gohlke to deal with the entrenched resistance at the Bundesbahn turned out to be woefully inadequate.

Several methods for dealing successfully with entrenched resistance to change have been identified from the observation of management practice by John Kotter and Leonard Schlesinger. These methods differ in terms of the power and resources that must be applied. Although one method does not exclude the other, the intervention paths favor certain combinations over others.

Negotiation

Negotiation typically involves the least power but can be very expensive with respect to the resources that have to be sacrificed to get an agreement. Pilkington Brothers was unable to offer the national union enough to get an agreement on work reorganization. However, by recognizing a different constellation of interests at the local level, it opened up a new negotiating process which became the bridge to its new culture. Negotiation is better suited to renewal and revitalization using the collaborative and cultural implementation approaches because of the high premium placed on participation and involvement relative to the other methods for dealing with resistance.

Manipulation

Manipulation can be relatively quick and inexpensive. It is often employed to deal with external status quo agents on paths of resistance. But manipulation requires the ability to structure information, events, and involvement in a manner desirable to the status quo agents without creating the feeling of manipulation. At Ford U.K., for example, quality circles were first introduced as a "structural remedy for poor productivity and quality" rather than as a genuine attempt to mobilize employee commitment. The unions dismissed the quality circles as a "heavy-handed attempt to short-circuit existing bargaining procedures."[10] It was only in 1985 that Ford was able to overcome its traditional confrontation with the unions and the bad taste of manipulation left by the quality circles, by negotiating an agreement that got rid of flat-rate earnings and exchanged productivity bonuses for flexible working practices.

Coercion

Coercion may be the only alternative when speed is essential on a restructuring path and when the status quo agents cannot be converted no matter what else is done. Here it is essential that the manager has enough power to "force people to accept change by explicitly or implicitly threatening them (with the loss of jobs, promotion possibilities, and so forth) or by actually firing and transferring them."[11] At the Deutsche Bundesbahn, some of the status quo interest groups were so entrenched that no amount of education, facilitation, participation, negotiation, or manipulation was likely to dislodge them. The only possibility would have been to force them to change. But Gohlke did not have the power to do so in all cases internally, and certainly not with respect to the external interest groups. His biggest mistake was to accept the appointment in the first place, without the power of a commander internally, and the backing of a political sponsor (party) to force the pace of change externally.

DEALING WITH MULTIPLE CHANGE FORCES

Several of the examples in this chapter suggest that a complete radical change process may involve several phases with different intervention paths and corresponding implementation styles. This may be because of pressure from more than one change force; for example, one strong established force and another weak and emerging. Alternatively, there may be a company-specific change force (typically financial) that differs in intensity from the competitive change force. Having more impact and being a greater threat to survival, the strongest change force is dealt with in the first phase of the change process, while the weaker change force(s) is/are dealt with in subsequent phase(s). Once the necessary resources and competence have been acquired to deal with the strong change force, competence can be added to deal with emerging forces.

At Pilkington Brothers, the strong competitive change force for cost reduction was associated with the sharp decline in growth and affected mainly the production and delivery side of the business. The weaker emerging change force was associated with the development of new specialty products and affected both marketing and production.

With adequate financial resources and a growing appreciation of the need to change, the managerial ranks were relatively open to change. In the first phase of the change process, top management used a cultural style to implement a revitalization path designed to acquire the cost reduction competence needed to deal with the corresponding strong change force. In the second phase, management used a collaborative style with the unions to acquire the flexibility for new product development needed to deal with the weaker emerging change force.

At Sisu, like at Pilkington, the strong competitive change force was for cost reduction necessitated by the sharp drop in demand and the weaker emerging change force was associated with the development of a new product. But in contrast to Pilkington, Sisu was under strong financial pressure to get its house in order and the ranks below management were closed to any change. As a first step, Jerkku dealt with the immediate financial pressure by getting the government to support a corporate change process.

In the first phase of the internal process, Jerkku used a commander style on a restructuring path to acquire the cost reduction competence for dealing with the strong forces of change and resistance. In the second phase, having broken the resistance to change, he initiated a collaborative style between the marketing department and the field sales force to provide the necessary competence for customized solutions to trucking problems.

At both Pilkington and Sisu, the phases of the change process were sequenced in the order of the strengths of the corresponding change forces. The intervention paths and implementation styles were consistent with the forces of change and resistance during each phase.

**KEYS TO PRACTICE: MOBILIZING
THE ORGANIZATION**

1. Select implementation style(s) consistent with the chosen intervention path(s) and corresponding interplay(s) between forces of change and resistance.
2. Motivate the change for key stakeholders on both a rational and an emotional level in order to develop commitment.
3. Trigger the organizational leap by giving key players implicit contracts in a new change organization with objectives, responsibilities, milestones, and follow-up.
4. Deal with status quo agents using negotiation, manipulation, coercion, or isolation, taking into account the strength of the related resistance and the change force.
5. Deal with multiple change forces by sequencing the different phases of the change process in the order of the strengths of the forces.

CHAPTER 9

Leapfrogging the Competition

"A T THE START of the 1980s few people gave Harley-Davidson much chance to survive. The last U.S. motorcycle maker was being battered by the Japanese. Its share of the super-heavyweight motorcycle market had fallen from 75 percent in 1973 to 25 percent." As Peter Reid pointed out in his book on Harley-Davidson: more than half the machines coming off Harley's assembly line had missing parts; the dealers had to fix them up before they could be sold.[1]

When Vaughn Beals took charge in 1975, at the behest of the owner AMF, he intervened immediately, merely to keep Harley in business. With the chief engineer, Jeff Bleustein, he set up a quality control program to repair the bikes before selling them to the dealers. But the cost of this program accounted for 25 percent of the final retail price of $4,000. At a strategy retreat in North Carolina, the senior managers decided that cost reduction had to be the number-one priority if they were to catch up with the Japanese. Yet catching up would take years.

To keep Harley in business meanwhile, the company drew on its greatest remaining asset; the Harley-Davidson product image of the macho biker's bike. William G. Davidson, grandson of one of the founders and styling vice president of the company, created a series of cosmetic innovations. "He performed miracles with decals and paint. A line here and a line there and we'd have a new model." The Super Glide was a factory-built custom bike that looked like the garage creations put together by do-it-yourself Harley fanatics. Together with other models, like the Low Rider and Wide Glide, it kept Harley in business.

After Beals and twelve other executives took control of Harley in a leveraged buyout in 1981, they visited Honda's plant in Marysville, Ohio. As a result of this visit and a successful pilot program, they decided to introduce just-in-time inventory control. Some of the workers laughed at the idea of replacing Harley's computerized control system, overhead conveyors, and high-rise parts storage with just-in-time push carts. To deal with the resistance, Harley executives spent months meeting with employees from all departments. The employees were involved in planning the system and working out the details. "No changes were implemented until the people involved understood and accepted them. It took two months before the consensus decision was made to go ahead. That was a Friday—and we started making the changes on Monday." The employees responded with initiative. The company followed up by teaching workers the use of statistical tools needed for quality control, training plant managers to become team leaders, and helping suppliers to use similar methods.

Having laid the quality and cost foundation for its comeback, Harley turned to the next phase, adding perceived value through marketing. First, it won five years of declining import tariff protection against the big Japanese bikes. Then a series of TV commercials announced Super Ride, a demonstration program inviting bikers to try out a new Harley at any of the 600 or more dealers. As a result, potential buyers were increasingly convinced that Harley had solved its quality control problems. Super Ride became so successful that Harley now takes a fleet of demo bikes to all motorcycle rallies. Money was also spent boosting dealers and forming the Harley Owners Group (HOG). The club sponsors bikers' events virtually every weekend from April to November all over the country and includes managers and their wives: "HOG is one way we differentiate ourselves from our Japanese competitors." Indeed, Honda tried and failed to create its own version of HOG.

In 1983, Harley moved from the red to the black in terms of profitability. Its market share started climbing again. By 1989, Harley had recaptured almost 50 percent of the super-heavyweight bike market, with profits of $26.9 million on sales of $810.1 million.

The Harley-Davidson comeback is a classic example of how a breakpoint can be exploited to leapfrog the competition. The change process at Harley-Davidson—and other companies like

Sisu the Finnish truck company that have successfully leapfrogged the competition—comprised three phases, which we focus on in this chapter:

- Buying time to stay in the game
- Catching up with the competition
- Outperforming the competition

In addition we look at the

- Sequencing and timing of the phases

BUYING TIME

A leapfrog involves coming from behind competitors that are further along in adapting to radical industry change. This competitive disadvantage shows up in poor financial performance. Since companies have limited financial resources and financial stakeholders with limited patience, poor performance puts a constraint on the time available to improve the situation, before the company is forced into a takeover, bankruptcy, or possibly liquidation.

In effect, the poor financial performance gives rise to a force for financial change from the shareholders and bankers. If the latter are unwilling to support the change needed to restore the company's competitive position, the financial pressure becomes an obstacle to the needed competitive change. Either the company deals with the financial force by somehow buying time for the competitive change, or it is prevented from implementing a competitively viable intervention path and is eventually forced into a bankruptcy or liquidation by the financial pressure.

Several alternative measures of financial performance can be used as a proxy for the time available. The market-to-book ratio (the stock market value of the company relative to its book value) is a sensitive measure of investors' opinion about the firm's current and future performance. A declining market-to-book ratio indicates eroding investor confidence. Several statistical studies have found that the market-to-book ratio is one of the better indicators of the chance of a takeover. The ratio of return on equity to cost of equity (interest rate plus a risk premium) is a related measure of performance for unlisted companies or divisions. If the company is earning and expected to earn a lower return than investors can get elsewhere, it will generally sell for less than its book value. A minimally acceptable level of performance would be a long-run ratio of 1 to 1 for both the market-to-book and the return to cost of equity ratios.

If the company or business unit is still earning an acceptable return, the external breakpoint has not yet affected its performance. Other things being equal, the company potentially has the time available to deal with the external discontinuity. Once the performance begins to decline and erode the resource base under the impact of the breakpoint, there is not enough time left for a slow process of change; only intervention paths with intermediate and short time horizons remain feasible. Finally, when the adaptation gap between the environment and the company reaches crisis proportions, there is not even enough time for resistance and still less for time-consuming intervention.

The larger the resource base, the longer the company can stave off the need for drastic action in the face of declining performance. Large companies in particular often have accumulated large hidden resources over time that can be either activated or sold off to provide a cushion against the need to do something about declining performance. When the resources are finally depleted, however, the performance is often so bad that little can be done with the existing organization. This was very much the story of Société Générale de Belgique. Unfortunately, the same is true of many large companies. Instead of monitoring their situation and reacting in time, they were shocked into action only by a financial crisis.

To buy time to stay in the game, the resistance and restructuring paths are commonly employed. In this context, the resistance path involves getting the dissatisfied stakeholders to buy into the proposed changes and reduce the pressure they could apply. Or, alternatively, they may be asked to provide temporary protection against the forces of change. Most commonly, the government is asked for some form of assistance or the financial stakeholders supply additional funds to get the company back on its feet.

Using restructuring to buy time typically involves downsizing, selling, or liquidating unprofitable business, to improve the overall performance of the assets and to provide capital for repositioning the company. Alternatively, dissatisfied financiers are bought out by others in a restructuring of the liabilities.

At Harley-Davidson, it was only after Beals took charge that the full implications of the shift in the motorcycle industry were accepted, including the threat to the company's survival. By this time, however, Harley faced not only dissatisfied financiers, but also a high level of customer dissatisfaction manifested in the plummeting market share. To provide the necessary time for staying in the game at the eleventh hour, Harley appealed to the banks for financial support and drew on intangible assets in the form of William G. Davidson's design skills to stem the erosion of market share.

The change process took so much time, however, that the Harley executives continually had to deal with dissatisfied stakeholders. For example, when the success of the catch-up phase was still in the balance, AMF Corp., the parent company, decided to pull out. The executive team gained more time by taking control with a leveraged buyout and appealing successfully to the government for temporary tariff protection.

CATCHING UP

This involves the successful adoption of one of the new strategies that competitors are using to deal with the new industry environment.[2] Here, correct assessment of the unfolding strategic change scenario, together with the related competence gap, are essential.

An audit of existing resources and competencies, relative to the key success factors in the competitor's approach, is needed to estimate the size of the competence gap. The stock of resources and competencies is affected by the organizational capability available to develop them.

- Tangible Resources: human skills, finance, supplies, technology, information.
- Intangible Resources: customer loyalty, corporate image, employee motivation, supplier and stakeholder relationships.
- Functional Competencies: R&D, technology know-how, purchasing, production, marketing distribution, service.
- Organizational Capabilities: environmental scanning (which affects access to information), management of stakeholder relationships (which affects access to resources), management of internal learning (which determines ability to develop competencies).

To close the competence gap, the revitalization, renewal, or restructuring paths are employed, depending on the strength of the change force implicit in the unfolding industry scenario and the strength of the resistance. Revitalization and renewal imply a largely in-house approach to acquiring the necessary competence, whereas restructuring in this context tries to inject that competence by acquisition from the outside.

Beals and his team at Harley-Davidson went for revitalization with a focused product strategy and a companywide effort to introduce continual quality and cost improvement. The organizing approach was centered around quality circles. This intervention path was consistent with the strong force for quality and cost reduction created by the Japanese competition.

However, the initial resistance to the quality circles and just-in-time management was considerable. Before the revitalization could take hold at Harley, this resistance had to be reduced dramatically. To motivate change, months were spent meeting with employees from all departments to explain how it would work and how the survival of the company depended on it. Without this important preparation, the revitalization would have been rejected by the organization. As it turned out, with the preparation period included, the revitalization took so long to produce results that some of the financiers, most notably the parent company, got cold feet and withdrew.

For workers on the shop floor, however, the key to their change commitment was intense involvement in the design of the change process. About three weeks after the introduction of the just-in-time system, Beals got the following reaction from workers when asking how the conversion was going: "Well, we have some problems, but it's a lot better than it was before, and we'll get these problems fixed." "That reaction," said Beals, "demonstrated the true value of employee involvement."

Another intervention path more consistent with the strong forces of change and strong resistance might have been some form of restructuring implemented with a commander style, designed to break the resistance. But restructuring often has an adverse effect on the morale of the organization and makes employees dependent on the decisions of the commander. This is opposite to the kind of attitude and behavior required for the revitalization later on. A restructuring phase would have simplified matters early in the change process in exchange for complicating them later. Harley's management decided to tackle the resistance the other way around: by convincing the status quo agents about the desirability of the change early on in order to facilitate matters later during the third phase of the leapfrog.

OUTPERFORMING

Getting ahead of the competition in the third phase of the leapfrog was crucial for Harley, as it is for all companies trying to exploit a breakpoint. In most cases, catching up is not too difficult; the leading competitors provide living role models of what has to be done and the organization can still tap the motivation generated by the threat of discontinuity. Outperforming the competition is another matter; competitors can no longer merely be copied, and the original motivation for change has often dissipated.

The key to outperforming is finding a way to create a competitive advantage by offering a superior value-cost package to the marketplace. To deliver a superior value-cost package, the company has to get its resource inputs on better terms, transform them more effectively, or sell the output on better terms. In the case of a successful leapfrogger, this is most frequently done by taking as a base the competitor's formula during the second catch-up phase of the leapfrog and then in the third phase improving on it. Or more succinctly, by piggybacking on the competitor's formula.

After bringing its product and production quality up to Japanese standards using revitalization and the related continual improvement techniques, Harley-Davidson took this formula as a basis for developing a special relationship with its customers. Management shifted to an intervention path of renewal, with the marketing department as a large task force, which was consistent with the weak change force implicit in the development of a customer relationship and the low resistance implicit in marketing's support of William Davidson's designs.

An incremental approach was followed with the Super Ride Program, first communicating the fact that Harley had solved its production problems and then the owner groups creating an intangible benefit for Harley owners. The biking events were rooted in American biker culture. They gave owners an opportunity to celebrate the use of their bikes and socialize together at big jamborees. This cultural factor was a unique Harley advantage which foreign competitors could not easily duplicate. Honda's failure to set up a competing network of clubs for its bikes underlined the uniqueness of Harley's outperforming advantage.

Piggybacking possibilities typically are greater early on in a technology or product cycle. Scarce resources have yet to be fully exploited, competitors have yet to fully refine their competence across the whole set of key success factors, and the full range of extensions to the product offering has yet to be explored. To identify piggybacking opportunities, latecomers to a breakpoint should keep the following standard possibilities in mind.

Value. A new layer of perceived value can be added by enhancing or customizing the competitor's product offering. A complete strategy encompasses not only an innovative product or service idea but also the way it is promoted, distributed, supported, and used by the customer. The leading Japanese competitor in heavyweight bikes stopped short of offering users a relationship, thereby providing an opportunity for someone else to add this and enhance the product. Alternatively, when there is only one dominant product, customized applications become attractive. This is what Honda, Yamaha, and Kawasaki did to the old standard American bikes by adding new sizes and simple controls which made them accessible to different users.

Cost. Lowering delivered cost by streamlining the production and delivery process is another way of improving on the competitor's offering. Peter Drucker points out that opportunities to lower delivered cost are often presented by pioneering firms that "skim the most profitable business off the top of the market, leaving large but unsatisfied demand underneath." The possibility of offering the new formula at a price competitive with that of previous offers provides a crucial advantage. Rationalization and improvement are seen as a way to offer more value by making the whole organization closer and more responsive to the market. As a result, more perceived value can be offered at lower cost.

Time. Speeding up response time to market needs and product development cycle times often allows successful piggybackers to put together a complete and competitively priced formula faster than the innovator. In particular, early formulas often lack a suitable approach to distribution, which gives followers a chance to address this aspect first. A major European toy manufacturer rationalized and then developed a partnership with retailers which allowed it to capture sales information at retailer level. As a result, it was able to reduce stock in the whole system, limit retailers' year-end carryover of unsold toys, and get quicker feedback on customer response.[3]

SEQUENCING AND TIMING

Leapfrogging involves adding layers of resources and competence to the organization to stay in the game, catch up, and outperform. For the leapfrog to succeed, these layers of competence must be reflected in an improving and eventually superior value-cost package relative to the competition. This strategic side of the leapfrog can be summarized graphically in a value-cost diagram (Exhibit 9-1) for Harley-Davidson.

Harley fell behind the Japanese in the 1970s when the latter entered the heavy bike market with cheaper machines which they

EXHIBIT 9–1   **Harley-Davidson Leapfrog: Strategic Moves in Value–Cost Terms**

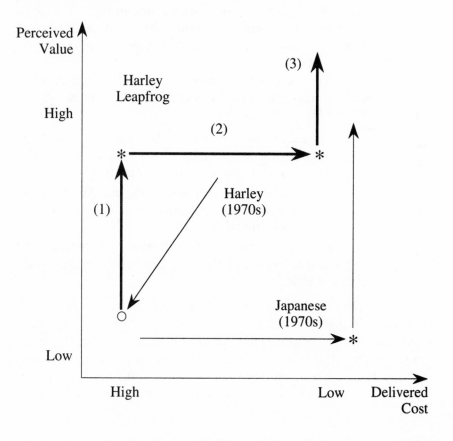

subsequently upgraded. By the time Harley woke up, the Japanese were selling better quality bikes at lower prices. Harley then embarked on what turned out to be a leapfrog with three strategic moves.

Phase 1   Stay-in-the-game by adding value with W. Davidson's designs.

Phase 2   Catch up by lowering delivered cost with production improvements.

Phase 3   Outperform by adding value with marketing and customer relationships.

The key to the success of the leapfrog was the integration of the strategic moves with appropriate intervention paths. The intervention paths were sequenced to deal with the stronger change forces first, thereby clearing the way for dealing with the weaker ones. Moreover, each phase was used to create the organizational platform for launching the next phase. If this is not carefully done, the whole process can be aborted. British Steel, for example, cut costs so heavily during a phase of convergence in the early 1980s that it had no financial or human flexibility left to enhance its product range when the industry diverged with a rejuvenation breakpoint a few years later.

The overall change process can be summarized graphically by mapping out the intervention paths in the change arena as shown in Exhibit 9-2 for Harley-Davidson.

Phase 1   Resistance path to stay in the game by shielding operations from competitive change forces with financial restructuring and W. Davidson's designs.

Phase 2   Revitalization to catch up with the Japanese by reducing resistance and moving production toward continuous improvement.

Phase 3   Renewal to outperform the Japanese by incremental addition of value through marketing (Super Ride and HOG programs).

The timing of the transition between the phases is crucial. If the process moves too soon from one phase to the next, the basis for supporting the next phase may not be sufficient. On the other hand, if the process is too slow, the company may miss the window of opportunity that often opens up after an industry breakpoint. Although competitors can take advantage of the new conditions to

EXHIBIT 9–2 **Harley-Davidson Leapfrog: Change Process in Terms of Intervention Paths**

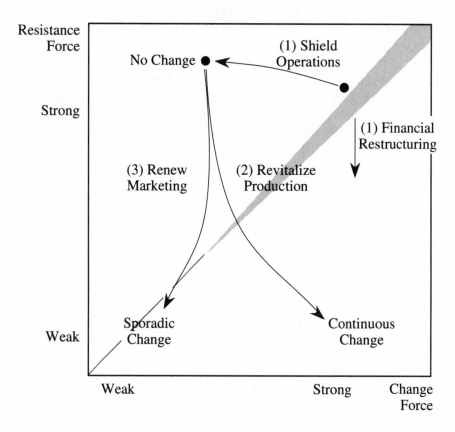

reposition themselves, the time available is not unlimited. The more competitors pursue the new opportunities, the less will be available for latecomers. Competitors begin participating in the inexorable economic process that gradually equates supply with demand, thereby eliminating all opportunities with superior returns. Moreover, the demand can only support a certain number of players with normal returns on the supply side. Those that take too long getting their act together will be shut out of the game.

At Harley-Davidson, the timing problem was not so much the window of opportunity as the way in which the slow pace of the change process continued to undermine support from the financial stakeholders. The second phase of the leapfrog almost collapsed when Citibank withdrew in 1989 because it could not see any financial value being created.

The company only survived the transition to the third phase because it found an alternative source of finance from Heller Financial Corp., where the number-two man was a Harley fan. In 1986, Harley refinanced the debt again, this time with a public stock offering of $26 million. This provided the support needed for outperforming the competition with the HOG program. Yet this third phase of the leapfrog was so successful that, by 1989, the share price had almost tripled. Harley-Davidson celebrated its eighty-fifth birthday with a jamboree attended by 24,000 bikers who were witnesses to the culmination of one of the most dramatic examples of how the forces of change and resistance can be exploited to leapfrog the competition.

KEYS TO PRACTICE: LEAPFROGGING THE COMPETITION

1. Choose an initial intervention path that is capable of addressing the strongest force of change and the related resistance.
2. In the next phase, move to an intervention path for dealing with the resistance (especially the competence gap) relative to the change force implicit in the behavior of competitors.
3. Look for a way of outperforming the value-cost offering of competitors (possibly by piggybacking on their approach) and move to an intervention path for doing so.
4. Time the transition between phases of the leapfrog to ensure that an appropriate basis is in place for the next phase, while still allowing enough time to capitalize on the window of opportunity.

PART III

Creating Breakpoints

A NTICIPATION GIVES A COMPANY the oppor- tunity to shape a competitive breakpoint to its advantage. The first competitor to see and act on an oppor- tunity becomes the change agent that embodies the force of change in the industry. As such, the company strongly influences the inter- play between the industry's forces of change and resistance. In par- ticular, the company can lead the industry in crossing the boundary between old and new competitive behavior. If the market accepts the new direction, the company and the market together can trigger a breakpoint.

In this part of the book we look at the proactive change capa- bilities, or organizational behavior patterns, that can give the com- pany the opportunity of creating a competitive breakpoint (see Exhibit III-1). In most cases companies that create competitive breakpoints have been working on their change capabilities for years. The competence and organizational behavior needed to cre- ate breakpoints can only be acquired through a process of learning which takes time.

In the context of the corporate change arena, there are three types of change capability, or three behavior patterns capable of changing the industry. Each of these change capabilities is dealt with separately in one of the chapters that follow. At this stage it will come as no surprise that the most appropriate behavior pattern for creating an industry breakpoint will reflect the interplay of forces confronting the company.

EXHIBIT III–1 **Proactive Change Capabilities for Creating Competitive Breakpoints**

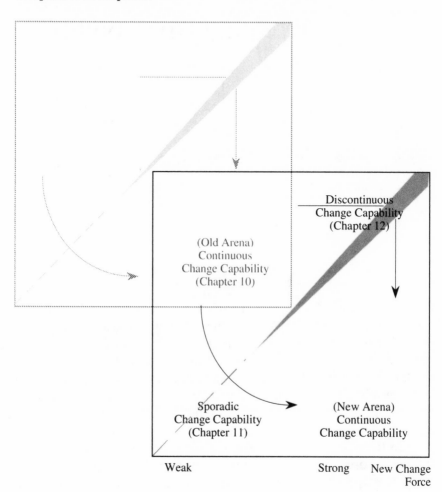

In Chapter 10, we discuss the continuous change capabilities needed to capitalize on strong forces of change, represented by well-established external trends. Continuous change capabilities, however, have to be initiated and nurtured by top management; they do not emerge on their own. A proactive organizational turning point or breakpoint is often used to prepare the ground for the development of continuous change, which follows the transition from old to new behavior.

Once continuous change capabilities are in place, they can serve as a base for creating competitive breakpoints in a new change area. However, crossing the behavior boundary in the new arena often requires a more directive approach in the form of a sporadic, or discontinuous change capability.

Chapter 11 looks at the strategic option, or proactive turning point capability, needed to deal with weak change forces corresponding to uncertainty in the direction of external trends. Chapter 12 discusses the organizational realignment, or proactive breakpoint capability, required to deal with the high resistance in internal change running counter to an anticipated external turning point.

Few, if any, companies are masters of all three proactive change capabilities. Most companies that create breakpoints can only do so in certain environments. But the environment itself is always changing. Hence, the excellent companies of the future will be those that can draw on all three of these change capabilities to create breakpoints whenever the opportunity presents itself.

CHAPTER 10

Nurturing
Continuous Change

W HEN THE LEADING EXECUTIVES of Canon's Copier Division saw the worldwide success that the Camera Division was having with the AE-1 camera, they were keen to duplicate that success. The director of the Copier Division raised the idea of a small, $1,000, maintenance-free copier for the small-business and home-use markets with the Copier Development Center. Within a few months, the task force had been created. Within three years, the sales launch was held for Canon's dramatically new PC-10 and PC-20 cartridge-type copiers which triggered a breakpoint in the marketplace.[1]

The rapid response to internal competition and a perceived market need did not occur in a vacuum. Canon had been implementing a six-year "Premier Company Plan" initiated by its president, Ryuzaburo Kaku. The plan ambitiously called for Canon to become a leading company in Japan within the first three years and a world leader in the second three years. Previously, Canon had often beaten the competition to the market with attractive new products, but soon fell back behind the pack again. The company couldn't turn its new products into growth opportunities because its operations ran in an uncoordinated fashion without effective long-range planning.

In a typical restructuring move, plants were consolidated and the company was reorganized into three product groups: cameras, business machines, and optical products. Atypical were the management systems used to coordinate the product groups. These are described by the Japan Management Association in a compilation of the Canon Production System. Three study committees were formed with companywide members to implement and improve three different management systems: the Canon Development System (CDS), the Canon Production System (CPS), and the Canon Marketing System (CMS).

> The system study committees were asked to build management systems based on long range planning that would give Canon the ability to move ahead quickly and to withstand any unforeseen market changes. The development system (CDS) committee was to foster the development of new products, high in performance and quality, matched to consumer needs, and timed for the market. The production system (CPS) committee was to eliminate waste so the company could manufacture higher quality products at lower costs and withstand both a stronger yen and intensified competition. The marketing system (CMS) committee was expected to expand and strengthen Canon's independent domestic and overseas sales network by building a high quality service and sales force.[2]

The development system that emerged was based on a standard procedure for multifunctional task forces with mandates to develop new products. The first phase of the procedure was to come up with a product concept that transformed the product "goal" into an "honest design"; the second phase was a feasibility study to lay out how the company could come up with the technology and features needed for the new product; and the third phase involved the development of a prototype and mass production trials. An important task of the CDS committee was to keep improving the approach to new product development. Among its programs, one that was most beneficial to the product groups was TS 1/2, designed to cut product development times in half.

The production committee set three companywide goals: "To strive for the best quality, the lowest cost, and the fastest delivery anywhere." To achieve these objectives, the committee developed three systems: Quality Assurance in all stages of development, production, and sales; Production Assurance to lower costs and improve delivery times with the JIT system and the Signal (visual control) system; and Personnel Training for Canon's employees through a life-long educational program.

CPS was designed to create an ongoing process of improvement. At the outset, a sequence of plans was drawn up to coordinate implementation in each factory. The first plan from 1976 to 1978 was aimed at eliminating waste of materials, machines, and human effort throughout the production process, with the help of visual standards that allow "anyone to tell at a glance whether an abnormality has occurred." The second plan from 1979 to 1981 was intended to get everyone to adhere to all plans, schedules, and rules. When this was not possible, the supervisor and worker had to determine whether the problem was with the work standard or the way it was done. This led to small group activities and projects that clarified responsibilities and established standards that everyone could follow. The third plan from 1982 to 1984 focused on improving productivity and shortening the cycle times of all activities to attain "higher levels and higher speed." The ultimate objective was a trouble-free, stockless, and flexible production system.

When the goal of a small copier was raised by senior executives, Canon's Development System swung into action, providing a rapid response. Once the new copier line was launched, the marketing and production systems ensured that Canon could build market share and reap the share and benefit of its product breakthrough. Canon's market share and production experience made it difficult for competitors to catch up.

The Canon approach illustrates several aspects of the breakpoint-creating process. On the one hand, there is the use of systems to develop a capability for continual improvement. On the other hand, there is the conscious strategic choice of the small-copier market segment. In this chapter we shall explore the former, those capabilities that give a company the necessary flexibility to capitalize spontaneously on strong forces of change. The more developed these continuous change capabilities, the greater the chance that the organization will seize on the forces of change to create a breakpoint from the bottom up.

A number of continuous change capabilities are apparent in companies that have initiated competitive breakpoints from the bottom up. The first of these is critical to anticipating the forces of change. The other three are suggested by the approaches to organizing continuous change discussed in Chapter 7 (see also Exhibit 10-1).

- Information and intelligence capability to gather and evaluate the information for sensing the forces of change.
- Continuous (process) improvement capability. The planning

Exhibit 10–1   **Continuous Change Capabilities**

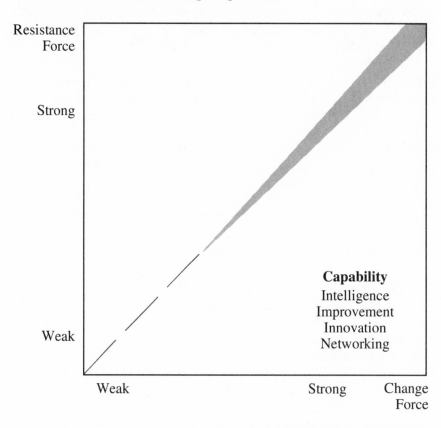

and management systems that promote what the Japanese call "kaizen."

- Spontaneous (product) innovation capability. The self-designing approach to organization that stimulates intrapreneurship.
- Stakeholder networking capability that provides access to critical tangible resources and leads to the development of intangible assets.

These are all continuous change capabilities which are crucial for leadership in industries where the change forces are strong. Important for creating breakpoints is the way in which these capabilities can be deployed to provide first-mover advantages that preempt the moves of competitors.

INTELLIGENCE CAPABILITY

Many companies put themselves at a disadvantage by operating in the dark. Quantitative forecasts prove so unreliable that executives prefer to use their intuition. However, it is an intuition that is hobbled by closed attitudes and an emaciated information system. No matter how creative such intuition, it cannot possibly hope to sense the potential for a breakpoint, except by luck. As a result, no matter how well endowed the company may be in other capabilities, competences, or resources, it cannot possibly create a breakpoint in its industry, except by chance.

To create industry breakpoints, a well-developed information and intelligence capability is essential. In leading companies, this comprises two essential building blocks: first, open attitudes throughout the company, especially on the part of leading executives; second, an information-gathering approach to develop intelligence for competitive advantage.

Open Attitudes

Flexible attitudes are not natural. To loosen closed attitudes, several steps can be taken: it is important to be aware of one's mindset, to become a student of the business environment, and to engage in creative thinking.

Be aware of your mind-set. Peter Senge suggests several techniques that can be used to surface and test the hidden models that make up our mind-sets and shape our intuition.

Looking for assumptions that have become facts in our minds. These block the questions needed to properly diagnose problems.

Balancing advocacy with enquiry. Strong arguments for one's positions often reflect a hidden model.

Advocacy has to be tempered with enquiry, that is, listening and questioning to tap the views of others.

Distinguishing what we really believe from what we think we believe. Actions speak louder than words. What we do is usually a better guide to our deep beliefs than what we say.

Recognizing defensive routines. We use masks and habits to protect ourselves from exposing what we are thinking. These defensive mechanisms have to be loosened if we are to open our minds to the potential impact of emerging forces. Once we are more aware of our mind-set, we can begin to update it with respect to some of the external developments that otherwise might have been ignored as irrelevant.[3]

Become a student of the business environment. Leo Esaki, the Japanese Nobel-Prize winner in physics in 1973, observed that through fierce competition, the United States produces many outstanding teachers in the form of politicians, executives, and professionals, but relatively few serious students. By contrast, "Japan is a nation of avid students." The apprentice ethos in Japan produces an excellent rank and file, but few superior leaders. In Esaki's view, "the Japanese must shed their apprentice mentality and become capable instructors; Americans should tone down their missionary spirit and learn from others."[4]

James Fallows pointed out that the Japanese don't work with abstract principles.[5] But they pay a lot of attention to the forces of change. Adaptation to competitive pressure and external forces is part of daily business life. "Gaiatsu" (outside pressure) is a widely used construct. Public speeches by Japanese CEOs and senior executives invariably start with the five or ten most important forces affecting their companies; Western executives more typically discuss their firm's historical financial performance. The quick reaction to endaka is vivid testimony to the studious attention that successful Japanese companies pay to the forces of change. Above all, Japanese executives are obsessed by the competitive pecking order expressed in market shares. So sensitive are they to the moves of their competitors that a guide to business in Japan, by one of the Big Six accounting firms, recommends against any mention of the competition during a first visit.

To anticipate breakpoints, executives must copy their Japanese peers and constantly study the environment. Current trends and resistance factors, possible turning points, and cycles should always be in the back, if not the front, of their minds. As should the evolution of the 5 Cs: customers, competitors, supply chain, channels, and the company itself. In particular, competitors have to be followed to see what kind of capabilities and competencies they are adding.[6] And the market should be monitored, as perhaps the most important source of ideas for innovation, for the possibilities of adding an extra layer of value, or otherwise improving the current offering in the marketplace.

ICI's executive directors, for example, engage in a whole range of intelligence-gathering activities that make them de facto students of the business environment: meetings with customers and government officials, frequent trips to subsidiaries, meetings with planning department futurologists, annual two-day meetings with the top fifty executives in the company to share ideas and information, plus a continual flow of reports and ideas from the businesses and staff departments.[7]

Engage in creative thinking. An open, well-informed mind has to be supplemented with creative thinking if a breakpoint is to be initiated. Analytic techniques based on logic and deduction are not enough because the idea is to change the rules of the game. Lateral thinking can be useful as a way of giving more play to one's intuition.[8] Lateral thinking suggests several techniques that fit in with the anticipation of breakpoints:

> The recognition that ideas and behaviors often come in pairs of polar opposites, as they cycle between divergence and convergence. The old behavior has to be abandoned before the opposite pole can be embraced.

> The search for varying viewpoints. The strategic change scenarios provide a framework for exploring alternative views of the future.

> The suspension of logical thinking by not requiring correctness at every stage of the discussion, by not tackling every problem head on, by not labeling or classifying everything, and by assuming everything is possible.

> The incorporation of chance into the process of imagining and into the content of future scenarios. Chance plays a critical role in creative thinking and has been credited as a key element in many innovations.

Simple approaches have the best chance of accessing the creative, intuitive, right side of the brain. Most managers have had their own experience with personal creativity. For example, sleeping on a problem often allows the subconscious to work on it overnight, so that on awakening, one has a potential solution in mind. It is also important to break the habit trap, the daily routine that stifles creativity. New ideas are invariably an extrapolation or combination of existing concepts: new places, new people, new experiences increase the chance of creative synthesis.

According to a journalist who tried to interview them, truly creative idea people are continually moving around, hopping from one plane to another. Moving around can help in engaging in activities that the left brain has difficulty dealing with, simple activities that only the right side of the brain can perform. Simple activities like "blind contour drawing," which entails close intense observation as one draws the edges of a form without looking at the drawing while it is in progress. The more one can use simple activities to become aware of the sensation associated with right-brain activity, the more one can bring it into play at will when trying to see through a breakpoint.

Corporate Intelligence Systems

Individual information and ideas need to be combined and exchanged to produce intelligence that is more than the sum of the inputs. Corporate experience in this area suggests a role for formal and informal information-gathering systems, such as: environmental scanning systems, intelligence centers, existing information sources, insights of employees, and integrated intelligence consciousness.

Environmental scanning systems. Formal scanning systems manned by experts have a mixed record. On the one hand, companies like Kirin Beer of Japan report that their corporate planning department plays a major role in monitoring the environment and helping executives respond to competitor's moves. On the other hand, Shell reports that its planning department's $15 a barrel scenario for oil, when the price was double that, had little impact on managers' decisions and competitive behavior. Shell is certainly correct when it says that without active and heavy participation by line managers, a scanning system is dead. Indeed, the head of Kirin's planning department is also a key line manager. To work, scanning and scenarios must become part of the line executive's tool kit and not the preserve of an ivory tower staff. Indeed, every employee must become part of the corporate intelligence system.

Intelligence centers. These centers are one of the more effective ways of getting everyone involved. The model is the intelligence headquarters of an espionage service. Intelligence centers do not build intricate quantitative models of the world. Rather they act as gathering and sifting centers for all the information supplied by the company's people.

During one beer war (not in Japan!) the largest competitor was being challenged by a new imported beer. Every salesperson was instructed to collect information from customers and outlets about where and how much of the new beer was being bought and with what reaction from consumers. A huge chart of the country and sales districts was put up on the wall in the "War Room." The competitor's every move was recorded and countermeasures and initiatives launched. Within six months, the large competitor's executives believed they knew more about what was moving the imported beer than did the competitor himself. Their marketing campaign was altered and then fine-tuned to upstage and, where possible, preempt the competitor's every move, using selective price discounting, promotions, and distribution relationship management. Once the War Room began to function, the outcome of the war was never in doubt.

An electronics company uses a competitor-information center to serve its sales force. They can call in to find out about competitors they are bidding against. The salespeople are not compensated for information supplied to the center. Rather they supply information, because they know that similar information provided by their colleagues will help them.[9]

Existing information sources.   Even without an intelligence center, virtually every company has unused repositories of potentially valuable information. Sales and marketing executives typically have more competitive information than they share. A marketing executive at a large medical supplies company took the president of a data search company into a colleague's office with a full bookshelf and an empty desk. "Joe just retired," said the marketing executive. "There are over $50,000 worth of market studies in his office, and no one else even knew they were here until now." The same president of the data search company believes that libraries and senior executives are hopelessly underutilized as intelligence sources.[10]

Insights of employees.   Some companies have explicit processes for drawing on the insight and intelligence of employees with a natural bent for creative thinking, especially with respect to technology intelligence.

Philips N.V. has a good track record of identifying and developing emerging technologies, if not always commercializing them. Peter Van Laarhoven, one of their strategic planners, has developed what he calls the "opposing expert" approach to ferreting out nascent technology trends within the Consumer Electronics Division. He uses word of mouth to seek out the number-one expert in the company with respect to a particular technology and get an opinion on future trends. He then looks for the most acclaimed expert with an opposing view of the technology's development and synthesizes both opinions for division planning. Already in the early 1980s he was able to identify the key products that will shape consumer electronics in the 1990s: video-graphics, ESP photography, high-definition TV, integrated home entertainment systems, and the 128 related technologies. Van Laarhoven's essential contribution was to get the knowledge of experts out into the mainstream of the company's planning system.

Betting on established forces of change is at the heart of the methods used by several companies, especially in Japan. To ensure that new trends are recognized on all levels, the Asahi Chemical company

> put together groups of young employees in their twenties and thirties to study possible areas of diversification. A powerful motivation for group members is that business derived from the areas they choose must be capable of supporting them later in their careers. Asked to determine the most profitable business in the next century, two such groups came to the same conclusion: biochemicals and electronics. Asahi Chemical is accordingly channeling 40 percent of its research and development money into these areas. In 1988 the company had already organized a microelectronics subsidiary which is moving aggressively into design, production, and sale of custom semiconductors.[11]

Tenneco, Inc., one of the youngest of the *Fortune* top 20 companies, uses a "brain skill management program" to look beyond new product breakpoints. In the first step, a diagnostic test is administered to identify highly "intuitive executives," who are given the task of listing high-potential, new product ideas. A second group of "logical executives" are asked to evaluate the ideas of the first group, with special attention to feasibility and ease of implementation. In the third step, the two groups meet to assess and add to the list of recommended project ideas. One of the advantages of the program is the systematic manner in which intuitive individuals are put into contact with one another across departmental lines. Another apparent payoff is the respect each group develops for the critical role of the other in the strategic planning process.[12]

Integration of intelligence consciousness. An intelligence system is not complete until all executives are involved. This message is at the heart of the approach of several leading companies. At Shell, planning has been turned into a process for learning how alternative strategies play out in different environmental scenarios. Executives are encouraged to make their view of the market, the environment, and the competition explicit, either through an interview, or by participating in a team effort to develop a new common model. After the views and models have been laid out and, usually, put on a computer, the executives use them for planning trials to find inconsistencies and draw conclusions, which are matched against information from the planning department and elsewhere. The models are improved and the cycle repeats itself. In the process, the executives learn about what is happening in the environment, build scenarios, and develop plans for the next year.[13]

In numerous industries, especially those involving service and distribution, such as fast-food chains, hotels, car rentals, distribution, department stores, and banking, the computer has been used to build an integrated information system that extends beyond the company to suppliers, distributors, and in certain cases the customers themselves. The entire system acts as an integrated information and intelligence network that, in many cases, is crucial to competitive advantage.

For IKEA, the international Swedish furniture company, fast and effective logistics are a key success factor. The company uses an integrated information system to link its stores to the specialized subcontractors that manufacture furniture kit parts. To respond to market demand as quickly as possible, the parts have to be ordered, shipped, and re-grouped in the right store at the right time—"not too early, and not too late." Various operating information systems are integrated under the umbrella of a competitive information system. The integrated information system provides real-time intelligence on how customers are responding to different forms of promotion and new lines of furniture. The intelligence has allowed IKEA to track the shifting profile of its young, suburban customer groups. On several occasions, IKEA has altered the product mix and layout of its outlets ahead of competitors to maintain its market share momentum. Together with the rest of the competitive formula, the information and intelligence capability have created a competitive breakpoint that followers in Europe have had difficulty copying.[14]

CONTINUOUS (PROCESS) IMPROVEMENT CAPABILITY

This is kaizen, the Japanese-inspired capability to involve the entire work force in improvement-oriented planning and control. Kaizen, which means improvement, evaluates and rewards everyone from the bottom to the top of the company, not merely on the basis of their output, but also in terms of their ability to improve what they are doing and help others to improve. "One of the features of our workers," according to Eiji Toyota, chairman of Toyota Motors, "is that they use their brains and their hands. Our workers provide 1.5 million suggestions a year and 95 percent of them are put to practical use."[15]

A continuous improvement capability is not something unique to Japanese culture. In its sample of auto plants, the MIT International Motor Vehicle Program found two that provide a striking contrast. In one assembly line, workers had multiple tasks; robots were used only as part of a careful plan, and the entire plant was in the midst of a relentless corporate drive to increase efficiency and quality, while wringing unnecessary cost out of "every facet of the operation." In the second plant, 10,000 miles away, robots were more widespread, but the housekeeping was not very good; parts inventory and scrap were scattered around, and a special building was used to correct defects in the cars that came off the main assembly line. Not surprisingly, the first plant was more productive than its more highly automated competitor. Yet, the first highly successful plant was a forty-year-old facility run by one of Detroit's Big Three, while the second was a much newer Japanese plant a few hours outside Tokyo.[16]

Japanese Approach

Notwithstanding the American plant mentioned above, Japan still provides the leading role models. At Canon, for example, the kaizen activities are embodied in the Canon Production System (CPS), which has the following elements: improvement targets on every level of the organization built into the planning cycle; workplace "vitalization" programs involving small-group improvement teams (quality circles), a suggestion system, safety and health announcements, and recognition of progress and special effort; three production improvement systems aimed at quality, cost, and delivery time, a support system comprising intensive training, R&D in management and production technology, and publicity and coordination for the entire effort.[17] The CPS effort is supported by top-management involvement, detailed planning, self-management and mutual monitoring, and an emphasis on process improvement.

Top-management involvement. Top management is heavily involved in CPS. The managing director makes "house calls" to each of the plants monthly. During these "doctor's rounds," the plant manager and his team report on the progress of the improvement effort: goal achievement plans, profits realized from CPS, and solutions used to solve specific problems. The visitor comments, suggests new initiatives where necessary, or points out problems that seem to have gone unnoticed. In addition, "Operation Catchball" provides a discussion forum, with the director of production technology, for section chiefs running similar operations, where they can catch up with the approaches used by others and help solve each other's problems.

Detailed planning. Kaizen has a heavy built-in emphasis on planning at every level. All CPS operations are supported by a broad three-year plan and an annual goal achievement plan for day-to-day implementation. CPS set out to make planning an automatic activity: "Planning is worked into everyone's daily routine through a variety of structured activities that are essential to the continuous improvement process—level-by-level improvement targets, managing the gap between actual and target to achieve goals, and the self-management drive."[18] To focus individual, team, and group effort, the CPS identifies nine areas where waste can be eliminated such as in defects, work-in-process, start-up times, idle equipment, and so on.

Self-management and mutual monitoring. In contrast to Western planning systems, Kaizen emphasizes self-management and mutual monitoring on all levels. Problem identification is a continuous process in every work section. Workers are expected to develop their own improvement achievement plan, incorporating repeated learning cycles of "plan-execute-observe-reflect." Regular meetings are set up to discuss problems and progress. "Open achievement records are maintained for all workers to chart their progress in planning, productivity, merit eligibility based on skill examinations, number of work improvement proposals, and attendance rate."[19]

Emphasis on process improvement. Kaizen also differs from traditional Western performance appraisal in its emphasis not only on results, but also on process improvement. In the words of Mayumi Olsubo of Bridgestone Tires Co. Ltd., "When the sales manager evaluates a salesman's performance, that evaluation must include process-oriented criteria such as the amount of the salesperson's time spent on calling new customers, time spent on outside customers' calls versus time devoted to clerical work at the office, and the percentage of new enquiries successfully closed. By paying attention to these measures, the sales manager hopes to encourage the salesperson to produce good results sooner or later. In other words, the process is considered just as important as the obviously intended results: sales!"[20]

Continuous Improvement in Non-Japanese Settings

How can continuous improvement be introduced in a non-Japanese setting? Part of the answer seems to have a lot to do with the choice of the right motivating theme. In the United States, Paul O'Neill, the new CEO of Alcoa, has introduced continuous improvement into that mature company by focusing on safety. A strange choice for some because Alcoa already had the industry's best safety record: injuries were going down by almost 50 percent every five years. But on his first day, O'Neill told his safety director that the only goal he would accept was zero injuries: "The wish to be injury free isn't something people can debate, so it was a good place to drive a stake into the ground . . . (even more importantly) you can't get safety unless you really understand your processes." In effect, the focus on safety is impossible without total quality control. To reinforce the change, O'Neill also introduced a profit-sharing program based on performance-related goals, including targets for safety and energy conservation. Even Wall Street has been impressed. According to one analyst, "This is the first time Alcoa is coming to the end of a business cycle [in October 1990] with lower costs than it had at the beginning."[21]

British Telecom, following the Japanese model, has linked quality management to the business-planning process to make it part of the normal working environment: "Customer requirements are identified, goals agreed, and responsibilities allocated. Progress is then monitored against these benchmarks." In addition, senior managers continually establish improvement projects to tackle specific problems in a structured way. One of the early successes was increasing the in-service level of the 80,000 phone booths around the United Kingdom from 60 percent to 90 percent.[22]

Tools for Continuous Improvement

Among the many tools that can be used in the process of continuous improvement, two stand out as central to the whole process—the problem frequency chart and the improvement half-life.

Problem frequency chart. This is an issue frequency chart (in quality control jargon, a Pareto diagram) that is useful for identifying the highest-priority issue for improvements. If the objective is lower downtime, then a chart is kept to record the number of times each different causal factor is responsible for a breakdown. The problem-solving team then focuses on the factor responsible for most of the breakdowns. Once that factor has been fixed, the exercise is repeated to find the next target for improvement.

Improvement half-life. The second tool is the improvement half-life, or the time needed to improve the quality of performance by 50 percent. The improvement half-life tends to be the same for a particular company, no matter what the issue, because it depends on the company's rate of learning. The shorter the improvement half-life, the better the organization is at the entire improvement process. By monitoring the time taken to improve performance (such as defects, failure rates, production throughput times, delivery times, market response times, receivable collection times) the company can follow its progress and set targets to enhance its continuous improvement capability.[23]

The power of the improvement cycle time to increase the speed of operations and thereby create a competitive discontinuity is striking. In the United States, GE has cut the order to finished goods time for circuit breaker boxes from 3 weeks to 3 days; Motorola has cut the same time for pagers from 3 weeks to 2 hours. Honda has cut the new product development time for cars from 5 years to 3 years, while Hewlett-Packard has cut the development time for printers from 4.5 years to 22 months. Given the time and effort needed to develop a continuous improvement capability, this can soon become an enormous competitive advantage for the fastest company.[24] The shorter the improvement time, the better the quality, cost, and delivery time and, hence, the greater are the profits. Higher profits, in turn, can be invested to lower the improvement time further, thereby creating a "winner's cycle."[25]

SPONTANEOUS (PRODUCT) INNOVATION CAPABILITY

Stimulating continual innovation and intrapreneurial activity has been turned into a fine art by some American companies. Among the most renowned for this capability are 3M, Hewlett-Packard, and Texas Instruments.

Ingredients for Stimulating Innovation

Observers of the corporate masters of innovation have identified several ingredients needed to stimulate innovation:[26]

An incentive structure that rewards people for identifying opportunities and that lessens the negative consequences of failure when an opportunity is pursued;

A corporate environment that encourages communication and the exchange of information and ideas by providing random access to information, creating cross-functional contact, moving people around, supporting informal multifunctional teams, and, above all, facilitating interaction with the marketplace; and

An organization with multiple centers of power-reporting relationships, loosely defined positions, and an easily accessible resource and competence base.

At 3M, intrapreneurs have been given free rein for decades. Everyone, from the president down, prides themselves on being or having been involved as an intrapreneur or sponsor of intrapreneurs. New product champions are the company heroes. Allowance is made in the portfolio of innovative projects for failures. Alternate channels are available for securing approval and support of a project should one's superior not be willing to take it on: an idea generator can look for a sponsor anywhere in the division, the R&D department, or the new ventures group. The company is a beehive of ideas, teams, projects, and products in various stages of gestation and development. The famous yellow Post-it pads came from an idea one of the development engineers had while he was singing at church; he thought that removable markers would be ideal for his hymn book. But making a product that wouldn't stick properly was the opposite of what 3M was all about, making products that stick. After quick and laborious work in his lab, he had what he wanted. Then came the task of selling it to the marketing department. For this he involved the secretaries of the top-management team. They received samples for their bosses and for their bosses' friends. When the secretary on the top floor could no longer keep up with the demand, the product was on its way to commercialization.

Numerous companies began to decentralize and delegate decision making to autonomous business units in the late 1980s in a search for more entrepreneurial behavior and innovation. Even a renowned innovator like Texas Instruments began to feel that its intricate matrix organization could do with some loosening up. Originally, Texas Instruments had subdivided itself into market-focused, product customer centers (PCCs). In 1980, there were already more than eighty of these PCCs, designed not only to reflect customer groups, but also to provide the firm's middle managers with some entrepreneurial experience. The PCCs were consolidated into divisions and groups and held together by the company's OST (objectives, strategies, and tactics) system. For any one innovation project, several tactical action plans might be needed for implementation; the resources for these were pulled in from wherever necessary in the company. By assigning both a line (PCC) and a strategic responsibility (OST), managers were forced to take into account the long-term innovative needs of the company. In the mid 1980s, however, profits suffered from lack of initiative and innovation. To correct the balance, groups of PCCs were consolidated into even more autonomous units. According to Fred Buey, TI's president at the time, "The manager of a PCC controls the resources and operations for his entire family. . . . The PCC manager is to be an entrepreneur."[27]

Self-Designing Organizations

Is the search for a greater innovation capability in the late 1980s and early 1990s merely a reflection of the cyclical oscillation between opportunities for innovation and efficiency? Or does this signal a longer-term shift in the balance between tightness and looseness? One factor supporting a longer-term shift is the widespread use of new computer-networking technology to hold together these looser, more spontaneously innovative organizations. Nowhere is this more apparent than in parts of the financial services industry.

The rapidity of change in the financial services sector can be so great that a highly developed spontaneous innovation capability is essential for any firm aspiring to market leadership. The life cycle of financial products is so short, that only frontline executives and employees can possibly identify the opportunities early enough to capitalize on them. According to Philip Purcell, CEO of Dean Witter and a former partner at McKinsey & Co., "McKinsey's techniques of strategy don't work. Things move too fast. We have had three different key products in four years, so what is strategy? You simply get great people and back them. And even then they can't tell you what they'll be doing next year."[28]

Dee Hock, the head of VISA International, the credit card company, regarded the business as so vulnerable to unpredictable shifts in the market that the only protection was a highly flexible and opportunistic team of managers who could initiate change whenever conditions were favorable. Hock kept his top executives on their toes with continual job rotations, ad hoc project teams, and an ambiguous, loose structure. "There is so much change in VISA," he said, "that most employees have to flail about frantically to keep their balance. They become tight rope walkers so good at anticipating change that they adjust to it before it occurs."[29]

Dwight Crane and Robert Eccles argued that to support this level of innovation capability, the leading investment banking firms have become self-designing organizations. Their description included the following distinguishing features:

Grass roots strategy formulation. Within broad guidelines established by top management, people throughout the organization, including those at fairly junior levels, contribute to the business strategies that shape future corporate strategy. In the words of Joe Perella, co-head of Investment Banking and Mergers and Acquisitions at First Boston, "First Boston has a breadth of culture that enables a lot of people to thrive. We get a lot of things percolating—the hot house concept. Sometimes you get strange things growing. There are product areas that exploded from a junior person who was given lots of room. The secret is that senior management recognizes what it takes to be creative and does not suffocate people."[30]

A flexible network of specialized departments. The strategic decision, about which business areas to compete in, is translated by top management into a structural design of corresponding organizational units. To exploit changing market conditions, people on all levels have a high degree of autonomy to create new specialized subunits, determine how to organize their unit, as well as manage the relationships with other units. As a result, a lot of spontaneous re-organizing occurs on the lower levels of the firm. Several types of networking devices are used to coordinate the organization: customer-focused units, combined responsibilities and reporting relationships, special integrating roles and units, lateral processes, personnel flows, and physical proximity.

An example of how a self-designing organization can create a competitive breakpoint is provided by First Boston. In asset-backed securities, First Boston preempted the competition by creating the first unit dedicated to this market. Anthony Dub, head of the unit, explained that its creation was "a conscious bet that we can get technologically ahead of the market place by putting six to eight people on this." In his view, the specialization was one of the reasons why First Boston had a 90 percent market share in 1986, including a $4-billion auto receivables deal with General Motors Acceptance Corporation.

STAKEHOLDER NETWORKING CAPABILITY

Networking is based on the capability to reduce the cost of transactions between the firm and its stakeholders. Carlos Jarillo points out that transaction costs may be higher than necessary because of the limits to rationality, uncertainty about the future, a small number of players, and/or opportunistic behavior on the part of some. The key to reducing these effects is the ability to build trust between the parties. Trust eliminates opportunistic behavior and permits the exchange of sensitive information that can reduce uncertainty and soften the limits to our rationality. Trust building is the fundamental skill behind the longer-term "special" relationships that make up a network.[31]

Building trust requires an investment of effort into learning about the values and motivations of the other party, and developing confidence that neither party has an incentive to engage in opportunistic behavior. Time is essential for both of these. Having a track record or reputation that cannot survive charges of opportunistic behavior can help in building the other side's confidence about the relationship.

Two types of networking activity can be distinguished. The first involves improving the relationship with existing stakeholders to enhance the company's access to the resources that they provide. The second has to do with the creation of new networking partners by subcontracting out the noncore activities of the company.

Improving Access to the Resources of Stakeholders

A stakeholder relationship that goes beyond the normal arm's-length interaction in the marketplace is an intangible asset that can create value and, in certain cases, help trigger a breakpoint.

Market networks. First Boston's Asset Backed Unit is an example of how external networking can create an intangible asset that is difficult for competitors to imitate, in this case, a leading reputation and relationship with major clients in the marketplace. In the heavy motorcycle market, Harley-Davidson used customer relationships to leapfrog the competitors.

Supplier networks. In the automobile industry, the Japanese competitors are well known for the way in which they have nurtured the relationship with their suppliers as part of the low-cost turning point they created in their industry.

Financial networks. The governance relationship between active owners and managers is becoming more and more widely recognized as a potential source of value. Close oversight reduces the costs associated with opportunistic behavior on the part of managers and uncertainty about what's going on in the firm. Examples include the numerous corporate breakpoints triggered by leveraged buyouts designed to capture the value implicit in active ownership. The same is true of certain acquisitions by holding companies in Europe and the relationship between German and Japanese banks and the companies in which they hold shares.

Developing New Networking Partners

Subcontracting and networking are central to shaping the scope of a company's vertical integration, that is, those segments of the industry chain in which the company chooses to be active. When IKEA decided to subcontract the production of furniture kits to a network of East European plants, and the final transport and assembly to the customers who put the kit together at home, the company triggered a discontinuity by redefining the rules of the game. This is an example of one of several ways in which networking can be employed to create a competitive breakpoint.[32]

Subcontracting noncore activities.   Focusing on core activities, the way IKEA did, can be used to trigger a breakpoint. In the 1960s and 1970s, in the college textbook publishing industry, companies like McGraw-Hill and Prentice-Hall initiated a fundamental shift by concentrating on the editorial activities and subcontracting out the printing and binding activities. Some publishers also cut back their art, graphics, and design activities. In addition, key editors were allowed to create autonomous subsidiaries for experimenting with new publishing approaches. McGraw-Hill focused on its distinctive competence in product development, while Prentice-Hall emphasized sales. These new rules of the game were superior in both efficiency and flexibility to the old rules. Those who couldn't play the new game were shut out in the restructuring of the industry.

Networking to share risk.   Networking can facilitate the creation of a breakpoint by spreading the risk around. When IBM decided to introduce a personal computer, the PC development task force under Don Estridge bought the microprocessors from Intel, while developing external networks of software suppliers and distribution outlets. The external networks gave the PC unit the speed and flexibility to get an IBM product onto the market within eighteen months. After establishing itself in the market, when the risk was lower, IBM drew some of the software and distribution back in-house.

Creating synergy.   The joint value created by the partners in a new network can be large enough to trigger an industry breakpoint. In the Italian knitwear (or wool textile) industry, around Prato, strikes caused sharp increases in labor costs that, together with declining demand, forced more and more subcontracting in the 1970s. The manufacturing process consisted of a series of technologically different operations, with distinct specializations, that made subcontracting attractive and easy to implement. Observation of the resulting industry network over twenty years revealed a gradual progression of three phases, beginning with an initially dominant role for the leading firm in coordinating its network. In the second phase, there was greater self-organization within the network. More interaction between the subcontractors and franchises reduced the leading firm's coordinating function, thereby allowing it to concentrate more on innovation. Eventually, in the third phase, the interplay among all the players began to drive the innovation process; innovative ideas emerged from everywhere, diffused rapidly throughout the network, and propelled the Italian industry into global leadership.[33]

Perhaps the best-known company in the industry is Benetton, which started in a typical entrepreneurial way: Guiliane Benetton made boldly colored sweaters in her spare time.[34] When she was seventeen and her brother Luciano was twenty, he had the idea of selling her sweaters wholesale. They bought a used knitting machine for 30,000 lire from the sale of younger brother Carlo's bicycle and Luciano's accordion. Before long they had sold a collection of eighteen sweaters, and within a year they began hiring local girls to help meet the growing demand. Luciano decided to sell the products to retailers at a 10 percent discount, provided they paid cash. He promised small knitting subcontractors exclusive rights, provided they put up the money for the machines. The retail distributors evolved into franchises that were managed in areas controlled by agents, known as "centurioni." By 1989, there were eighty agents, who were in turn coordinated informally by five senior agents. The knitting subcontractors grew to 700. In 1989, they were coordinated by the ten largest subcontractors who dealt directly with Benetton.

Benetton had discovered that color was the critical fashion factor. So Benetton's output was manufactured in unbleached off-white wool and dyed later, in accordance with information on the most popular colors of the season. In 1989, despite numerous manufacturing sites outside Italy, garments were still dyed on a month's notice. The flexibility and productivity of the Benetton network established new standards in the global industry, with output reaching 50 million pieces a year, distributed through a worldwide network of 4,500 shops. Benetton clearly had created an industry breakpoint by using networking to change the rules of the competitive game.

LIMITS TO CONTINUOUS CORPORATE CHANGE

Two limits to continuous change stand out: the first reflects the risk that spontaneous processes can become counterproductive when the forces of change switch direction; the second has to do with the apparent difficulty of combining continuous improvement and spontaneous innovation.

Counterproductive Spontaneous Change

What may be preemptive flexibility in one environment can become resistance to change in another. The spontaneous change capabilities described in this chapter can run a firm off the tracks if left unchanneled for too long. They may pull the company so far in one direction that the company cannot adapt when the forces of change switch direction. Spontaneous innovation, for example, can become a huge obstacle to efficiency and cost reduction, so much so that when the environment favors efficiency, the company is lost.

At Drexel Burnham Lambert, the junk bond business was a classic example of an innovative strategy that grew spontaneously out of the activities of highly talented employees. DBL's innovation generated an industry breakpoint and changed the rules of the competitive game in its favor, making the company an industry leader. But the very same spontaneous activity became part of the resistance to change, when interest rates shifted and the junk bond market weakened. Missing at Drexel was timely intervention by top management to realign the firm.

Combination of Continuous Improvement and Innovation

Continuous change capabilities are indispensable for companies that want to capitalize on strong external forces of change and lead the competitive pack by creating breakpoints. In the presence of strong change forces, leading competitors invariably have either a well-developed kaizen or intrapreneurship capability. Yet few, if any, have been able to combine both; we have been unable to identify a company with both a continuous improvement and a spontaneous innovation capability in the same business unit. The tight disciplined planning at the heart of continuous improvement is antithetical to the loose, self-organizing environment of spontaneous innovation.

American practitioners of spontaneous innovation often have

no complementary process of cost reduction, not to mention continuous improvement. As a result, they are unable to reap the life cycle benefits of their innovations; 3M has had difficulty making money with its computer diskettes; Apple Computer talks about reducing its hardware business; innumerable Silicon Valley start-ups sell out; Route 128 around Boston converts to software. The number of industries that Far Eastern competitors have taken over with their continuous improvement capability grows every year. Although spontaneous innovation is more fun, the longer-term cash flows accrue to Japanese-style continuous improvement.

From time to time, however, the Japanese combine continuous improvement, not with spontaneous innovation, but with dedicated task forces to deal with the need for fundamental product innovation. Although the teams within these task forces may be self-organizing, the entire process is initiated by, or cleared with, and tightly monitored from the top. This process of structured innovation, which we discuss in the next chapter, is completely different from the free-wheeling, bottom-up process of spontaneous product innovation so appropriate for capitalizing on strong external forces of change.

KEYS TO PRACTICE: NURTURING CONTINUOUS CHANGE

1. To lead in creating discontinuities, you must first become a student of the business environment and participate in corporate intelligence-gathering.
2. When forces of change are developing strongly, stimulate spontaneous innovation by encouraging risk taking within clear guidelines, exchange of ideas and people, and multiple access to resources.
3. When forces of change are strongly established, build continuous improvement into corporate planning and into the performance appraisal and reward systems. Be careful to avoid the clash within the same organizational unit of a tight improvement process and a loose innovation process.
4. Develop a networking capability to enhance access to stakeholder resources and to increase flexibility by subcontracting out noncore activities.

CHAPTER 11

Developing
Strategic Options

A<small>N</small> A<small>MERICAN</small> <small>JOURNAL</small> provided Messrs. Akio Morita, Masaru Ibuka, and their engineering colleagues with an introduction to the tape recorder. Because the tape recorder was not being made by the large Japanese companies, they decided it would be their first manufactured product. From the very beginning, however, the founders of Sony took a more pioneering approach than the traditional large Japanese companies. As Akio Morita recounts they developed their own tape recorder and magnetic tape, without any help from the outside.[1]

Not unlike many other engineering entrepreneurs, Morita and company thought their product would sell itself. But prospective customers said the price for their "toy" was too high. So Morita did some practical research on marketing by walking around stores. When he saw a customer pay good money for an apparently useless antique, he realized that a sale can occur if the customer understands the value of the merchandise. As a company offering products with which the public was not familiar, Sony's marketing had to communicate information about the products to the customer effectively and accurately. "The fewer intermediaries in the chain of communication, the better." So instead of relying on third parties for distribution, which is customary in Japan, Sony set up its own sales outlets throughout Japan.

Sony's management also noticed that sales and collections on sales were difficult in one of the areas, a depressed coal-mining district. If Sony had been dependent on this area alone, it would have gone bankrupt. Since Japan's economy was going through serious fluctuations at the time, Sony concluded that to offset regional and national business risk, it had to be international. Once again, instead of going through the trading companies, Sony set up its own marketing system in various countries. Like other Japanese companies at the time, its competitive advantage was based mainly on low labor costs.

Defective products exported from Japan became very expensive to repair. To improve quality and reliability, Sony applied quality control techniques learned from the United States, including the zero-defect concept. The resulting total quality control circles generated improvements not only in quality and reliability, but also in productivity and costs. So while Western companies were choosing between differentiation and low cost, Sony was improving both simultaneously.

With growing sales and reputation, Sony moved toward world-scale plants. In 1970, the company established its first color television factory in America in San Diego. Production facilities spread through the United States, Europe, Brazil, and Venezuela. Throughout the 1970s, Sony invested heavily in market development, creating its worldwide brand franchise. The growing market share led to further process improvements and reductions in costs.

To leverage and maintain the investment in brand name, Sony put more emphasis on innovative new product development. Management played a key role in encouraging innovation by coming up with innovation targets and putting together task forces to develop the products. "We always have an image of how an ideal product would look and perform in our minds. This is not wishful thinking on our part, but a concrete plan for which exact product specifications have been drawn up." This includes a target price. Management then carefully selects and challenges a small task force, or design team, to produce a prototype with step-by-step creative engineering.[2]

Morita himself gave the go-ahead to the Walkman design team, overriding the objection of sales and marketing, which were not convinced that a portable tape player would sell. Competitors also held back for the same reason. Meanwhile Sony introduced the Walkman and immediately began making improvements, introducing new models, and establishing a strong position as market leader. "Since the prototypes of future models are already developed, our marketing is quite flexible. We are prepared to launch new products into the market when the need arises." With eighty-five models on offer, sales of the Sony Walkman accounted for 40 percent of portable tape player sales in the United States and 50 percent in Japan in 1987.

Sony not only gives itself the option of introducing a new model whenever needed, but also immediately improves manufacturing: "Developing an innovative product is only the first step in keeping a successful business going. The second is developing innovative manufacturing." Manufacturing facilities are initially set up in Japan where top management can directly monitor the improvement effort. Quality circles are asked to find ways of eliminating waste and simplifying the production process. Only when the production line has been improved "as much as is humanly possible" is automation introduced to further enhance product quality and reduce labor costs.

Sony has also made some big errors. The huge commitment to the Betamax video recorder was unable to beat back the challenge of the alliance supporting the VHS system, largely because of the software available for the latter. Digital Audiotape was launched in 1990 as the magnetic tape response to the compact disc, but only sold a fraction of what was planned; it was repositioned for the professional market. Once again lack of software was part of the problem.

In the 1980s, Sony established positions in semiconductors, home video games, and laptop computers. The latter was extended by an alliance with Apple to produce a miniature Apple laptop. As the decade closed, Sony made the most dramatic move since its founding. It acquired CBS Records and Columbia Pictures Entertainment, two of America's largest companies producing audio and visual software. With the international battle over HDTV standards looming in the background, Sony integrated forward to acquire downstream competence in the apparent belief that these activities would dominate the future of the consumer electronics industry. Having been burned by the lack of software for the Betamax video recorder, Sony was determined not to make the same mistake again.

The Sony story illustrates how a global industry leader is willing to make large commitments to new technology on certain occasions, while at other times it hedges its bets by taking only a small position, a strategic option, in several alternative business activities. During the early years when Sony was a follower, the way ahead was more clearly marked by competitors; there was less need to hedge the future with strategic options. Later, when Sony faced the full brunt of industry uncertainty as a leading player, it turned naturally to strategic options as a way of managing the risk.

The development of strategic options is typically a three-step process of structured innovation management.[3] Viewed from within the company, it is a process of sporadic change often involving a corporate turning point. Viewed from outside, the final step in the process can trigger an industry breakpoint. Doing so requires a proper understanding of

- Structured innovation management and corporate mastery of the following three steps:
- Sourcing new competencies (technological, functional, operational) that will be crucial for the future.
- Selecting strategic options to explore the potential payoff to promising competencies in the form of new products and processes.
- Timing the full commitment of resources to the exploitation of the new products and processes.

STRUCTURED INNOVATION MANAGEMENT

The path in the change arena traced out by a structured innovation process as a competence moves from the sourcing step, through the option selection step, to full commitment, is shown in Exhibit 11-1. At the sourcing step, the company retains the flexibility of developing the competence in several different directions, along with the flexibility of committing no significant resources. But from the sourcing step the company can only respond very slowly to the market. At the option selection step, resources are committed to a team or project assigned to create pilot processes, or prototype components and products. If the company decides not to go ahead, only this limited commitment of resources will be lost. The phase of option selection is intermediate in the time required to get to the market. At the full-commitment step, a dedicated organization is put in place to exploit the competence in terms of new processes and/or products. Flexibility is very low but the response time to the market is quick.

Strategic options are valuable when the environment is highly uncertain, for example, prior to a turning point in a trend. Options are especially valuable when the change forces are weak, when the turning point is not expected for some time. Under these condi-

EXHIBIT 11–1   **Sporadic Change Capability:**
Structured Innovation Process

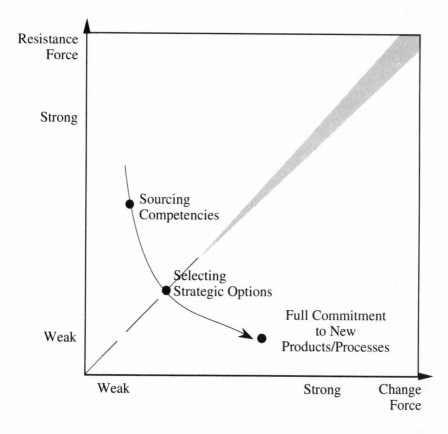

tions, it makes no business sense to make a full commitment of resources to new competence, the utility of which is impossible to assess. This is especially so when the resources have other uses with high payoff. By contrast, it makes a lot of sense to reduce the risk inherent in the uncertainty by exploring several alternatives first.

The path from competence sourcing to full commitment may involve an investment of small-resource increments in a series of steps. For example, in the development of a new product, the basic technology competence is developed in the laboratory; followed by prototype design, component engineering, design and engineering simplification, pilot production, product offering development complete with marketing and distribution, and market testing, prior to full commitment to production, distribution, delivery, and service. In many companies these steps get lost between the laboratory and ongoing operations. Neither is willing to manage the series of optional commitments to the next steps. R&D doesn't have the financial and management resources, and operations can't afford the risk.[4]

Alcan set up a dedicated design and demonstration organization to test the feasibility of the more risky aspects of new manufacturing processes, products, and materials. This unit was separate from both the existing mainstream organization and the new business units that evolved from the new competence. It linked the definition of process and product specifications to the creation of a commercial technology that could be handed over to the business units. The design and demonstration unit had to integrate "business, technical, market, social, and cultural factors" into the development of the new process competence or product prototype. Its output included detailed engineering specifications, new methodologies of operation, and the market testing of new products. For example, in its first five years of existence, this small unit directed the commercialization of a new continuous aluminum sheet production process and a new reduction cell technology.[5]

In this kind of unit numerous initially promising ideas that are not feasible have to be killed; to reject infeasible projects is part of the unit's mission. To make sure the unit fulfills this sifting role, the reward and incentive structure has to be set up so that manager and team encounter no career risk when rejecting impractical projects. At Canon, the feasibility testing of a strategic option is built into the mandate of the new product development process. The initial product concept is handed over to a team of bright young engineers to flesh out how it might be manufactured. They are expected to draw in other experts as needed and consider a wide range of alternatives before narrowing in on the final component, product design, and production engineering technologies.[6] At Sony, the design team performs a very similar function. In effect, it determines whether an initial concept can be converted into a viable, commercial product.

SOURCING NEW COMPETENCIES

Where do new competencies originate? In the first place, they emerge from business intelligence, management's judgment that the company should explore new product offerings, technologies, and other functional competencies useful in exploiting emerging forces of change. For example, a task force such as the one set up to explore the Sony Walkman is given the mandate to explore a new product or competence. Sony, Canon, and innumerable other firms that use task forces to explore new possibilities have well-defined milestones at which the project can be discontinued if necessary.

A second source of strategic options are the processes of continuous improvement and spontaneous innovation. Of the many proposals and suggestions addressed to management by potential intrapreneurs and quality circle members, some are implemented right away, some are discarded, and some become candidates for incremental development of new competence and eventually new products. At Sony, the prototypes of future models held in reserve for market introduction fall into this category.

A third increasingly common source of new competence is the external network of special partnerships and alliances. Sony's moves into semiconductors and home video games have all the earmarks of new competence development, designed to create strategic options that can be exploited should the opportunity arise. Most partnerships and alliances are temporary. Management can either terminate the activity or bring it in-house. Although alliances have a variety of forms and purposes, many are used to develop experience with a new technology (as Olivetti has done with small high-tech companies), to penetrate a new market (laptop computers for Sony in the case of the Apple alliance), and to gain access to resources (as in the case of Gillette). Even IBM is developing a dense network of alliances to increase its exposure to possible new developments and to spread the cost of development.[7]

Fourth is traditional R&D, still a key source of new technological competence, especially in the pharmaceutical and biotech industries. As an illustration, the Janssen research teams at Johnson & Johnson synthesized some 68,000 original molecules in the years from 1953 to 1986, which were developed into 66 new pharmaceutical compounds. At Philips Consumer Electronics, R&D has continued to provide management with options on breakthrough products and technologies such as the videocassette recorder, the compact disc, and the digital compact cassette.

No portfolio of strategic competencies is complete without volume production and delivery competencies. Apple Computer has been widely admired for the spontaneity of its innovation process. But Apple was unable to drive home the competitive advantage implicit in its MacIntosh line because it did not have the process competence needed to market and deliver the MacIntosh cost effectively. "For fiscal 1990, analysts estimate, Apple spent a stunning 24 percent of sales, or $1.4 billion, on sales and marketing costs, compared with 12 percent at Compaq Computer Corp."[8] Silicon Valley, in general, has been criticized for having no sense of how to improve the production and delivery process. Without a complete and renewable portfolio of competence that spans the whole process from intelligence to innovation, to mass production and product enhancement, product breakthroughs are mere staging platforms for competitors to leapfrog the innovators.

SELECTING STRATEGIC OPTIONS

Which options should be developed further? Which options would be the most valuable for the creation of a competitive discontinuity? The most valuable are options that have the highest future payoff and the lowest need for resources. The payoff depends on how much the company's value-cost offering can be improved in the marketplace.

To develop a breakpoint in competitive advantage, the value-cost offering must be improved radically. Either resources are obtained under significantly more favorable terms, or the competencies must be leveraged, that is, brought to bear in a way that is significantly more effective. The advantages of sticking to one's knitting and of related rather than conglomerate diversification indicate that leading-edge competence is built most effectively and economically on previously developed abilities. The payoff to linked competence development is higher, because of the application of experience, and the cost is lower, because of the partial use of resources in place. Thus, the most valuable strategic options are those where sustainable leverage can be obtained by projecting existing organizational capability and functional competence into new arenas.[9] To sustain the advantage, the leverage must make it difficult for competitors to buy, imitate, or replace the new product with a substitute.

Business System Leverage

Special functional competence in one or more of the activities of a business system provides a point of leverage into other industries and markets where the same activities are the key to success. By facilitating access to other industries, business system leverage can create a breakpoint in a saturated market. Bic, the French ballpoint pen manufacturer, leveraged its competencies in the low-cost manufacturing of plastics and in mass merchandising and advertising from the maturing pen market into disposable razor, disposable lighter, and wind surfboard breakpoints. In all cases, it quickly created a high-volume, low-cost position by concentrating on the manufacturing, assembly, and distribution activities and by buying new nonplastic raw materials and components such as the sails for windsurfers.

Downstream extension is another way of leveraging business system competence. Lego, the Danish producer of plastic construction toys, anticipated the growing forces of imitation when its patents expired in 1984, as well as the rising power of the large toy distribution chains. Lego's brand name and toy system had made it Europe's largest toy company. In addition, Lego considered itself the lowest-cost producer for its type of toy. To turn the change forces to its advantage, Lego extended its information system into the distribution outlets. With this extra market intelligence and its completely integrated manufacturing system, Lego not only outpaced its low-labor-cost rivals with shorter and shorter product renewal cycles, but also strengthened its bargaining position relative to its distributors.[10]

A powerful source of competence leverage is the accumulated business system experience behind a high market share. The importance of market share was discovered in the United States, but is most fervently applied in Japan. Whenever the related experience can be projected to the other side of a breakpoint, it provides a highly potent source of competence leverage. When Sony introduced the Walkman radio, the experience gained building its existing market share could be applied immediately to the new formula, opening up a large first-mover advantage which competitors are still struggling to close.

Product Market Leverage

Competence in dealing with existing customers and markets can provide leverage through the repackaging of existing offerings, or the sale of new and expanded product offerings. Sony has used its brand name and know-how in the consumer electronics market to launch a stream of new products that have created periodic breakpoints. Harley-Davidson's understanding of what bikers were looking for was the key to its development of new models, as well as to the extension of its customer relationships. Similarly, Whirlpool's understanding of what people are looking for in user-friendly household appliances has provided a point of leverage for an expanding product range and geographic coverage that has left most competitors behind.

Restructuring in mature markets around new market segments also can create a competitive breakpoint. SKF Bearings, the world's largest bearing company, having rationalized and automated production, was still unhappy with its performance. Looking at their markets, Mauntz Sahlin, the CEO, and his executive team, began to realize that the industry had ignored the enormous difference between the needs of the original equipment manufacturers and those of the after-sales markets. Whereas bearings were vital components in the OEM market, they were simply spare parts in the after market. But the after market contributed 41 percent of SKF sales. Sahlin set up a new Bearing Services Division to sell "trouble free operations," to provide customers with solutions to production problems that involved bearings. For example, to help customers anticipate when a bearing should be replaced, SKF developed a "planned maintenance package." Customers were more than willing to pay for the service; price was no longer the main buying criterion. When the June 1989 financial results came out, two years after the reorganization, SKF profits had increased two-thirds over the previous year and the share price shot up by 50 percent.[11]

The other dimension of product market leverage is expertise in a particular end-use. Classic examples include armament manufacturers that provide a wide variety of ever more sophisticated arms to a wide range of customers, or the medical equipment divisions of companies like Siemens and General Electric that compete with one another to create breakpoints in state-of-the-art diagnostic-imaging equipment (X-ray, ultrasound, CT scanners) for all kinds of health care institutions.

Network Leverage

A global network of selective, functional competencies can provide the base for a competitive breakpoint. The idea is to exploit the comparative advantage of different locations. If the coordination problem can be managed, this provides the best possible business system, while enhancing intelligence. Logitech, the leading producer of the computer mouse, was started in 1982 by two Stanford graduates, one of whom was Swiss and the other Italian, plus another Italian from Olivetti. From the beginning, the holding company, financial headquarters, and hardware development were in Switzerland, while the operational headquarters, marketing, and software development were in Silicon Valley. The first commercial contract was with a Japanese company. After a few years, most of the manufacturing was based in Taiwan, with smaller factories in the United States and Ireland. The comparative advantages of these locations are evident: Silicon Valley was the world's lead market for PCs and PC software, Switzerland provided mechano-electronic skills from the watch industry, and Taiwan and Ireland had low labor costs in relative proximity to large markets.

Logitech not only developed the mouse, but has since come up with two other important innovations, a small scanner, and the immobile mouse attached to the side of the computer keyboard. According to Giacome Marini, one of the founders, "Our strength has been in building innovative products based on a product idea of an outside innovator. We always go to Akhihabara, when we go to Japan. . . . Furthermore, Daniel Borel [another founder] spends more than 30 percent of his time with customers." In effect, Logitech's real innovation is the way it has used a global network to leverage the speed and flair of a start-up into several product breakpoints.[12]

Technology Leverage

The leverage of technological experience, according to several studies, is key to the success of high-tech companies. "Developing a distinctive competence in a core technology is critical to the long-term growth of technology-based firms." In the twenty years after its start-up in the late 1960s, a New England computer printer manufacturer released eighteen new products. Its second product was one of the first small matrix printers. A refined version of the printer was sold with the Apple microcomputer. From then on, the company focused on printing technology in the personal computer marketplace, with enhancement designed to provide more speed and better printing at lower costs. The company was highly successful in creating the basis for a jump to a new copying technology.[13]

By contrast, a rather small company that had created the first graphics terminal for use with minicomputers in newspaper composition followed up, not with a better terminal, but with a tablet for engineering workstations, and then a text-editing workstation incorporating new microcomputer architecture, followed by text-editing software. This company tried to initiate successive discontinuities involving different technologies from a skimpy base, couldn't get the necessary leverage, and stagnated.[14]

Technological competence can provide a springboard for moves into otherwise unrelated industries. Japanese companies, in particular, are adept at following the technology trail wherever the opportunities look most attractive. Kao, for example, moved from soap to cosmetics using the end-user as a link. Then it moved into floppy computer discs and digital audio tape because the surface tension technology of coating a disc has similarities to what's needed for a cosmetic to spread on the human face.

Yamaha's technology trail has taken it even further afield. Yamaha started out in wood carpentry before moving into pianos in 1941. During World War II, the company was asked to produce wooden propellers for aircraft. Wooden propellers led to steel propellers. After the war, Yamaha applied its steel casting know-how to making motorcycle engines for which there was a huge demand. In 1955, there were many Japanese motorcycle manufacturers. After the shakeout in the early 1960s, only four remained: Yamaha, Kawasaki, Honda, and Suzuki. When the price pressure continued, Honda moved into cars while Yamaha went into power boat motors where it captured a 50 percent market share. And once in the leisure industry, Yamaha expanded its product range to include water skis, snow skis, tennis rackets, swimming pools, and in the late 1980s, plastic bathrooms.

TIMING THE FULL COMMITMENT OF RESOURCES

Timing is the most difficult part of managing a process of structured innovation. The greater the uncertainty about a rapidly evolving environment with weak change forces, the greater is the advantage of delaying a full commitment of resources to a particular product or process strategy until the situation unfolds. But the trade-off is a greater risk of missing the window of opportunity in the market place. By the time the situation has revealed itself sufficiently with an identifiable strong change force, more daring rivals may have guessed correctly and taken over the market. The art of timing the full-scale commitment of resources involves avoiding premature commitment on the one hand, and being too late on the other hand.

Sony committed itself prematurely to the Betamax technology and also to the introduction of digital audio tape. But its success with numerous other pioneering products like the Walkman and camcorder more than offset these lapses. Whereas Sony sometimes jumps the gun, Philips has the reputation of not getting off the starting blocks. Its VCR 2000 technology was perfected to make it the best available, but by the time it got to the market, the VCR race was half over. However, the joint launch of compact discs by Philips and Sony worked out extremely well, the combination of Sony's speed with Philips's perfectionism apparently providing just the right timing.

In many cases, the timing dilemma can only be solved, if at all, by the informed judgment of experts in the technology. Key to successful timing is consistency with the evolving interplay between industry forces of change and resistance. New competence cannot be added successfully to the firm's portfolio of competencies, nor layers of value to the product offering, without regard to the life cycle evolution of the product and its underlying technology. Sensitivity to cyclical patterns can be used to shape the timing decision.

Competitive Turning Point Sensitivity

The oscillation between periods of intense product innovation and periods of process improvement can be useful for timing purposes. In the idealized competitive cycle, after the introduction of new (product) technology in the market, the addition of competence in low-cost production, and then global distribution, becomes crucial in the quest for growth and market share. Thereafter, differentiation and variety-creating skills become important, to be followed by rejuvenation of the business system with product enhancement and customization. None of this proceeds in a predetermined fashion. Rather each new layer of value opens up the option of creating the next layer. The competitive cycle suggests the sequence of strategic options that might be exploited to maintain an advantage or create a new discontinuity.

After Ricoh developed an innovative desktop copier, it exercised the option provided by alliances with cost competitive suppliers of standard parts, assemblers, and distribution channels to trigger a shift in the international rules of the game toward low-cost competition. Xerox, without a stakeholder networking capability, did not have this option.

The Finnish company, Nokia Cable Machinery, had 2.5 percent of the world cable machinery market in 1982. The pursuit of differentiation with product quality and then geographic spread doubled Nokia Cable's global share to 5 percent in 1985. Thereafter, however, possibilities for further product range and geographic spread dried up. Sensing convergence of its products with those of competitors, Nokia Cable began to prepare for price competition by tightening up its operations. This gave it the option of lowering prices if necessary. When a price war indeed broke out with the Swiss competitor Maillefer, Nokia knew the timing was right to apply its low-cost advantage. After softening up Maillefer, Nokia proposed a merger. Maillefer had little choice and the merger was rapidly consummated. To consolidate the merger, Nokia–Maillefer reorganized quickly to develop a global network of specialized functional sites. With this competitive advantage, it had 15 percent of the global market by 1989.[15]

Technology Turning Point Sensitivity

The shift from one phase of a technology life cycle to the next is used by the consulting firm A.D. Little to determine when to move from emerging technology to an option on its further development, and thence to full commitment. Emerging technology embraces concepts and experiments in the R&D labs with promising potential in the mid to distant future. These turn into technologies worthy of development and selective exploitation as strategic options when they start affecting competitive advantage by showing increasing potential for promoting product differentiation. Full commitment to aggressive exploitation of a technology is called for when feasibility studies show it is becoming key to new product development.

Honda is well known for the way in which it entered the global markets for motorcycles, power mowers, and automobiles, by developing technology and products for segments just beyond those of the leading competitors. While marketing small, 50 cc. cycles in the United States, Honda was creating design and technology options for expansion across the entire range of the motor business. The most visible aspect of this investment in pacing the technology were the big European Honda bike races. Once the competence was in place and the markets were resisting price increases on existing products, Honda knew the timing was right to convert its technological options into key commitments to the automobile, lawn mower, marine engine, and generator markets.[16]

Socio-political Turning Point Sensitivity

Shifts in the socio-political cycle can also be used to time the full commitment of resources. When the Berlin Wall fell in 1989, VAW (Vereignigte Aluminum Werke), Germany's largest aluminum company, was faced with two breakpoints in its markets.[17] First, the sudden surge in demand for flexible packaging materials from West German groups selling food in East Germany, plus rising demand for aluminum from the construction industry which began modernizing shops in East Germany. Second, partially in response to the ecological problems in East Germany, the Bonn government drafted a proposal to make retailers and producers responsible for the burning or recycling of all packaging. Demands also were increasing to make automobiles more and more recyclable.

VAW had been developing its strategic options for some time. After rationalizing its smaller operations and developing low-cost primary capacity in areas with cheap energy, like Tomago in Australia and Alouette in Quebec, VAW used a joint venture with Alcan of Germany to develop its Norf plant in Reuss for aluminum foil and strip. According to Jochen Schirner, head of the management board, the Norf plant gave VAW the option of moving into higher-value-added products such as the packaging business with its lucrative niche of flexible packaging. In addition, VAW opened up its new research center in Bonn, which soon came up with another strategic option, a method of shaping flexible aluminum for car components.

When the implications of the collapsing Berlin Wall became clear, VAW began to exercise its strategic options. It quickly committed DM980 million to develop the capacity of the Norf packaging plant and greatly expanded the sales force to cope with the new orders from East Germany; in addition, a crash laboratory program was started to ensure that flexible aluminum packaging would be recyclable. On a much lesser scale, it expanded its commitment to aluminum car components, thereby developing a further strategic option in the auto component market. In effect, VAW was exploiting the East German socio-political breakpoint to create a market share breakpoint for itself in flexible packaging, while positioning itself for a potential competitive breakpoint in the European car component market.

Outpacing the Competition

The timely development of strategic options allows a company to outdistance its competitors.[18] How far depends on how frequently strategic options are used to create industry breakpoints.

In the watch industry, once it had caught up with the competition, the restructured Swiss watch company SMH used its newly developed value and cost options to trigger an industry breakpoint and then a turning point that allowed it to outpace the competition. First, to catch up with Seiko and other Far Eastern competitors, SMH developed a completely new, automated production process in which the time-keeping mechanism was built into the watch casing. Then, looking for market segments where this low-cost technology would provide the best advantage, it found the youth market. Ernst Thomke, the managing director, sensed that this market had evolved beyond cost competition and that the timing was right for something with excitement. The resulting Swatch triggered a value-based breakpoint that introduced fashion into the watch market. But Thomke and his team didn't rest on their laurels. Once the Swatch took off, the timing was right for completing the competitive cycle with a dramatic streamlining of the advertising, logistics, and distribution systems. And, most recently, Swatch designs of limited series created by well-known artists have added new perceived value by making these Swatches into collectors' items. Taken together, these proactive breakpoints have allowed the Swiss to outpace their competitors and recapture the number-one position in the value of international watch exports.

SMH's deployment of successive strategic options can be depicted graphically on a value-cost diagram in numbered sequence, along with the related moves of Japanese competitors (see Exhibit 11-2).

In the same vein, Sony was able to pull ahead of Philips, its long-time rival in consumer electronics, by regularly exercising its value and cost options. Sony maintains a stock of prototype future models which are ready for launch when market conditions warrant. It is also capable of driving down costs with its innovative manufacturing programs. By contrast, Philips, with excellent R&D capability, tends to go for the big new product breakthroughs. These have been frequent, but Philips has been unable to capitalize

EXHIBIT 11–2   **Swatch: Outpacing the Competition in Value–Cost Terms**

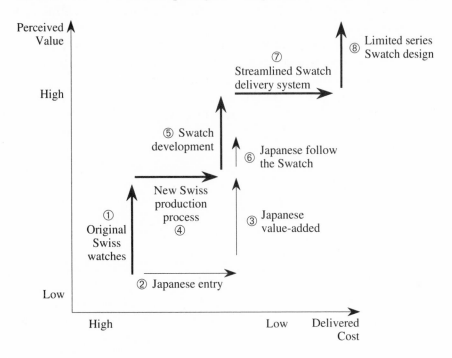

on them for lack of market-driven value options for further development, above all options to deliver the new products cost effectively.

Sony's move into Hollywood software fits the pattern of developing strategic options to outpace the competition. Ideally, when the HDTV turning point finally occurs, or even before that when new products like programmable compact discs emerge, Sony will have its software options ready to go. But Sony must still prove it can exercise those options by marrying the Japanese and Hollywood management cultures.

KEYS TO PRACTICE: DEVELOPING STRATEGIC OPTIONS

1. When the forces of change are uncertain, their impact delayed, and resources expensive, ensure that the company can create options on new competencies.

2. Other things being equal, assign task forces to develop further those options that leverage existing corporate strengths into products and processes.

3. Time the full commitment of resources to new products and processes to create competitive breakpoints by exploiting turning points in the forces of change and resistance.

4. Use the periodic deployment of strategic options to outpace the competition and lead the industry.

CHAPTER 12

Realigning the Corporation

JOHNSON & JOHNSON turned Sir Joseph Lister's breakthrough into a thriving business.[1] They did so in much the same way Honda and Canon, almost a century later, built businesses on breakthroughs made elsewhere. Lister founded modern antiseptic surgery by proving Pasteur's theory that bacteria cause infection. Johnson & Johnson figured out how to produce antiseptic dressings in quantity and then continually improved both the product and the process. So much so that when Lister wrote for details, he found that the American technology was ahead of his own.

To make the transition from medicinal plasters to antiseptic dressings, the Johnsons teamed up with a local New Brunswick pharmacist, Fred Kilmer. While the Johnsons experimented with the sterilization of their plasters, Kilmer surveyed American physicians and put together the first booklet on "Modern Methods of Antiseptic Wound Treatment," with a catalog of Johnson's products in the back pages. Within months, 85,000 copies were in circulation, Johnson's sales took off, and the antiseptic bandage breakpoint was in full swing.

But J&J did not stop there. Despite the company's rapid growth, Robert W. Johnson, the founder and eldest of the three brothers, insisted on quality, perfection, and customer service. Dedication to solving customers' problems continued to generate new product ideas. When a physician wrote to say that one of his patients was complaining of skin irritation, Kilmer suggested sending a small container of Italian talc. From then on, the talc was always included with certain plasters. As customers began to ask for more of the powder, Johnson's Baby Powder was born.

During the first decade of the twentieth century, when workers across the United States were protesting poor working conditions, J&J pioneered worker welfare. The company was one of the first to come up with a comprehensive program of medical care, legal advice, housing, and a mutual benefit fund, followed by pensions and insurance. J&J's attitude toward its employees went beyond benevolent paternalism. When Earle E. Dickson, a cotton mill worker, came up with the Band-Aid breakthrough (his wife was constantly cutting herself in the kitchen), he was made a vice president.

The Spanish-American War, the Galveston storm of 1900, the San Francisco earthquake, and World War I all saw J&J align itself with the nation's needs. The company provided free and low-cost medical supplies and encouraged its employees to volunteer and enlist. Richard Gwathney, a salesman from Virginia, was the first employee to volunteer for military service in the Spanish-American War. Robert Johnson wrote him personally, promising to continue his full pay and hold his job open.

When advertising emerged before and during World War I, J&J became one of the leading practitioners of the art. An advertising alliance was formed early on with J. Walter Thompson. One of the most successful early campaigns was for a kidney plaster. It featured a boy and girl sitting together at the beach, his arm around her back, with the caption: "Feels good on the back." The ad spawned countless variations by amateur and professional artists and ran for an amazing thirty years.

J&J followed closely and often led developments in the health care industry. After Kilmer's book on wound treatment it came out with the first complete book on first aid, "Johnson's First Aid Manual," which was soon adopted as the nation's most popular guide to health care. The "Red Cross Messenger" was developed to help druggists sell their products; and J&J's testing department was to lead the way to the Pure Food and Drug Act. The company also pioneered the use of the Red Cross symbol for health care products, and was copied by competitors. Long, sometimes acrimonious discussions with Clara Barton, founder of the American Red Cross, took place, resulting finally in legislation passed to protect the American Red Cross's use of the mark, but reserving Johnson's rights to it.

J&J dealt with the external breakpoint of the Great Depression in the 1930s, not with forced layoffs, but by reducing the hours worked by employees and the salaries of all senior executives, including the CEO. In 1935, Robert Johnson, Jr. wrote and sent a pamphlet—which later became the credo of the company—to the chief executives of other companies, challenging them to take a broader and longer-term view of the crisis.

> Out of the suffering of the past few years has been born a public knowledge and conviction that industry only has the right to succeed where it performs a real economic service and is a true social asset. Such permanent success is possible only through the application of an industrial philosophy of enlightened self-interest. It is to the enlightened self-interest of modern industry to realize that its service to its customers comes first, its service to its employees and management second, and its service to its stockholders last. It is to the enlightened self-interest of industry to accept and fulfill its full share of social responsibility.

During the first decade after World War II, the company devoted most of its resources and effort to plant and sales office expansion, taking advantage of the postwar upswing. Strong cash reserves permitted continual plant expansion despite periodic dips in the U.S. economy. New facilities were added in five states, and by 1956, J&J had twenty-five international affiliates. In the second decade from the mid-1950s, as organic growth slowed, the emphasis shifted to product diversification. Many acquisitions were made, not all of them related to the company's traditional product lines.

J&J decided to move into the high-growth pharmaceutical market, but was to fail in its efforts to develop a pharmaceutical business from within. So the search began for an acquisition. In 1959, McNeil Laboratories of Philadelphia was acquired, thereby bringing sedation and relaxant drugs and eventually Tylenol into the J&J product range. The Swiss firm Cilag Chemie was taken over in the same year, and Janssen Pharmaceutica, run by the brilliant Belgian pharmacologist Paul Janssen, in 1961.

Meanwhile the company stayed close to customer trends. Johnson granted funds to Northwestern University to start the country's first hospital administration program. Some years later it sponsored the first Conference on Child Nurturing. And when TV broke through in the 1950s, J&J was one of the first major sponsors, becoming known for its "good taste" in advertising. In 1986, the company was one of the top ten advertisers on TV.

When the social responsibility of business emerged as a major societal concern, on disclosures in the 1970s of illegal payments by other companies overseas, J&J launched a series of Credo Challenge conferences for its top executives. The challenge was to criticize and improve the statement of corporate mission and values. In the end, only minor changes were made with the credo, but with a strong sense of renewed commitment. And in 1975, when Richard Sellars stepped down as the third CEO, he led the effort to revitalize the city of New Brunswick for the next ten years. J&J had decided against leaving the city, in part because this would have violated its code of social responsibility. Instead, it built a new headquarters downtown and assigned a senior executive to assist Sellars in his campaign.

In the decade from 1976 to 1986, under the leadership of James Burke, the highly decentralized business units were grouped into three loose, market-oriented segments: consumer, pharmaceutical, and professional (hospital health care). Johnson's sales expanded from $2.5 billion to $7 billion with more than 50 percent from products with market share leadership. In the consumer products area, 25 percent of the sales were from new products created over the previous five years. Between 1953 and 1986, Janssen's R&D team developed sixty-six new pharmaceutical compounds after synthesizing 68,000 original molecules; three of the compounds were additions to the World Health Organization's list of essential drugs.

Exploding health care costs triggered an aggressive acquisition campaign by J&J in the professional hospital segment. Some thirty companies were acquired between 1976 and 1985, which was more change than the company could support. Some acquisitions didn't work out, like Technicare, which cost $74 million and lost $110 million over the next five years before being sold at a huge loss. Moreover, J&J had increasing difficulty coordinating its professional activities and lost ground in the marketplace, because of a corporate culture that prized autonomy and decentralization.[2] In an attempt at a more convergent approach, the Johnson & Johnson Hospital Services Division was set up to provide a corporate interface with the emerging, integrated, health care delivery systems. As part of this interface, Coast, an on-line computer procurement system, was developed for J&J's professional customers.

But breaking the old habits of independence and learning how to cooperate was not easy and continues to challenge the company.

In 1982 and 1986, the Tylenol disaster struck twice. The first time Johnson & Johnson moved immediately to cooperate with the media in keeping the public informed, withdrawing Tylenol television advertising, and removing and destroying 31 million capsules from stores and homes across the country. Within six weeks Tylenol was re-launched in new "triple safety sealed packaging"; within a year it had recaptured its leading market position. On the second occasion, in 1986, Johnson replaced all capsules in the hands of retailers and consumers at cost and urged users to convert to solid dosage caplets. Within a week there was evidence of strong consumer support. Five months later the brand was again the country's leading pain reliever. J&J received widespread recognition as "a company that cared."

The Johnson & Johnson story illustrates the crucial role of top management in realigning the corporation as soon as possible with major trends as they emerge in the business environment. No matter how effective the organization's capabilities for spontaneous change from the bottom up, or in turning strategic options into new business from the middle, from time to time most companies have to be realigned from the top down to take advantage of a fundamental new trend. These trends reflect socio-political and economic turning points, shifts in the positions of the company's different stakeholders and access to the resources they control, or alternatively, major shifts in the competitive environment that cannot be adequately dealt with from the bottom up.

Observation of how excellent companies like Johnson & Johnson, Sony, and Canon realign their organizations points to the following common features:

- Creating a strategic goal that is simple but challenging, combined with absolute, companywide commitment to a clearly articulated set of values.
- Reallocating resources to the new task(s) most crucial to attaining the strategic goal.
- Redirecting effort to sustain the corporate energy needed for the realignment.
- Redistributing the value created by the company toward the stakeholders with the most valuable resources as a result of the new trend.

All of this requires harmonizing the roles of those who can create breakpoints by developing and positioning managers who can lead the change process.

Realignment is a process of discontinuous change appropriate to companies facing a strong force running counter to existing internal change (see Exhibit 12-1). The companies successful at realignment have learned how to turn the new trends, or trend reversals, to advantage. Within the guidelines created by a long-run goal, they mobilize their organizations by drawing on the strong tension between existing internal change and the direction of the new trend.

Realignment differs from restructuring in several important respects: realignment is carried out *before* the company gets into trouble, while it has ample time available for internal change; com-

EXHIBIT 12–1   **Discontinuous Change Capability:**
Realigning the Corporation

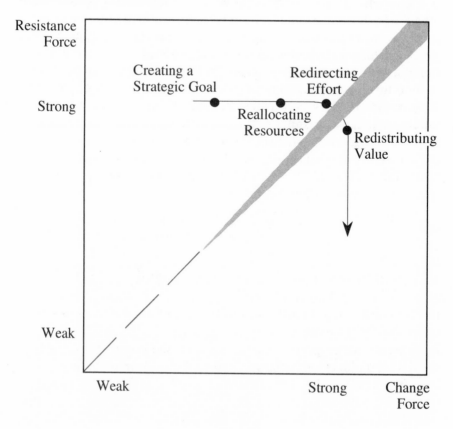

panies that realign typically have some intelligence capability and can often draw on a learning capability in the form of experience with continuous or sporadic change; and since the strategic goal remains, little if any change is needed in vision, values, and beliefs. In brief, provided motivation is clearly established, realignment can be carried out more quickly, with fewer aftereffects than restructuring. And whatever ripple effects there may be in learning new behaviors, they play themselves out in the absence of survival pressure.

CREATING A STRATEGIC GOAL

Companies that create competitive breakpoints, be they entrepreneurial start-ups, Japanese entrants, or Johnson & Johnson, are frequently characterized by strategic ambitions that go well beyond their existing capabilities and competence.[3] These ambitions reflect the firm's strategic goal. Behind the goal is an emerging agenda for how existing competence is going to be stretched and complemented to fulfill the ambition.

From its inception, the goal of Johnson & Johnson has been to play a leading role in the health care products industry. This goal, together with the vision and values embedded in its credo, has provided the context for most of its strategic decisions. In the early days, the operating task was to produce antiseptic dressings. Publications, conferences, and other activities to help the medical profession use its products were a natural part of the mission. Close association with medical practice led easily into professional products. Although the decision to go into pharmaceuticals was more difficult for J&J to accomplish, it was the inevitable extension of the competence required to pursue the strategic goal.

The strategic goal provides the framework within which a company can react to external shocks and pursue the continuous change capability and strategic options that create competitive breakpoints. Apart from a flirtation with diversification into industrial products based on some of its in-house technology, virtually all of Johnson & Johnson's key decisions have been consistent with the goal of playing a major leadership role in the health care products industry. Commitment to the accompanying credo was crucial in shaping the response to the Tylenol tragedies. Top management's rapid reaction to honor the J&J's commitment to its customers not only showed the outside world but also, more important during the early days of the crisis, signaled to everyone within the company what the appropriate response would be. The Tylenol crisis "highlighted as never before the unique value of the Johnson & Johnson Credo in defining responsibilities. . . ."

Organizational realignment only works if employees identify with the expectations of management. When the organization is changing, employees have difficulty knowing whether they are getting accurate information, and even more difficulty monitoring the behavior of top management to determine whether the new organization will be in their best interests. Hence the importance of a corporate mission and philosophy like Johnson & Johnson's that means something in the day-to-day life of the company. Anecdotal evidence from around the world suggests that employees commit when management is perceived to be providing direction to deal with business shifts and driven by a larger set of values beyond pure personal gain. According to Kozo Ohsone, a director of Sony and leader of the breakpoint creating design teams for the Walkman, Compact Disc, and the Watchman: "The key to improvement and innovation is a respectful and trusting relationship between management and workers. It means creating an environment in which everyone realizes the importance of working together to achieve common goals."

Japanese competitors have been particularly effective at combining their overall vision and values with a focused, strategic goal. Often this goal is made concrete, and is therefore much easier to communicate; for example, using the company's most dangerous competitor as the objective. The products of the competitor can be seen and examined. Its strategies can be analyzed. The gap between its performance and the challenger provides an ongoing measure of performance. In the late 1970s, Komatsu implemented its famous Maru-C, or "Surround Caterpillar" program. Toyota started with Chrysler as the target to be beaten. Once this had been achieved it moved up market until, in the 1990s, its objective was to catch Mercedes through continual improvement of the Lexus. Sony focused on Philips from the early days when Morita visited the Philips complex in Eindhoven and decided that if a company situated in a small Dutch town could be a major world player, so could Sony.

Persistence is key to the successful pursuit of a strategic goal.[4] An important sign of strategic persistence is the continual willingness and capability to act on emerging forces. Komatsu's Maru-C program started in 1960 with the acquisition of technology from

International Harvester, Cummins Engine, and Bucyrus-Erie. A quality program was the immediate next step, followed by a volume expansion program, a cost reduction program, an innovation program, and a distribution network expansion effort. In the mid-1980s, Caterpillar came back through its joint venture to attack Komatsu in Japan. Komatsu lost ground with the high value of the yen and its CEO was fired for not being able to press the advantage. Yet, Caterpillar's strategy was essentially a unidimensional one based on high-value machines and good service. When the market began to swing toward smaller machines in the late 1980s, Komatsu regained the competitive advantage and Caterpillar was forced to revitalize in a belated attempt to control costs.

REALLOCATING RESOURCES

The Komatsu experience shows how opportunities arise from time to time to anticipate and trigger breakpoints in the competitive rules of the industry game from the top of the company. These anticipatory shifts often involve the repositioning of entire companies. Even though the signal that a change is needed may come from the front line, such shifts can only be satisfactorily coordinated from the top. They provide the ultimate test of top management's strategic skill, its ability to realign the company by reallocating resources in the direction of emerging change forces ahead of the competition.

Reallocating for a Turning Point

A common form of reallocation is designed to stimulate the shifts between convergent and divergent forms of competitive behavior. Convergent competition typically requires the special allocation of resources for continual improvement in sourcing, manufacturing, logistics, and distribution. Divergent competition requires extra resources for spontaneous innovation, customization, marketing, and local operations. When it comes to resource reallocation, those firms with well-developed continuous change capabilities and strategic option portfolios have a huge advantage. Even with these attributes, however, overall realignment cannot occur without the guiding hand of top management.

Seiko's decision to move into scientific instruments was triggered by a planning department report on global watch prices and their tendency toward increasing weakness. As the watch industry matured, the time was approaching for a divergent move. But it was the CEO, Ichiro Hattori, who combined this report with one on Matsushita's plans for a TV watch to initiate a realignment of the company. Even though profits were still healthy, Hattori began questioning the company's direction, starting with the board and working down to the shop floor. When the reassessment, reallocation of resources, and implementation were over, Seiko had moved away from watches into a quite different industry.

Reallocating for a Leapfrog

The leapfrogs discussed in Part II typically involve a reallocation of resources by top management which ultimately may produce a further competitive breakpoint. After catching up, a firm has to reallocate resources to provide a platform for creating the competitive advantage needed to outperform the competition. At ICI, it was the board that realigned the company during the 1980s. Although alarmed by poor financial results, the board found that ICI was backing the wrong trends. Forty percent of group volume was produced in the United Kingdom, which had lower growth rates than other industrial countries and accounted for only 4 percent of the world chemical market; 60 percent of sales were in cyclical, commodity, bulk chemicals with low margins; ICI productivity was low compared to its competitors'; and the product mix was aging because of too few new products. The diagnosis defined the tasks around which the realignment would take shape: first, convergence around production efficiency and lower personal costs; second, divergence toward higher-value specialty chemicals, pharmaceuticals, biologicals, and agrichemicals; plus a special drive for increased market share in continental Europe and fast-growing Asian countries.

To improve productivity, overlapping divisions were consolidated into the £5 billion Chemicals and Polymers group. Then resources were allocated to the development of new business by setting up the ICI Acquisitions group to look for promising business in the targeted specialties. International business groups were set up for most activities in a move away from U.K.-centered geographic businesses toward global product lines. Between 1982 and 1988, £2.5 billion was invested in 150 acquisitions and divestitures related to the core business; there were no big acquisition failures. Between 1980 and 1987, high margin, less cyclical products grew from 38 percent to 50 percent of the company's portfolio, while

U.K. sales declined from 38 percent to 25 percent. This realignment propelled ICI into the *Fortune* ranking of the world's top five chemical companies based on sales.[5]

Timing Reallocation

Realignments produce the same timing dilemma as do strategic options. Those who wait too long miss the window of opportunity. On the other hand, moving later rather than sooner, learning from the mistakes of others, can be an advantage.

In 1985, after observing its competitors for some time, the top management of Marks and Spencer (M&S), the U.K. clothes, food, and household retailers, decided to switch from a paper-based information and communications system to an electronic system.[6] By no means the first major British retailer to put in information technology, M&S, unlike its competitors, concentrated on getting information rather than merely putting in the technology. M&S capitalized on the strong relationships it enjoys with suppliers. As a result, it was one of the first retail chains in Europe to introduce electronic ordering and invoicing. The system allowed M&S to outpace the competition by introducing a wide variety of specialized products in a disciplined manner. In addition, a computerized warehousing system allows shop assistants to avoid stockouts. All of this increased M&S's market share significantly. M&S keeps the "customer happy by putting the right merchandise on the right store shelf at the right time." In 1989–1990, when most British retailers were being dragged down by high interest rates, M&S announced a 14 percent rise in pre-tax profits to £604 million. By timing its allocation of resources to information technology, Marks and Spencer was able to shift rapidly toward a divergent variety of specialized lines, while the rest of the industry was still struggling to control costs.

REDIRECTING EFFORT

Building the organizational energy needed to support realignment and to continually develop new capabilities and strategic options is crucial to creating breakpoints. As opposed to leapfrogging, where survival is often used to motivate change, creating breakpoints means leading companies have to tap other sources of organizational energy. This is especially so when an external trend reversal makes existing internal change counterproductive.

Exploiting Organizational Tension

Some executives have learned how to turn a new trend, or trend reversal, to advantage. They mobilize their organizations by drawing on the tension between the opposing poles of behavior:[7] the organizational looseness needed for spontaneous innovation and the tightness associated with continual improvement; the differentiation needed for local customization and the integration associated with global product lines; the openness associated with competitive, assertive, more individualistic behavior and the coordination associated with cooperative, team-oriented behavior, sensitive to the group environment.

In shifting the emphasis from one pole to the other, on these or other dimensions of behavior, management not only alters structure, systems, and process, but also opens up a gap between where the organization is and expectations about where it should be. It is this expectations gap that provides the energy for change.[8] The gap opens up during what is typically a discontinuous shift in emphasis from one pole to the other. Thus, the life of a dynamic organization is often characterized by periods of relative continuity in either a tighter or looser configuration, punctuated by periodic breakpoints that mark the shift from one configuration to another.

The high-tech and financial services industries in the United States, both of which are characterized by rapid change, provide examples of companies with strong cultures that go through cycles of continuity separated by brief periods of organizational discontinuity. In the investment banking industry, top management intervenes periodically to close down some activities and emphasize others.[9] During the intervening periods the organization operates in a very decentralized spontaneous fashion in close symbiosis with evolving market needs. The management intervention has been described as a process of "annealing," during which the organization is reshuffled and heated up, and after which it cools down in a more autonomous mode.

A study of U.S. high-tech firms identified two contrasting sets of success factors, one set associated with continuity, the other with discontinuity: "On the one hand, business focus, organizational cohesion, and integrity imply stability and conservation. On the other hand, adaptability, entrepreneurial culture, and hands-on top management are synonymous with rapid sometimes precipitous change."[10] Hewlett-Packard, 3M, Apple, and DEC, all originally famous for their loose, innovative cultures, were forced to

tighten up at several points during the 1980s, in pursuit of greater coordination and lower costs.

Exploiting the Tension between Improvement and Innovation

Japanese high-tech companies like Sony and Canon maintain a continual tension between innovation and improvement. Whereas there are no available examples of continuous improvement co-existing with spontaneous innovation in the same organization unit (the disciplined teams used for improvement being incompatible with loose, individually driven intrapreneurship), there are examples of teams for structured innovation co-existing with improvement teams. The possibility of using the team structure as a basis for both continual improvement and structured innovation seems to have been overlooked by those who argue that improvement and innovation are contradictory.[11] In this type of organization radical innovation is triggered by periodic task forces selected by top management with a challenging new product objective in mind. Canon not only has a finely tuned continuous improvement capability, but is also capable of discrete task force innovation, as demonstrated by the development of the personal copier.

Another approach to maintaining the innovation-improvement tension is the one followed by Carnaud, the French packaging company, now part of Carnaud Metal Box.[12] Jean-Marc Descarpentries changed the priority operating ratios from year to year to fit shifting corporate priorities. The number of organizational levels between himself and the shop floor was limited to a maximum of four. Quality circles were in place throughout the company. For innovation, complementary product development networks were created which drew the needed resources from throughout the company. Descarpentries encouraged a flexible mind-set by avoiding formal strategic planning with a central staff and by using the shifting ratio priorities to maintain the tension between innovation and improvement.

Exploiting the Tension between Global and Local

The tension between global and local, between the loose control of geographic subsidiaries and the tighter coordination of integrated global product lines, is common in most multinationals. Many companies put themselves through periodic reorganizations that shift the balance of power between different arms of their matrix structure, between geography on the one hand and product lines on the other hand. Here again most of the examples come from American and British companies, some of which have reorganized several times in the space of a few years. In some cases, it is difficult to discern the purpose. Reorganizations not coupled to a new strategic task have an air of desperation about them.

On the other hand, a well-timed reorganization can play a crucial role in redirecting effort toward a new strategic task. Helmut Maucher of Nestlé anticipated the coming consolidation of the food industry and began to revitalize by pressuring status quo agents early.[13] Procedures were streamlined and power shifted from the head office on Lake Geneva into the field. Then the company was exposed to new ways of doing things through reorganization by acquisition, the most notable being the Rowntree takeover. Instead of being distributed across Nestlé's geographic zones, Rowntree became the first center for a global product line, in this case confectionery. The effort put into resolving the tension between this new global product line and the zonal structure lead to the creation of two strategic product groups, as part of a realignment from a local to a global orientation in an increasingly brand conscious industry.

Internal differentiation between business system functions is another approach to accommodating the tension between local and global needs. Upstream activities like R&D, product policy manufacturing, and logistics tend to be integrated and run on a global basis. Downstream activities like marketing, distribution, and personnel are decentralized to satisfy local needs which vary across regions and countries. Procter & Gamble has consistently used strong product and brand managers to explore the advantages of global reach, while remaining very sensitive to the differences in tastes and eating habits expressed by the regional sales organizations.

McDonald's prides itself on being not only global and local, but also coordinated. McDonald's is highly integrated on certain dimensions with globally standardized menus, restaurant layouts, quality control, and training programs. It is highly localized with respect to franchise management, staffing, marketing, and sourcing. It is also highly coordinated, with a computer system that exchanges information between franchises, many meetings, and conferences. As a truly integrated global network, it quickly benefits from progress made in any one of its operations. But McDonald's lacks a spontaneous innovation capability. When the chain began to lose U.S. market share in the early 1990s, it didn't have a mechanism for fundamental, bottom-up experimentation. It thus found itself without any relevant strategic options.

Exploiting the Tension between Cooperation and Competition

The tension between cooperation and competition has been symbolized for centuries by the continual interplay between the yin and the yang in Chinese culture. The yin is the more supportive, group-oriented side; the yang the more assertive, individualistic side. Accumulating survey evidence supports the casual observation that the competitive yang tendency is more prevalent in the Anglo-Saxon business world, while the cooperative yin tendency is more pronounced in Northern Europe and certainly in Japan.[14]

Yet companies need both types of behavior to take advantage of the opportunities created by new trends. The Japanese, embedded in a largely cooperative culture, encourage competition between teams to get the organizational energy for continual improvement and realignments. At Canon, work centers compete with one another for the accolade of the Premier Work Center, factories compete with one another, and so on. In the Japanese economy at large, the keiretsu, or industrial groups, compete ferociously; the in-group cooperation is in constant tension with the between-group competition.

At the other end of the spectrum, U.S. companies, in a highly competitive and individualistic national culture, must consciously build coordination mechanisms into their organizations to balance the competition between units with some cooperation. The four most common approaches involve the use of structure, systems, socialization, and people.[15] The structural solutions typically involve matrix management, committees and task forces, and/or centralization of certain functions. On the systems side, the information system is playing an increasingly important coordinating role, together with the performance measurement and reward systems. Socialization includes career rotation, geographic proximity, and shared facilities. Finally, there is the choice and promotion of people with broad perspectives, experience, and an ability to work with other departments or functions. In a well-managed organization, these coordinating mechanisms generate a creative tension between competition and cooperation.

Dee Hock, the head of the VISA credit card company, kept his executives on their toes with continual job rotations, ad hoc project teams, and structural amorphousness. Contrasting with the

competitive spirit created by Hock's visionary and somewhat auto-
cratic style was the president, Chuck Russell, "one of the nicest
men in the company. He's one of those guys who will just pop into
your office with cup of coffee in his hand, take a seat, and say
'How are you today?' But he's not just a nice guy who occupies
space—he's brilliant about this business."[16] During VISA's golden
years in the 1980s, these two top men incarnated the tension
between competition and cooperation, thereby providing complementary poles of inspiration for the entire organization.

The tension created by Johnson & Johnson's Hospital Services Division is a classic example of what is missing in many
decentralized and highly creative companies: cooperation to get
the most out of the internal competition. J&J initially did not see
the competitive turning point and did not realize what was needed
to serve the emerging integrated health care market. Only when
declining performance set in did the company react. The creation
of the Hospital Services Division was a move toward cooperative
behavior that would allow J&J to exploit economies of scale and
scope.

REDISTRIBUTING VALUE

In many companies the implicit assumption is that the stockholders come first. The customers, employees, and suppliers have
contracts that stipulate the terms of their exchange with the company, typically in terms of fixed payments. Any surplus goes to the
stockholders to compensate them for putting up the risk capital.
And yet, in many circumstances, capital is not the scarcest and
most valuable of the necessary resources. In well-developed financial markets, capital is readily available for attractive projects.
Especially in high-tech industries, certain types of competence
may be more difficult to obtain than capital. Companies that don't
have ready access to scarce capabilities and competence have a
competitive disadvantage. Companies that understand this invest
in maintaining their access to crucial resources. As part of realignment they distribute some of their surplus value to the stakeholders
that control the valuable resources, thereby investing in future
access to those resources.

Numerous widely admired Japanese companies are well
known for putting their employees and managers ahead of return
on investment and capital gain. Many of these firms are in high-
tech industries where the collective know-how of their employees

is a crucial resource built up through years of organizational learning. These teams cannot be simply downsized during lean years and then quickly reconstituted when demand picks up. To maintain and build commitment, as a first priority, value is distributed to those inside the company. In the automobile industry, for example, the trends of value-added per employee are remarkably smooth for Japanese, as compared to American competitors. By contrast, for the Japanese automakers, return on equity fluctuates far more than for their American counterparts. In the longer run, to the extent that the distribution of value to employees represents an investment in access to a scarce resource, the Japanese shareholders benefit. Without discounting other factors, the performance of Japanese auto share prices bears this out.

Redistributing to Stakeholders with Valuable Resources

When the forces of change shift the relative position of stakeholders, companies locked in to maximizing value for a particular stakeholder group cannot react. Others with more flexibility can redistribute value to enhance their access to the critical stakeholder resource. If they can develop privileged access, they may have the basis for creating a competitive breakpoint. For example, if workers with the right skills are readily available, it does not make economic sense to invest in anything more than the training needed to bring them on-stream, as McDonald's does. On the other hand, if for some reason the right profile suddenly becomes scarce, those companies that can retain crucial employees and attract new ones have an obvious competitive advantage.

Johnson & Johnson's pioneering of medical handbooks in the early days reflected the need to create a market for its products, a need far more important than any short-run profit maximization objective. (Customers were much more valuable than capital.) The company's tilt toward workers' welfare during the depression and toward societal and communal programs during national and local crises are examples of value distribution in line with shifts in the positions of stakeholders. In these cases, J&J was investing in the organizational commitment of these stakeholders during periods of realignment when the company's support would be most appreciated.

Monitoring the Returns to Stakeholders

Just as it is customary to monitor the return on equity to ensure that shareholders are getting a risk-adjusted return that exceeds interest rates, executives should monitor the "return" to the other stakeholder groups, especially when the forces of change are active. Although not as widely studied as financial measures, non-financial data are available for assessing whether other stakeholders think they are getting a fair return: declining sales and customer loyalty are obvious indicators that the product/price offering is inadequate; absenteeism, turnover, and strikes reflect employee dissatisfaction; recurring legal claims for pollution violations indicate an unsatisfactory relationship with the environmental protection authorities; and so on.

Waiting to be forced into action by one of the stakeholder groups is tantamount to giving up the initiative and being constrained to turn the situation around. Rather, as part of realignment, management should ensure access to valuable resources by altering the pattern of value distribution.

HARMONIZING ROLES TO CREATE BREAKPOINTS

Creating breakpoints in different environments demands organizational capabilities covering no less than three types of basic change: continuous change, sporadic change, and discontinuous change. Within the change arena, each of these is appropriate for a different mix of industry forces and resistance. To create breakpoints, no matter what the mix of forces and resistance, excellent companies require proactive access to all three change types.

Top management has to identify and develop managers capable of leading the three different types of basic change process. Change managers develop by being "jolted" out of their daily routines with challenging assignments that stretch their abilities and then allow time for integrating the experience into their managerial repertoire.[17] Sustained excellence requires nothing less than the capability to create breakpoints by developing and positioning managers so that those on the front line can improve and innovate, those in the middle can develop new business from strategic options, and those at the top can change the corporate direction when they sense a major turning point in the forces of change. The successful management practice discussed in Chapters 10, 11, and 12 falls naturally into the domain of these three levels of manager:

Frontline managers. Intrapreneurs and improvement team leaders drive the engine of continuous change that allows a company to take continuous and spontaneous advantage of strong industry trends. They are on the frontline of the intelligence, improvement, innovation, and networking capabilities. Since few companies have all of these properly in place, those that do create breakpoints by continuously outperforming the competition.

Middle managers. Middle managers manage the company's portfolio of strategic options that is so crucial to the creation of breakpoints when industry trends are uncertain. Middle managers have to bridge the gap between the vision of top management and the uncertain reality of the marketplace.[18] Together with frontline managers, they decide which options to pursue. With top management, they decide which options to convert into a full-scale corporate commitment and when. With timely implementation, strategic options lead to outpacing of the competition.

Top managers. Top management has to provide the strategic goal and shape the corporate culture within which the frontline and middle managers can pursue continuous and sporadic change. To deal with major trend reversals in the business environment that make existing bottom-up change counterproductive, top management has to realign the organization from time to time. A new business direction may be needed to trigger a competitive breakpoint, together with a reallocation of resources, redirection of effort, and possibly a redistribution of the value created.

The future belongs to companies that can create competitive breakpoints by drawing on the talent and commitment of their people to capitalize on continuous change when the forces are strong, strategic options when the forces are uncertain, and organizational realignment when a major trend reversal is in sight. Sustained excellence in today's global markets requires nothing less than the capability not only to create a pricing breakpoint by continually improving the cost performance of the Canon Copier, but also to create a product breakpoint by developing the option to launch a Sony Walkman when the market's ready, and to create a market breakpoint by realigning J&J with the converging market for professional hospital services. In brief, a company is truly topflight when it can create breakpoints, no matter what the industry environment.

**KEYS TO PRACTICE: REALIGNING
THE CORPORATION**

1. Use a long-run goal to motivate realignment from the top down when a major shift in the direction of the change forces is anticipated.
2. Use the leading indicators of turning points to time the reallocation of resources.
3. Use the tension between opposing poles of behavior to mobilize the organizational energy for realignment.
4. Use the value of the resources provided by stakeholders to guide the redistribution of the value created by the company.
5. Provide leadership for the creation of competitive breakpoints by developing and positioning managers on the frontline to lead continuous organizational change, in the middle to lead sporadic organizational change, and on the top to realign the company.

Notes

Preface

1. Thomas J. Peters and Robert H. Waterman, Jr., *In Search of Excellence* (New York: Harper & Row, 1982).
2. Jolie Solomon, "The Tom Peters Cult: Has It Changed American Business?" *Boston Sunday Globe,* March 10, 1991, pp. 39, 45.
3. Joseph A. Schumpeter, *Capitalism, Socialism and Democracy,* 3d ed. (New York: Harper & Row, 1950).
4. Richard Nelson and Sidney Winter, *An Evolutionary Theory of Economic Change* (Cambridge, MA: Harvard University Press, 1982).
5. Danny Miller and Peter H. Friesen, *Organizations: A Quantum View* (Englewood Cliffs, NJ: Prentice-Hall, 1984).
6. Richard N. Foster, *Innovation: The Attacker's Advantage* (New York: Summit Books, 1986), Chapter 4 and Appendix 2.
7. Modesto A. Maidique and Robert H. Hayes, "The Art of High-Technology Management," *Sloan Management Review* (Winter 1984), pp. 17–31.
8. Henry Mintzberg, "Crafting Strategy," *Harvard Business Review* (July–August 1987), pp. 66–75.
9. René Thom, *Structural Stability and Morphogenesis* (New York: Benjamin, 1975).
10. Kurt Lewin, "Frontiers in Group Dynamics, Concept Method and Reality in Social Science; Social Equilibria and Social Change," *Human Relations,* vol. 1 (1947), pp. 2–38.

Chapter 1

1. Interview with the chairman of a former Georges Meyer affiliate.
2. The sales growth rates were calculated from data in "Analyse Markten Consumentensector en Marktpositie" (Eindhoven, Nederland: Philips Gloeilampen N.V., Consumer Electronics Division, 1989), Table 1.
3. W.J. Abernathy and J.L. Utterback, "Patterns of Industrial Innovation," *Technology Review* (June–July 1978), pp. 41–47.
4. Michael E. Porter, *Competitive Strategy* (New York: Free Press, 1980).
5. Xavier Gilbert and Paul Strebel, "From Innovation to Outpacing," *Business Quarterly* (Summer 1989), pp. 19–22.
6. Paul Strebel, "Competitive Turning Points: How to Recognize Them," *European Management Journal* (June 1989), p. 141.
7. Most of the information on Kirin and all of the quotations are from Dominique Turpin, "Kirin Brewery Co., Ltd. (A)," IMD Case Study M366 (Lausanne, Switzerland: IMD International, 1990).
8. "The Shiseido Story" (Tokyo: Shiseido Co., Ltd., 1990).
9. Larry E. Greiner, "Evolution and Revolution as Organizations Grow," *Harvard Business Review* (July–August 1972), p. 37.

Chapter 2

1. For more information on the U.S. construction machinery industry in the 1980s see Clare C. Swanger and John R. Berthold, "A Note on the Construction and Earthmoving Equipment, Lift Trucks and Engine Industries" (San Francisco: The Altos Group, 1987).
2. F. William Barnett, "Four Steps to Forecast Total Market Demand," *Harvard Business Review* (July–August 1988), pp. 28–37.
3. R. Nelson and S. Winter, *An Evolutionary Theory of Economic Change* (Cambridge, MA: Harvard University Press, 1982).
4. George Taucher, "Mehr Schein als Sein," unpublished presentation (Lausanne, Switzerland: IMD International, 1990).
5. Richard N. Foster, *Innovation* (New York: Summit Books, 1986), Chapter 4.
6. Gerhard D. Mensch, *Stalemate in Technology: Innovations Overcome the Depression* (Cambridge, MA: Ballinger, 1979), Chapter 2.
7. Paul Strebel, "Dealing with Discontinuities," *European Management Journal* (December 1990), pp. 434–442.
8. Wang Chung quoted in Fritjof Capra, *The Turning Point* (London: Fontana paperbacks, 1983), pp. 17–19.
9. Frank E. Manuel, *Shapes of Philosophical History* (London: George Allen and Unwin, 1965), Chapters 2 and 3.
10. Paul Samuelson and William D. Nordhaus, *Economics* (New York: McGraw-Hill, 1985), Chapter 36.

11. N. Kondratiev, "The Major Economic Cycles," *Review of Economics and Statistics,* vol. 18 (November 1935), pp. 105–115.
12. Joseph A. Schumpeter, *Business Cycles: A Theoretical, Historical and Statistical Analysis of the Capitalist Process* (N.Y.: McGraw-Hill, 1939), Chapter 2.
13. For more information on the fast-food industry in the 1980s see Richard B. Robinson, "The Maturing Fast-Food Hamburger Industry: America's Culinary Masterpiece," Industry Note 239–267 (University of South Carolina, 1985).
14. P.L. Lawrence and D. Dyer, *Renewing American Industry: Organizing for Efficiency and Innovation* (New York: Free Press, 1983).
15. Paul Strebel, "Identifying Turning Points in Competitive Behavior," *Handbook of Business Strategy: 1989/1990 Yearbook,* Harold E. Glass, ed. (Boston: Warren, Gorham & Lamont, 1989), Chapter 13.
16. Michael E. Porter, *Competitive Strategy* (New York: Free Press, 1980).
17. Alex Taylor, "A Tale Dow Jones Won't Tell," *Fortune,* July 3, 1989, pp. 66–70.

Chapter 3
1. Most of the Société Générale story and all of the quotations are from David Hover and John Pringle, "Société Générale de Belgique (A)," IMD Case Study GM460 (Lausanne, Switzerland: IMD International, 1990).
2. "Who's Excellent Now?," Cover Story, *Business Week,* November 5, 1984, pp. 46–55.
3. Shoji Sakuma, "Media, Mergers, MCA and Matsushita," lecture at the Harvard Business School, January 30, 1991.
4. Carlo M. Cipolla, *The Economic Decline of Empires* (London: Methuen, 1970), pp. 1–15.
5. Paul Strebel, "Ford of Europe (A) and (B)," IMD Case Studies GM321, 322 (Lausanne, Switzerland: IMD International, 1984).
6. "Auto Slump Hits Honda and Production Is Cut," *New York Times,* January 30, 1991, p. D4.
7. Alfred M. Jaeger and B.R. Baliga, "Control Systems and Strategic Adaptation: Lessons from the Japanese Experience," *Strategic Management Journal* (April–June 1985), pp. 115–134.
8. Most of the information on Gillette and all of the quotations are from David Mehegan, "Mockler's Legacy," *Boston Globe,* January 27, 1991, pp. 81, 83.
9. Alfred D. Chandler, *Scale and Scope: The Dynamics of Industrial Capitalism* (Cambridge, MA: Harvard University Press, 1990).
10. B. Schweizer and T. Radja, "The Swiss Watchmaking Industry,"

Union Bank of Switzerland Publications on Business, Banking and Monetary Topics (Zurich: Union Bank of Switzerland, 1986), No. 100.

11. James C. Ellert, "Banking Industry Strategies: A Global Perspective," unpublished presentation (Lausanne, Switzerland: IMD International, 1990).

Chapter 4

1. The information on the Finnish softwood industry is from an IMD International Consulting Project carried out by Odd Anderson, Willow Forsyth, Philip Gentry, Alfonso Ordonez, and Cornelia Sailer under the direction of Tom Vollmann and Paul Strebel.

2. For a conceptual discussion of steady state behavior see, for example, J.G. March and H.A. Simon, *Organizations* (New York: John Wiley, 1958) or R.M. Gert and J.G. March, *A Behavioral Theory of the Firm* (Englewood Cliffs, NJ: Prentice-Hall, 1963).

3. For a discussion of how organizations are a function of their environment, and in particular a rapid growth environment, see, for example, P.R. Lawrence and J.W. Lorsch, *Organization and Environment* (Boston: Harvard Business School, 1967).

4. See, for example, J.B. Quinn, "Strategic Change: Logical Incrementalism," *Sloan Management Review,* vol. 20 (Fall 1978), pp. 7–21.

5. See, for example, S. Miller and P.H. Friesen, *Organizations: A Quantum View* (Englewood Cliffs, NJ: Prentice-Hall, 1984).

6. Paul Strebel, "Dealing with Discontinuities," *European Management Journal* (December 1990), pp. 434–442.

7. Xavier Gilbert and Paul Strebel, "Taking Advantage of Industry Shifts," *European Management Journal* (December 1989), pp. 398–402.

8. Gerhard Aschinger, "Reflections on the Crash," *Swiss Bank Corporation, Economic and Financial Prospects* (August–September 1988), pp. 1–4.

Chapter 5

1. The information on the Swiss alarm systems industry and the quotations such as the one on pp. 89–90 are from an IMD International Consulting Project carried out by Hans Bachmann, Daniel Crasemann, Jean-Yves Goumaz, Heinz Haller, Steve Morrell, and Ole Skov under the direction of Paul Strebel. See Amy W. Webster, Kurt Schaer, and Paul Strebel, "Securiton AG (A) and (B), and the Alarm Systems Industry in Switzerland," IMD Case Studies GM409, 410, 411 (Lausanne, Switzerland: IMD International, 1987).

2. Steven C. Wheelwright and W. Earl Sasser, Jr., "New Product De-

velopment Map," *Harvard Business Review* (May–June 1989), pp. 112–125.

Chapter 6

1. The material in this chapter on the robotics industry and ASEA Robotics and all of the quotations from ASEA executives are taken largely from J.-P. Jeannet and R.C. Howard, "ASEA Robotics AG, (A) and (B)," IMD Case Studies M342 and 343, as well as "The Worldwide Robotics Industry 1987," IMD Case Study GM415, (Lausanne, Switzerland: IMD International, 1988).
2. Bruce Greenwald, "MCI Communications Corp., 1983," Case Study 284–057 (Boston: Harvard Business School, 1984).
3. Tim Smart and John J. Keller, "MCI's New Problems, How to Spend All This Cash," *Business Week,* August 21, 1989, p. 33.
4. The material on SAS is taken largely from Sandra Vandermerwe, "Scandinavian Airlines System SAS (A)," unpublished case study (Lausanne, Switzerland: IMD International, 1989).
5. Janet Guyon, "Nabisco's New Cookie Line Marks the Beginning of a Fierce Sales War," *The Wall Street Journal,* October 19, 1983.
6. J.Ph. Deschamps, A.R. Shapiro, and D.J. Symnes, "The Great Chocolate Chip Cookies War (A)," IMD Case Study GM383 (Lausanne, Switzerland: IMD International, 1988).
7. George Thurrow, "Anglo American Sees Changes It Supported Growing into a Threat," *The Wall Street Journal Europe,* July 31, 1990, p. 1.

Chapter 7

1. Most of the Olivetti story and all of the quotations are from Juliet Taylor and George Taucher, "Ing. C. Olivetti & Co. S.P.A.," IMD Case Study GM352 (Lausanne, Switzerland: IMD International, 1986).
2. George Taucher, "The Challenge of International Alliances," unpublished presentation (Lausanne, Switzerland: IMD International, 1987).
3. Paul Strebel, "Organizing for Innovation over an Industry Cycle," *Strategic Management Journal,* vol. 8 (1987), pp. 117–124.
4. Kurt Bleicher, Franck Bleicher, and Herbert Paul, "Managerial Frameworks for Innovative Responses in High-Tech Organizations," *Business Horizons* (November–December 1983), pp. 69–78.
5. Teruo Yamanonchi, "Breakthrough: The Development of the Canon Personal Copier," *Long-Range Planning,* vol. 22, no. 5 (1989), pp. 11–21.

6. Percy Barnevik, "ASEA in Transition: Restructuring and International Expansion," proceedings of the EFMD (European Foundation for Management Development), Annual Conference, Helsinki, June 10–13, 1984, pp. 6–10.
7. Peter R. Richardson, *Cost Containment, the Ultimate Advantage* (New York: Free Press, 1988).
8. Paul Strebel, "Ford of Europe (A)," IMD Case Study GM321 (Lausanne, Switzerland: IMD International, 1984).
9. J.G. Miller and Thomas E. Vollmann, "The Hidden Factory," *Harvard Business Review* (September–October 1985), pp. 142–150.
10. Richardson, "Cost Containment, the Ultimate Advantage."
11. Francis J. Aguilar and Richard Hammermesh, "General Electric: Business Development," Case Study 382–092 (Boston: Harvard Business School, 1981).
12. G.F. Hardymon, M.J. DeNino, and M.S. Salter, "When Corporate Venture Capital Doesn't Work," *Harvard Business Review* (May–June 1983), pp. 114–120.
13. Ivor P. Morgan, "The Purchasing Revolution," *IMD Perspectives for Managers,* no. 7 (August 1986), pp. 1–4.
14. Jacques Bouvard, "Making the Most Out of Mergers," presentation to the IMD Corporate Planners Workshop (April 28, 1989), p. 24.

Chapter 8
1. The information on the Sisu story and all of the quotations are from Pierre Casse and Suzanne de Treville, "Sisu Auto (A) and (B)," IMD Case Studies OB214 and 215 (Lausanne, Switzerland: IMD International, 1990).
2. For example, see L.J. Bourjeois and David R. Brodwin, "Strategic Implementation: Five Approaches to an Elusive Phenomenon," *Strategic Management Journal,* vol. 5 (1984), pp. 241–264.
3. Most of the information on Pilkington's approach and all of the quotations are from Alan McKinley and Ken Starkey, "Competitive Strategies and Organizational Change," *Organizational Studies,* vol. 9, no. 4 (1988), pp. 555–570.
4. The information on Seiko's approach and all of the quotations are from Dominique Turpin, "Seiko (A) and (B)," IMD Case Studies GM396 and 397 (Lausanne, Switzerland: IMD International, 1988).
5. For example, see John P. Kotter and Leonard A. Schlesinger, "Choosing Strategies for Change," *Harvard Business Review* (March–April 1979), pp. 106–114.
6. All of the quotations on ASEA are from Percy Barnevik, "ASEA in Transition: Restructuring and International Expansion," proceedings of the EFMD (European Foundation for Management Development), Annual Conference, Helsinki, June 10–13, 1984, pp. 6–10.

7. Timmer's quotes are from Philips, "Operation Centurion: Movement for Change," quoted in the *Nederlands,* October 30, 1990.
8. Casse and de Treville, "Sisu Auto (A) and (B)."
9. More on the Deutsche Bundesbahn story can be found in Paul Strebel and George Taucher, "Deutsche Bundesbahn (A), (B), and (C)," IMD Case Studies 0B214, 215, 216 (Lausanne, Switzerland: IMD International, 1990).
10. McKinley and Starkey, "Competitive Strategies and Organizational Change."
11. Kotter and Schlesinger, "Choosing Strategies for Change."

Chapter 9

1. Most of the information on the Harley-Davidson story and all of the quotations are from Peter C. Reid, *Well-Made in America: Lessons from Harley-Davidson on Being Best* (McGraw-Hill, 1990), mainly as excerpted in *Fortune,* September 25, 1989, pp. 155–164.
2. For more on the analysis of competitive strategy in different environments see Michael E. Porter, *Competitive Strategy* (New York: Free Press, 1980).
3. Xavier Gilbert, "Information Technology for Speed-Based Strategies," *IMD Perspectives for Managers,* no. 3 (1990), pp. 1–4.

Chapter 10

1. Teruo Yamanouchi, "Breakthrough: The Development of the Canon Personal Copier," *Long Range Planning,* vol. 22, no. 5 (1989), pp. 11–21.
2. The material on Canon's production system and all of the quotations are from Japan Management Association, *Canon Production System,* (Cambridge, MA: Productivity Press, 1987).
3. Peter Senge, "The Leader's New Work: Building Learning Organizations," *Sloan Management Review* (Fall 1990), pp. 7–23.
4. Leo Esaki, "Student Bytes Teacher," Nippon Advertising Supplement to the *New York Times,* March 24, 1991, p. 2.
5. James Fallows, "Containing Japan," *The Atlantic Monthly* (May 1989), pp. 40–54.
6. C.K. Prahalad and Gary Hamel, "Core Competence of the Corporation," *Harvard Business Review* (May–June, 1990), pp. 79–91.
7. David B. Zenoff, "How ICI Got Its 'Second Wind': Transforming a Major Multinational," unpublished manuscript (San Francisco: D.B. Zenoff & Associates, 1989).
8. Edward de Bono, *Teaching Thinking* (Hammondsworth, England: Penguin Books, 1978).

9. Leonard M. Fuld, "Learning to Cultivate Home-Grown Spies," Manager's Journal, *The Wall Street Journal,* April 8, 1986, p. 9.
10. Ibid.
11. Bob Johnstone, "Diversification Helps to Protect Profits," *Far Eastern Review,* October 13, 1988, pp. 54–56.
12. Weston H. Agor, "Intuition and Strategic Planning," *The Futurist* (November–December 1989), pp. 20–23.
13. Arie P. de Geus, "Planning as Learning," *Harvard Business Review* (March–April 1988), pp. 70–73.
14. Xavier Gilbert, "Information Technology for Speed-Based Strategies," *IMD Perspectives for Managers,* no. 3 (1990).
15. Masaaki Imai, *Kaizen: The Key to Japan's Competitive Success* (New York: Random House, 1986).
16. John F. Krafcik, "Triumph of the Lean Production System," *Sloan Management Review* (Fall 1988), pp. 41–51.
17. Japan Management Association, *Canon Production System.*
18. Ibid.
19. Ibid.
20. Imai, *Kaizen.*
21. Thomas A. Stewart, "A New Way to Wake Up a Giant," *Fortune,* October 22, 1990, pp. 70–76.
22. Andrew Fisher, "A Total Commitment to Quality," *Financial Times,* September 19, 1988, p. 12.
23. Ray Stata, "Organizational Learning—The Key to Management Innovation," *Sloan Management Review* (Spring 1989), pp. 63–74.
24. Brian Dumaine, "How Managers Can Succeed Through Speed," *Fortune,* February 13, 1989, pp. 30–35.
25. James C. Abbegelen and George Stalk, Jr., *Kaisha: The Japanese Corporation* (New York: Basic Books, 1985), Chapter 3.
26. For example, see Howard H. Stevenson and J. Carlos Jarillo, "A Paradigm of Entrepreneurship: Entrepreneurial Management," *Strategic Management Journal,* vol. 11 (1990), pp. 17–27; and Rosabeth Kanter, *The Change Masters: Innovations for Productivity in the American Corporation* (Simon & Schuster, 1983).
27. Modesto Maidique and Robert Hayes, "The Art of High-Technology Management," *Sloan Management Review* (Winter 1984), pp. 17–31.
28. Dwight Crane and Robert Eccles, *Doing Deals* (Boston: Harvard Business School Press, 1988), Chapter 6.
29. Dee W. Hock quoted in J. Stewart Dougherty and Robert C. Eccles, "VISA International: The Management of Change," Case Study 9-482-022 (Boston: Harvard Business School, 1981, revised, 1983).
30. Crane and Eccles, *Doing Deals.*
31. J. Carlos Jarillo, "On Strategic Networks," *Strategic Management Journal,* vol. 9 (1988), pp. 31–41.
32. For a conceptual treatment see Jarillo, "On Strategic Networks."

33. Gianni Lorenzonis and Oscar A. Ornati, "Constellations of Firms and New Ventures," *Journal of Business Venturing,* vol. 3 (1988), pp. 41–57.
34. Werner Ketelhohn and Robert C. Howard, "The Fashion Success Story of the 1980s: Benetton SpA," IMD Case Study GM438 (Lausanne, Switzerland: IMD International, 1990).

Chapter 11
1. Most of the history of Sony is from Akio Morita, *From a 500-Dollar Company to a Global Corporation: The Growth of Sony* (Pittsburgh, PA: Carnegie-Mellon University Press, 1985).
2. The quotations on Sony's product development are from Kozo Ohsone, "Innovation in Management: The Case of the Walkman," *Sony Innovation in Management Series,* vol. 1 (1988), pp. 3–21.
3. See, for example, William H. Matthews, "Kissing Technological Frogs: Managing Technology as a Strategic Resource," *IMD Perspective for Managers,* no. 5 (1990), pp. 1–4.
4. Ibid.
5. Gian F. Frontini and Peter R. Richardson, "Design and Demonstration: The Key to Industrial Innovation," *Sloan Management Review* (Summer 1984), pp. 39–49.
6. Teruo Yamanouchi, "Breakthrough: The Development of the Canon Personal Copier," *Long Range Planning,* vol. 22, no. 5 (1989), pp. 11–21.
7. SRI International quoted in George Taucher, "The Challenge of International Alliances," unpublished presentation (Lausanne, Switzerland: IMD International, 1987).
8. *Business Week,* October 15, 1990, pp. 40–46.
9. C.K. Prahalad and Gary Hamel, "Core Competence of the Corporation," *Harvard Business Review* (May–June, 1990), pp. 79–91.
10. Xavier Gilbert, "Competitors in the World Toy Industry—1988," IMD Case Study GM413 (Lausanne, Switzerland: IMD International, 1988).
11. Sandra Vandermerwe and Marika Taishoff, "SKF Bearings: Market Orientation through Services," IMD Case Study M376 (Lausanne, Switzerland: IMD International, 1990).
12. Matti Alahuhta, "Global Growth Strategies for High Technology Challengers," *Acta Polytechnica Scandinavica* (Helsinki, Finland: Electrical Engineering Series No. 66, 1990).
13. Marc H. Meyer and Edward B. Roberts, "Focusing Product Technology for Corporate Growth," *Sloan Management Review* (Summer 1988), pp. 7–16.
14. Ibid.

15. Alahuhta, "Global Growth Strategies for High Technology Challengers."
16. Gary Hamel and C.K. Prahalad, "Unexplored Routes to Competitive Revitalization," Working Paper Series, No. 14 (London: London Business School, 1986).
17. The information on VAW comes from Kenneth Gooding, "German Aluminium Group Shows Its Mettle; How VAW Is Coping with Dramatic Changes in Its Market," *Financial Times,* October 9, 1990, p. 29.
18. Xavier Gilbert and Paul Strebel, "Strategies to Outpace the Competition," *Journal of Business Strategy* (Summer 1987), pp. 28–37.

Chapter 12

1. The history of Johnson & Johnson and all of the quotations are from Lawrence G. Foster, *A Company That Cares: One Hundred Year Illustrated History of Johnson & Johnson* (New Brunswick, NJ: Johnson & Johnson, 1986); and Milton Moskowitz, Robert Levering, and Michael Katz, eds., *Everybody's Business, A Field Guide to 400 Leading Companies in America* (New York: Doubleday, Currency, 1990).
2. F.J. Aguilar and A. Bhambri, "Johnson & Johnson (B): Hospital Services," Case Study 9-384-054 (Boston: Harvard Business School, 1983).
3. Gary Hamel and C.K. Prahalad, "Strategic Intent," *Harvard Business Review* (May–June 1989), pp. 63–76.
4. Dominique Turpin, "Persistence and the Competitiveness of the Japanese Firm," *World Competitiveness Report* (IMD, Lausanne, and the World Economic Forum, Geneva, 1990).
5. David B. Zenoff, "How ICI Got Its 'Second Wind': Transformation of a Major Multinational," unpublished manuscript (San Francisco: D.B. Zenoff & Associates, 1989).
6. Della Bradshaw, "An Outfit Made of Durable Fibre," *Financial Times,* June 14, 1990, p. 26.
7. Paul Strebel and Christopher Parker, "Rebalancing the Organization; Key to Outpacing the Competition," *IMD Perspectives for Managers,* no. 3, (1988), pp. 1–4.
8. Michael Beer, *Organization Change and Development: A Systems View* (Santa Monica, CA: Goodyear, 1980); and L. Coch and F.r.P. French, Jr., "Overcoming Resistance to Change," *Human Relations,* vol. 1 (1948), pp. 512–532.
9. Dwight Crane and Robert Eccles, *Doing Deals* (Boston: Harvard Business School Press, 1988), Chapter 6.
10. Modesto Maidique and Robert H. Hayes, "The Art of High-Technol-

ogy Management," *Sloan Management Review* (Summer 1988), pp. 7–16.

11. See, for example, William J. Abernathy, *The Productivity Dilemma: Roadblock to Innovation in the Automobile Industry* (Baltimore: Johns Hopkins University Press, 1978); and Masaaki Imai, *Kaizen: The Key to Japan's Competitive Success* (New York: Random House, 1986).

12. Kevin O'Connell and Jan Kubes, "Carnaud S.A. (A) and (B)," unpublished case studies (Lausanne, Switzerland: IMD International, 1987).

13. Dana Hyde, James C. Ellert, and J. Peter Killing, "Nestlé Rowntree (A) and (B)" and Videotape, IMD Case Studies GM423, 424 (Lausanne, Switzerland: IMD International, 1989).

14. *World Competitiveness Report* (IMD, Lausanne, and the World Economic Forum, Geneva, 1989).

15. Benson P. Shapiro, "Functional Integration: Getting All of the Troops to Work Together," Note 9-587-122 (Boston: Harvard Business School, revised, 1987).

16. J. Stewart Dougherty and Robert G. Eccles, "VISA International: The Management of Change," Case Study 9-482-022 (Boston: Harvard Business School, 1981, revised 1983).

17. J.B.M. Kassarjian, "Jolt Your Managers Out of Their Comfortable Groove—They May Learn to Lead Change," *IMD Perspectives for Managers,* no. 4 (1991), pp. 1–4.

18. Ikujiro Nonaka, "Toward Middle-Up-Down Management: Accelerating Information Creations," *Sloan Management Review* (Spring 1988), pp. 9–18; and Paul Strebel and Christopher Parker, "Rebalancing the Organization: Key to Outpacing the Competition," *IMD Perspectives for Managers,* no. 3 (1988), pp. 1–4.

Index

About the Author

Paul Strebel is professor of Business Administration and director of the International Executive Program on radical change management at IMD, the International Institute for Management Development in Lausanne, Switzerland. His consulting and executive development activities have been in the areas of value-based strategic planning, acquisitions and mergers, and the anticipation and management of competitive turning points and breakpoints. Professor Strebel has extensive international experience in Europe, North America, the Far East, and South Africa. Among the companies he has worked with are ABB, AKZO, Caterpillar, Citibank, DEC, Grace, IBM, Nestlé, Philips, Price Waterhouse, Shell, and Standard Bank.

Prior to his present position, Strebel was director of Research at IMEDE, one of the founding institutions of IMD. He was recently a visiting professor at the Harvard Business School. Dr. Strebel received his Ph.D from Princeton University, his MBA from Columbia University, and his B.Sc. from the University of Cape Town, where he graduated with highest honors.